with CD–ROM/
Audio CD

face2face

Pre-intermediate Student's Book

Chris Redston & Gillie Cunningham

CAMBRIDGE
UNIVERSITY PRESS

V Vocabulary   **G** Grammar   **RW** Real World   **HwL** Help with Listening   **R** Reading   **W** Writing

3

1 Work, rest and play

1A Life stories

Vocabulary day-to-day phrases; question words
Grammar review of verb forms and questions

QUICK REVIEW ●●●
Introduce yourself to six other students. Find out their names and where they live. Tell the class about three people you spoke to.

Vocabulary Day-to-day phrases

1 Work in pairs. Are these phrases about family (F), work (W), free time (FT) or study (S)?

> be married *F*
> go to the cinema
> have an interesting job
> go shopping with friends
> play an instrument
> go to school/college/university
> be unemployed
> have brothers and/or sisters
> study other languages
> have children
> have a degree
> work for a company

2 **a)** Tick (✓) the phrases in **1** that are true for you now or in the past.

b) Work in groups. Tell other students about yourself. Use the phrases from **1** or your own ideas.

> I'm married and I've got two children.

> How old are they?

Reading and Grammar

3 **a)** Write the names of five famous British people. Why are they famous?

b) Work in groups. Compare names. Who is the most famous person, do you think?

4 **a)** Look at the photos. Why is Jamie Oliver famous, do you think?

b) [R1.1] Read and listen to the profile of Jamie Oliver. Match headings a)–d) with paragraphs 1–4.

a) An unusual restaurant
b) Family and free time
c) His early life
d) A famous chef

CELEBRITY PROFILE
Jamie Oliver

1

Jamie Oliver is one of Britain's favourite chefs – every week millions of people **watch** him on TV and use his recipes.

2

Jamie was born in Essex, England, in 1975. When he was only eight he **started** helping in his parents' restaurant. He went to catering college when he was sixteen and then worked at the famous River Café in London for three years. His first TV programme was called *The Naked Chef* and it was an instant success. Jamie quickly became famous and in 1999 he prepared lunch for the British Prime Minister.

3

Now Jamie has got his own restaurant in London called Fifteen. But it isn't a typical restaurant – every year Jamie takes fifteen young unemployed people and teaches them to become chefs. The programme about the restaurant, also called *Fifteen*, is on TV every week. He **is going to open** Fifteen restaurants in Australia and the USA in the future and at the moment Jamie **is writing** a new book of recipes. He's already very rich, of course – in 2003 he earned £3.8 million!

4

Jamie got married in 2000 and he lives in London with his wife, Jools, and their two daughters, Poppy Honey and Daisy Boo. He's so busy that he doesn't have much free time, but he loves riding around London on his scooter and he plays the drums in a rock band. When he's at home he likes making bread and cooking pasta – his favourite ingredients are olive oil and lemons from Sicily.

5 **a)** Read the profile again and find the answers to these questions.

1 How does he travel around London?
By scooter.
2 When did he get married?
3 Which instrument can he play?
4 What is he writing at the moment?
5 How often is *Fifteen* on TV?
6 How old was he when he started college?
7 How many children has he got?
8 Where is he going to open his new restaurants?
9 How much did he earn in 2003?
10 How long did he work at the River Café?
11 Who did he make lunch for in 1999?
12 Why is his restaurant called Fifteen?

b) Underline the question words in **5a)**.

c) Do the exercise in Language Summary 1 **V1.1** p119.

Help with Grammar Review of verb forms and questions

6 **a)** Match the words/phrases in **bold** in the profile to these verb forms.

Present Simple *watch*   Present Continuous
Past Simple   *be going to*

b) We usually use auxiliary verbs to make questions. Write questions 2–4 from **5a)** in the table.

question word	auxiliary	subject	verb	
How	does	he	travel	around London?

c) Look again at **5a)**. Then answer these questions.

1 Why don't we use an auxiliary verb in questions 5 and 6?
2 What is the verb in question 7?
3 Look at question 8. How do we make questions with *be going to*?

d) Check in Language Summary 1 **G1.1** p120.

7 **a)** Make questions with these words.

1 do / What / do / you ? *What do you do?*
2 you / got / brothers and sisters / have / How many ?
3 go / did / Where / you / to school ?
4 studying / Why / you / are / English ?
5 any other languages / you / Can / speak ?
6 going to / What / you / do / are / next weekend ?

b) **R1.2** **P** Listen and check. Listen again and practise.

c) Work in pairs. Take turns to ask and answer the questions.

Get ready … Get it right!

8 You are going to write a profile of someone in the class. Write ten questions to ask another student. Use these ideas or your own.

- personal details
- family
- work
- study
- free time
- last holiday
- future plans
- studying English
- home

9 **a)** Work with a student you don't know very well. Take turns to ask and answer your questions. Make notes on your partner's answers.

b) Write a profile of your partner.

c) Swap profiles with your partner. Check the information is correct.

d) Read other students' profiles. Who do you have a lot in common with?

1B Super commuters

Vocabulary work; questions about travel
Grammar subject questions
Help with Listening word stress
Review question forms

QUICK REVIEW ●●●
Work in pairs. Take turns to ask and answer questions and find six things you have in common.

Vocabulary Work

1 Work in pairs. Fill in the gaps in the diagram with these words/ phrases. Then check in **V1.2** p119.

a restaurant   a journalist
a newspaper   children
a receptionist   a department store
a multinational company
an office   old people   London
an accountant   teenagers
unemployed people   a charity
an editor   yourself

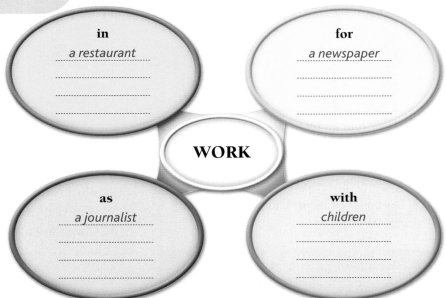

in
a restaurant

for
a newspaper

WORK

as
a journalist

with
children

Help with Listening Word stress

● In words of two or more syllables, one syllable always has the main stress.

2 **a)** **R1.3** Look at these words from **1**. Listen and notice the word stress.

óffice   joúrnalist   multinátional   cómpany
chíldren   depártment   péople   Lóndon

b) Where is the stress on these words?

unemployed   teenagers   accountant   charity
editor   receptionist   newspaper   yourself

c) **R1.4** Listen and check.

3 **R1.4** **P** Listen again and practise the phrases from **2b)**. Copy the stress.

4 **a)** Write the names of four people you know with jobs. Think of ways to describe their jobs. Use phrases from **1** or your own ideas.

b) Work in pairs. Tell your partner about these people's jobs. Who has the best job, do you think?

5 **a)** Match questions 1–4 to answers a)–d).

1 How do you get to work/university/school?
2 How long does it take you (to get there)?
3 How far is it?
4 How much does it cost?

a) (It's about) 15 kilometres.
b) (I go) by train.
c) (It costs) about £30 a week.
d) (It takes) about 40 minutes.

b) Work in pairs. Take turns to ask questions 1–4. Answer for you.

Reading, Grammar and Listening

6 **a)** Read about a new TV series. What is it about? What is *a commuter*, do you think?

b) Read about the series again. Then answer these questions.

1 Who lived in Bangkok?
2 How long did it take Mick to get to work?
3 How far was it to his office?
4 How long do people in Bangkok spend in traffic jams?
5 Who works for a multinational company?
6 Who is an editor?
7 Who lives in Spain?

SUPER COMMUTERS

ITV5, 8 p.m. ★★★★

Mick Benton's fascinating new documentary series looks at the enormous distances people travel to get to work. Mick got the idea for the programme when he worked for a TV company in Bangkok. He lived only four kilometres from his office but it took him over two hours to get to work every day. "The traffic in Bangkok is unbelievable," says Mick. "Often people sit in traffic jams for seven or eight hours a day. They even have their meals in their cars!"

In the first programme in the series, Mick interviews three 'super commuters' who work in London. Tony Rogers is an accountant for a multinational company, and travels from Liverpool and back every day. Andrea Price lives in Paris, but works as an editor for a London newspaper. And Ian Hicks is a fireman in Ealing, West London – he commutes all the way from Santander, in Spain!

So maybe your half-hour train journey to work every morning isn't so bad!

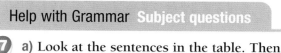

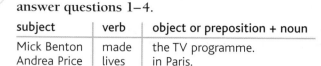
Help with Grammar Subject questions

7 **a)** Look at the sentences in the table. Then answer questions 1–4.

subject	verb	object or preposition + noun
Mick Benton	made	the TV programme.
Andrea Price	lives	in Paris.

1 Who made the TV programme?
2 Who lives in Paris?
3 What did Mick Benton make?
4 Where does Andrea Price live?

b) Which two questions ask about the subjects of the sentences in 7a)?

c) How are the question forms in 1 and 2 different from the question forms in 3 and 4?

d) Check in G1.2 p120.

8 **a)** Write questions for the words in **bold**.

1 **Mick** worked in Bangkok. *Who worked in Bangkok?*
2 Mick worked **in Bangkok**.
3 **Ian** lives in Spain.
4 Ian lives **in Spain**.
5 **Andrea** works for a newspaper.
6 The programme starts **at 8 p.m.**

b) R1.5 P Listen and check. Listen again and practise.

9 **a)** R1.6 Listen to part of the TV programme. Find one reason why Tony, Andrea and Ian live a long way from work.

b) Make questions with these words. Use the Present Simple.

1 Who / leave / home at 6.15 a.m.?
   Who leaves home at 6.15 a.m.?
2 How / Ian / travel to work?
   How does Ian travel to work?
3 Who / finish / work at 2 a.m.?
4 How long / it / take Ian to get to work?
5 Who / spend / £8,000 a year on travel?
6 Where / Andrea / stay when she's in London?
7 Who / commute / to London five days a week?

c) Work in pairs. Answer the questions in 9b). Then listen again and check.

Get ready ... Get it right!

10 Work in pairs. Student A → p102. Student B → p110. Follow the instructions.

1C Time to relax

Vocabulary free time activities; *do, play, go, go to*; frequency adverbs and expressions
Skills Reading: a newspaper article; Listening: a survey
Help with Listening sentence stress (1)
Review question forms

QUICK REVIEW ●●●
Work in groups. Find out who: gets up first, travels the furthest to class, spends the most on travel, watches TV the most, goes to bed last, sleeps the most.

Vocabulary Free time activities

1 Write the vowels (*a, e, i, o, u*) in these free time activities.

1 **do** judo   exercise
2 **play** v_ll_yb_ll   c_rds
3 **go** cycl_ng   r_nn_ng
4 **go to** c_nc_rts   the th__tr_

Help with Vocabulary
do, play, go, go to

2 **a)** Look at the phrases in **1**. Which verb do we usually use with these free time activities?

1 words that end in *-ing*
2 sports with a ball and other games
3 places and events
4 things you do in a gym or a health club

b) Match these words/phrases with the verbs in **1**. There are three words/phrases for each verb. Then check in **V1.3** p119.

> skateboarding   basketball   yoga
> art galleries   jogging   aerobics
> mountain biking   chess   sport
> the gym   museums   table tennis

TIP! • In these vocabulary boxes we only show the main stress in words and phrases.

c) Can you add any more words/phrases to the verbs in **1**?

3 Work in pairs. Ask questions with *Do you ever ... ?*. Find six things that you both do in your free time. Use the phrases from **1** and **2b)** or your own ideas.

> Do you ever go to art galleries?

> Yes, sometimes./No, I don't.

Reading and Vocabulary

4 **a)** Work in groups. How do people in the UK spend their free time, do you think?

b) Read the first paragraph of the article. Were you correct?

c) Read the rest of the article. Guess the correct answers a)–p).

d) **R1.7** Listen and check. Which answers do you think are surprising?

The British way of life?

A new survey on the free time habits of the British is published this week – and it shows that we still love football, shopping, going to pubs, watching TV, gardening and, of course, fish and chips! Here are some of the more surprising results from the survey.

● a)53%/(83%) of British families have a garden and b)15%/35% normally do some gardening every weekend.

● c)17%/27% of British people go swimming every week and d)26%/16% play football, but e)22%/32% watch football on TV at least once a week.

● 35% of adults go to f)the theatre/a rock concert at least once a year.

● British people watch TV for about g)two/four hours every day – and h)27%/47% of men have dinner and watch TV at the same time.

● The British are always happy when they're socialising. 46% of i)men/women and 23% of j)men/women go to a bar or pub every week.

● British people usually go on holiday once a year and 27% of these holidays are in k)Spain/France.

● l)30%/46% of adults go to a McDonald's restaurant every three months, but m)30%/46% go to a traditional fish and chip shop.

● The British spend £726 million on n)tea/coffee and £900 million on o)tea/coffee every year.

● And every British person eats p)9/16 kg of chocolate and sweets every year – more than any other country in the world!

Help with Vocabulary
Frequency adverbs and expressions

 a) Put these frequency adverbs in order.

> hardly ever   not (very) often   never
> sometimes   always *1*   occasionally
> usually/normally/generally *2*   often

b) Look at sentences 1–3. Then complete the rules with *before* or *after*.

1 The British are always happy when they're socialising.
2 British people usually go on holiday once a year.
3 35% normally do some gardening every weekend.

● Frequency adverbs go .... the verb *be*.
● Frequency adverbs go .... other verbs.

c) Put these frequency expressions in order.

> once every three months   twice a day *1*
> three times a week *2*   every Saturday
> once a month   once or twice a year
> every couple of weeks

d) Look again at sentences 2 and 3 in **5b)**. Where do the expressions in **5c)** usually go in a sentence?

e) Check in V1.4 p119.

 a) Put the word/phrase in brackets in the correct place in the sentence.

1 I go jogging on Sundays. (sometimes)
   I sometimes go jogging on Sundays.
2 He does yoga. (twice a week)
3 They go cycling at the weekend. (often)
4 I'm at home on Monday evenings. (always)
5 She goes mountain biking. (every weekend)
6 We go to the theatre. (once a month)
7 Do you go shopping at the weekend? (usually)

b) Write six sentences about your free time activities. Use frequency adverbs and expressions from **5a)** and **5c)**.

c) Work in groups. Compare sentences. Do you do the same things?

Listening

 a) R1.8 A researcher is interviewing Louise for this year's British free time survey. Listen and fill in the form.

FREE TIME SURVEY

activity	frequency
go to a bar/pub	once a month
do sport	
go to the theatre	
do some gardening	
go on holiday	
watch TV	

b) Compare Louise's answers with the newspaper article. Is she a typical British person, do you think? Why/Why not?

Help with Listening Sentence stress (1)

● We stress the important words in sentences and questions.

 a) R1.8 Listen to the beginning of the interview again. Notice the sentence stress.

We're doing a survey on the free time habits of British people.
Can I ask you a few questions?
How often do you go to a bar or a pub?

b) Look at R1.8, p145. Listen again and notice the sentence stress.

a) Work in pairs. Make your own free time survey. Write at least six questions.

How often do you watch sport on TV?

b) Work in groups of five or six. Ask your questions. Find out who does the things in your survey the most often.

1D Speed dating

QUICK REVIEW ●●●
Write your five favourite free time activities on a piece of paper. Work in pairs. Swap papers. Guess how often your partner does these activities. Ask questions with *How often ... ?* to check your answers.

Looking for someone special? No time to go on dates? Then speed dating is for you! Speed dating is quick, fun, and exciting – and you could meet the love of your life!

This is how it works: 25 men and 25 women get together in a friendly bar and sit at tables for two. They have three minutes to talk to each other. When the date is finished, a bell rings. Then all the men move to the next table. If you want to meet a person again, you tick his or her name on a card. At the end of the evening you hand in your cards. If there's a match, we send you the other person's email address. And after that it's up to you!

Call us now on 0800 975 4433 or check our website: www.quickmatch.co.uk

1 **a)** Read this advert for a speed dating company. Answer the questions.

1 How long is each speed date?
2 How many people do you meet?
3 What do you do if you like a person?
4 What happens if this person also ticks your name?

b) Work in groups. Discuss these questions.

1 Do you think speed dating is a good idea? Why?/Why not?
2 What questions do people ask each other on a speed date, do you think?

2 **a)** `R1.9` Becky is on a speed dating evening. Listen to her conversations with Chris and Marcus. Who does she want to see again, do you think? Why?

b) Listen again. What does Becky have in common with each man?

c) `R1.10` Listen and check who Becky wants to see again.

Real World Finding things in common

3 **a)** Look at these sentences and responses. Then choose the correct words in the rule.

A I really love travelling.   B So do I.
A I don't go out much.   B Neither do I.

● We use *so/neither* to agree with positive sentences and *so/neither* to agree with negative sentences.

b) Look at these sentences and responses. Do these people agree or disagree?

A I don't like cycling.   B Oh, I do.
A I'm a vegetarian.   B Oh, I'm not.

c) Fill in the gaps in the table.

	agree	disagree
1 I'm a bit nervous.		*Oh, I'm not.*
2 I can't speak Turkish.	*Neither can I.*	
3 I've got a dog.		
4 I don't go out much.		
5 I had a great time.	*So did I.*	

d) Check in `RW1.1` p120.

4 a) Look at R1.9, p145. Read and <u>underline</u> all the responses from 3.

b) [R1.11] [P] Listen and practise.

So am I.
Neither am I.

5 Write ways to agree and disagree with these sentences.

1 I don't like meat.
   Neither do I./Oh, I do.
2 I'm quite tired.
3 I went out last night.
4 I haven't got a mobile.
5 I hate getting up early.
6 I can speak Russian.
7 I didn't sleep well.
8 I'm not from this town.

6 [R1.12] Listen and agree with eight different sentences. Then listen again and disagree with them.

I'm not married.
Neither am I.

7 a) Write six sentences about you. Start each sentence with one of these phrases.

I love …	I don't like …
I went …	I didn't go …
I'm …	I'm not …
I've got …	I haven't got …
I can …	I can't …

b) Work in pairs. Take turns to say a sentence. Your partner agrees or disagrees. Continue the conversation if possible. What do you have in common?

I love eating out.

So do I.

What's your favourite food?

Pasta.

---

1 Review

1 a) Make questions with these words. [G1.1]

1 favourite food / 's / your / What ?
   What's your favourite food?
2 do / you / How often / cook ?
3 What / you / cook / can ?
4 How much / spend / you / do / on food a week ?
5 a favourite restaurant / got / Have / you ?
6 was / the last time / ate out / you / When ?
7 did / you / Where / go ?
8 going to / eat / What / you / are / this evening ?

b) Work in pairs. Take turns to ask and answer the questions.

2 a) Cross out the incorrect words/phrases. [V1.2]

1 work in *a school/an office/ a receptionist*
2 work as *a journalist/yourself/ a waiter*
3 work for *an office/a TV company/ a charity*
4 work with *children/unemployed people/a department store*

b) Work in pairs. Use the phrases in **2a)** and ask questions about the people your partner knows.

Do you know anyone who (works in a school)?

3 a) Megan and Bernie live in Birmingham. Look at the information. Then make questions 1–8. [G1.2]

	Megan	Bernie
works in	Leeds	Liverpool
works as	a doctor	a lawyer
journey to work	3 hours	1½ hours
cost per week	£200	£150
leaves home	6.30 a.m.	7.45 a.m.
gets home	8.30 p.m.	7.30 p.m.

1 Who / work / in Leeds?
   Who works in Leeds?
2 Where / Bernie / work?
3 What / Bernie / do?
4 How much / Megan / spend a week?
5 Who / spend / the most?
6 Who / have / the longest journey?
7 What time / Megan / leave home?
8 Who / get / home at 7.30?

b) Work in pairs. Take turns to ask and answer the questions.

4 a) Write six things you do in your free time. [V1.3]

b) Work in pairs. Ask questions about the things from **4a)**. Find things that you both do.

Do you watch TV?
Yes, I do./No, I don't.

c) Ask your partner how often he/she does these things. Who does them more often? [V1.4]

How often do you go to concerts?
About once a month.

Progress Portfolio

a) Tick the things you can do in English.

☐ I can ask people general questions about their lives.

☐ I can answer questions about my day-to-day life.

☐ I can talk about work and free time activities.

☐ I can ask and answer questions about travel.

☐ I can talk about how often I do things.

☐ I can agree and disagree with things people say.

b) What do you need to study again? See CD-ROM [● 1A–D].

2 Beginnings

2A Starting small

Vocabulary irregular verbs; past time phrases
Grammar Past Simple
Review question words; subject questions

QUICK REVIEW ● ● ●
Write five sentences beginning with *I'm (not)* … , *I've/haven't got* … , *I (don't) like* … , *I can/can't* … , *I went/didn't go* … . Work in pairs. Take turns to say your sentences. Agree or disagree with your partner's sentences.

Reading and Grammar

1 **Work in groups. Discuss these questions.**

1 What fast food companies are there in your country? What do they sell?
2 What are the good and bad things about fast food?
3 Do you ever go to fast food restaurants? Which ones? What do you usually buy?

2 **a) Read the article about KFC and Harland Sanders. Put these events in order.**

a) He travelled 250,000 miles a year.
b) His father died. *1*
c) He became the manager of a service station.
d) He sold the KFC business.
e) He developed his secret chicken recipe.
f) He learned to cook.

b) Read the article again. Then answer these questions.

a) Why did Harland Sanders learn to cook when he was a child?
b) How long did it take him to develop his secret chicken recipe?
c) When did the first official KFC restaurant open?
d) How old was Harland Sanders when he sold the company?
e) What happened in 1980?
f) Who bought KFC in 1986?

HOW FAST FOOD BEGAN

The man behind KFC

Harland Sanders was born in the USA in 1890, but his childhood wasn't a happy one. His father died when he was only six so his mother needed to find a job. She went to work in a shirt factory and Harland stayed at home to look after his younger brother and sister. That was when he first learned to cook.

He left home when he was twelve and worked on a nearby farm. After that he had a lot of different jobs and in 1930 he became a service station manager in Corbin, Kentucky. He started cooking meals for hungry travellers who stopped at the service station, and soon people came only for the food. Harland moved to a 142-seat restaurant across the street where he could serve all his customers. Over the next nine years he developed the secret chicken recipe that made him famous.

In the early 1950s he closed the restaurant and decided to sell his recipe to other businesses. The first official Kentucky Fried Chicken restaurant didn't open until August 1952 – by 1964 there were more than 600 KFCs in North America. That year Sanders sold the company for $2 million, but he continued to work as KFC's public spokesman and visited restaurants all over the world. He travelled 250,000 miles every year until he died in 1980, aged 90. Six years later PepsiCo bought KFC for $840 million.

There are now KFC restaurants in more than 80 countries and they sell 2.5 billion chicken dinners every year – and the recipe is still a secret!

Help with Grammar Past Simple

3 **a)** Read the article about KFC again. Find examples of the Past Simple forms of:

be	regular verbs	negatives
can	irregular verbs	

b) Answer these questions.

1 How do we make the Past Simple of regular verbs? Is there a rule for irregular verbs?
2 How do we make the Past Simple negative? How is the Past Simple negative of *be* different?

c) Look at the questions in 2b). Then answer questions 1–3.

1 How do we usually make Past Simple questions?
2 How do we make Past Simple questions with the verb *be*?
3 How are questions e) and f) different from questions a)–c)?

d) Check in G2.1 p121.

TIP! • There is an Irregular Verb List on p159.

4 **a)** Write the Past Simple of these regular verbs from the article about KFC.

die	need	stay	learn	work	start	move
develop	decide	continue	visit	travel		

b) R2.1 Listen to the Past Simple of these verbs. Tick the verbs that have an extra syllable /ɪd/ in the Past Simple.

died /daɪd/   *needed* /niːdɪd/ ✓

c) P Listen again and practise.

5 **a)** Read about McDonald's. Fill in gaps 1–11 with the Past Simple of the verbs in brackets.

b) Work in pairs. Check your answers.

Vocabulary Past time phrases

6 **a)** Put these time phrases in order.

in 1955	in the sixties	yesterday evening *1*
last week	the day before yesterday	eighty years ago
in the nineteenth century *8*	in July last year	

b) When do we use *ago*, *last*, and *in*? Check in V2.1 p121.

7 Work in pairs. Student A → p103. Student B → p111. Follow the instructions.

Do you want fries with that?

Ten years before KFC sold its first chicken dinner, the first McDonald's restaurant ¹ *opened* (open) in California. Dick and Maurice McDonald ² _____ (sell) burgers for 15 cents and milk shakes for 20 cents. People ³ _____ (not have) much time for lunch so they ⁴ _____ (not want) to wait long for their meal. At the first McDonald's, customers ⁵ _____ (can) get their food in 15 seconds! This ⁶ _____ (be) the beginning of cheap fast food.

In 1955 a man called Ray Kroc ⁷ _____ (become) an agent for McDonald's and ⁸ _____ (start) opening restaurants in other states. The McDonald brothers ⁹ _____ (not be) very ambitious and so Ray Kroc ¹⁰ _____ (buy) the company for $2.7 million in 1961. In the sixties he ¹¹ _____ (open) over 1,000 new restaurants and now there are more than 25,000 McDonald's in over 120 countries.

Get ready ... Get it right!

8 Think about the last time you had a special meal. Make notes on the meal. Use these ideas.

- reason for the meal
- where and when the meal was
- the people at the meal
- what time it started/finished
- what you wore
- the food and drink
- any other interesting information

9 **a)** Work in pairs. Take turns to talk about your special meals. Ask questions to find out more information.

> My special meal was last month, for my birthday.

> Where did you go?

b) Tell the class about your partner's special meal. Did anyone <u>not</u> enjoy their meal? Why not?

Vocabulary relationships (1)
Grammar Past Continuous: positive, negative and questions
Help with Listening weak forms (1): *was* and *were*
Review Past Simple; past time phrases

QUICK REVIEW ● ● ●
Make a list of eight things you did last week. Work in groups or go around the class. Ask questions with *Did you ... ?* and find one student who did each thing on your list.

Listening and Grammar

1 **a)** Look at the photos. Where are the people? Do they know each other, do you think?

b) Match sentences 1–3 to photos A–C. Guess who says each sentence.

1 I **was travelling** back from China and we met on the plane.
2 We **were standing** in a queue at the supermarket and he said hello.
3 When we first met, she **was going out** with my best friend.

c) R2.2 Listen and check.

Liam, Jenny and Ben

(A)

Help with Grammar Past Continuous: positive and negative

2 **a)** Look at this sentence. Then answer the questions.

*I **was travelling** back from China and we **met** on the plane.*

1 Which action started first?
2 Which action was shorter?
3 Which action was longer?
4 Did the 'travelling' continue after they met?
5 Which verb is in the Past Simple and which is in the Past Continuous?

b) Look at the Past Continuous verb forms in **bold** in **1b)**. Then fill in the gaps with *was, wasn't, were* or *weren't*.

POSITIVE
I/he/she/it + ... + verb+*ing*
you/we/they + ... + verb+*ing*

NEGATIVE
I/he/she/it + ... + verb+*ing*
you/we/they + ... + verb+*ing*

c) Check in G2.2 p122.

3 R2.3 P Listen and practise.

trávelling báck from Chína → I was /wəz/ trávelling báck from Chína → I was /wəz/ trávelling báck from Chína and we mét on the pláne.

4 **a)** Hilary is talking about how she met Ken. Choose the correct verb form.

1 I first *met/was meeting* Ken when we *waited/were waiting* in a supermarket queue.
2 It *rained/was raining* so he *offered/was offering* me a lift home.
3 While we *drove/were driving* to my flat, he *gave/was giving* me his phone number.
4 I *saw/was seeing* him in the supermarket again a few days later.

b) Put the verbs in brackets in the Past Simple or Past Continuous and complete Hilary's story.

5 He .... (talk) to a friend and he .... (not see) me.
6 So I .... (leave) while they .... (wait) to pay.
7 I .... (walk) home when a car .... (stop) next to me. It was him.
8 I .... (invite) him to dinner – and that .... (be) 20 years ago!

c) R2.4 Listen and check.

Vocabulary Relationships (1)

5 **a)** Tick the phrases you know. Then do the exercise in V2.2 p121.

go òut with someone   get engáged to someone   ask someone òut
go on a dàte   get márried to someone   fall in lóve with someone
meet someone for the first time   break úp with someone

b) Work in pairs. Put the phrases in **5a)** in order. There is more than one possible order.

Ken and Hilary

B

Linda and Colin

C

Listening and Grammar

6 **a)** [R2.5] Liam is talking about how he met Jenny. Listen and answer these questions.

1 Was Jenny at Ben's birthday party?
2 When did Liam ask Jenny out?
3 Why wasn't their first date very good?
4 What were they doing when Liam asked Jenny to marry him?
5 What was Liam doing when she said yes?

b) Listen again and choose the correct answer.

1 Liam and Jenny first met *last year/two years ago*.
2 They started going out in *March/September*.
3 He asked her to marry him *eight/eighteen* months later.
4 They got engaged a few *days/weeks* later.
5 They got married six *weeks/months* after that.

c) In which month did they get married?

7 **a)** [R2.6] Listen to the two different ways to say *was* and *were*.

	strong	weak
was	/wɒz/	/wəz/
were	/wɜː/	/wə/

b) [R2.5] Look at R2.5, p146. Listen again and notice how we say *was* and *were*. Are *was* and *were* usually strong or weak in: a) sentences? b) questions? c) short answers?

Help with Grammar **Past Continuous: questions**

8 **a)** Look at questions 4 and 5 in **6a)**. Then fill in the gaps in the rule.

● We make questions in the Past Continuous with: question word + _____ or _____ + subject + _____ .

b) Check in [G2.3] p122.

9 Work in pairs. Student A → p103. Student B → p111. Follow the instructions.

Get ready ... Get it right!

10 Choose a married couple you know well (yourself and your wife/husband, your parents, other relatives or friends). Make notes about the couple. Use these ideas.

● when, where and how they met
● where they went on their first date
● how long they went out together before they got married
● when they got engaged
● when and where they got married
● any other interesting or funny information

11 **a)** Work in groups. Tell other students about the couple you chose. Ask questions to find out more information.

My parents first met at work.

Where were they living at the time?

In Madrid. They were working for a ...

b) Which story is the most romantic, the most unusual or the funniest?

The 1001 Nights

Vocabulary connecting words (1)
Skills Reading: a book cover;
Reading and Listening: a story
Help with Listening weak forms (2):
the schwa /ə/
Review Past Continuous; Past Simple

QUICK REVIEW ● ● ●
Write five different times of the day. Work in pairs. Ask what your partner was doing at these times yesterday.

Reading

1 Work in groups. Discuss these questions.

1 Do you like reading? What kind of books or magazines do you read?
2 When is your favourite time for reading? Why?
3 What was the last book you read? Did you like it? Why?/Why not?

2 a) Read about the book. Then answer these questions.

1 What is *The Thousand and One Nights*?
2 How old are the stories?
3 Which countries are they from?
4 Were they for adults or children?

b) Work in pairs. Compare answers.

Reading, Listening and Vocabulary

3 a) **R2.7** Read and listen to Shahrazad's story, the first story of *The Thousand and One Nights*. Match paragraphs 1–3 to pictures A–C.

b) Read the beginning of Shahrazad's story again. Are these sentences true (T) or false (F)?

1 The King killed his first wife.
2 He was married to his next wife for three years.
3 Shahrazad worked for the King.
4 Shahrazad's father didn't want her to marry the King.
5 Shahrazad asked her mother to help her.

c) Work in pairs. Compare answers. Then correct the false sentences.

4 a) Which of these endings to Shahrazad's story is correct, do you think? Compare ideas in groups.

1 The King didn't kill Shahrazad and they lived happily together.
2 Shahrazad killed the King and became Queen.
3 The King killed Shahrazad and married her sister.

b) **R2.8** Listen and check.

c) Listen again and answer the questions.

1 Who listened to Shahrazad's first story?
2 Why didn't the King kill her the morning after the wedding?
3 What was Shahrazad's plan?
4 What did the King do in the end? Why?

The Thousand and One Nights is probably one of the most famous books in the world. It is a collection of stories first told by travellers from Persia, Arabia, India and China between the ninth and thirteenth centuries. In later years professional storytellers also told the stories in coffee houses in Turkey, Egypt and many other countries. *The Thousand and One Nights* contains well-known stories like Aladdin and Ali Baba and the Forty Thieves, so people often think they are just for children – but they were originally for adults.

This new edition of *The Thousand and One Nights* is fully illustrated and contains new versions of all the stories, translated from the original texts by Brian Woodhead.

Shahrazad's story

1 There was once an Indian king called Shahriyar. One day King Shahriyar found his wife with another man so he killed her and her lover. After that the King married a different woman every day and killed her the next morning before she could stop loving him. This continued for three years.

2 Shahrazad was the clever and beautiful daughter of the King's adviser. When her father told her what was happening, she decided to marry the King. Shahrazad's father tried to stop her because he knew she was going to die. But Shahrazad had a plan to save herself and all the women in the kingdom. The King and Shahrazad got married a few days later.

3 After the wedding, while the King was drinking with his friends, Shahrazad went to find her sister. "I need your help," said Shahrazad. "Come to the palace this evening and ask me to tell you a story."

Help with Listening Weak forms (2): the schwa /ə/

- In sentences we say many small words with a schwa /ə/ sound. These are called weak forms.

5 **a)** **R2.9** Listen to the difference between the strong and weak forms of these words.

	strong	weak
and	/ænd/	/ən/
to	/tuː/	/tə/
of	/ɒv/	/əv/
the	/ðiː/	/ðə/

b) **R2.8** Look at R2.8, p146. Listen again. Notice the sentence stress and weak forms. Are weak forms ever stressed?

Help with Vocabulary Connecting words (1)

6 **a)** **Look at sentences 1–5. Then fill in the gaps in the rules with the words in bold.**

1 The King found his wife with another man **so** he killed her.
2 The King killed his wife **because** he found her with another man.
3 **While** the King was drinking with his friends, Shahrazad went to find her sister.
4 Shahrazad was getting ready for bed **when** her sister came to visit her.
5 The King never heard the end of a story **until** the next evening.

- We use .... to give a reason why something happened.
- We use .... to say what the consequence of a situation is.
- We use .... to say something stops happening at this time.
- We can use .... and .... for things that happen at the same time.

TIP! • We don't usually use *while* with the Past Simple.

b) Check in **V2.3** p121.

7 **Choose the correct words.**

1 Shahrazad's father was very worried *while/when* she married the King.
2 *While/Until* she was telling the story, the King came into the room.
3 She didn't finish the story *so/because* the King didn't kill her.
4 The King didn't kill Shahrazad *so/because* he couldn't live without her.
5 Shahrazad wasn't sure the King loved her *because/until* he married her a second time.

8 **a)** **Work in pairs. Choose a story you both know. Make notes on these things. Ask your teacher for any new vocabulary.**

- the characters
- when and where the story happens
- how the story starts
- the main events of the story
- what happens at the end

b) Write the story. Use past verb forms and connecting words from **6a)**.

c) Read other students' stories. Which do you like best? Why?

Real World starting and ending conversations
Review Past Simple; Present Simple

QUICK REVIEW ●●●
Work in pairs. Tell the story of Shahrazad from *The Thousand and One Nights*. How much can you remember? *There was once an Indian king called Shahriyar. One day he …*

1 a) How do you greet: a family member, a friend, a person you work with, a man/woman you don't know, your teacher? Do you shake hands, bow, kiss, or just say hello?

b) Work in groups. Compare answers.

2 a) **R2.10** Listen to conversations 1–3. Match them to the people in the photo of David and Jane's party (A–C). Do the people know each other?

b) Listen again. How do these people know David and Jane? Match 1–6 to a)–f).

1	Sami	a)	is David's sister.
2	Celia	b)	is a neighbour.
3	Paula	c)	met David and Jane in Africa.
4	Simon	d)	is one of Jane's students.
5	Stephen	e)	works with David and Jane.
6	Carlos	f)	went to school with David.

Real World **Starting conversations**

3 a) **R2.10** Read the questions. Then listen again and tick the ones you hear.

1 **How do you know** David and Jane?
2 **Do you live** near here?
3 **Didn't we meet in** Milan last year?
4 **Do you know** Pam Jones?
5 **Where did you meet** David?
6 **You're** a student at the English Centre, **aren't you**?
7 **Are you a friend of** David's?
8 **What do you do?**

b) Match the questions in 3a) to the reasons we ask them a)–d).

a) people you know *1*
b) meeting someone in the past
c) where people live
d) people's jobs or studies

c) Check in **RW2.1** p122.

4 **R2.11** **P** Listen and practise the sentences in 3a).

Hŏw do you knŏw Dávid and Jáne?

5 a) Match these ends of conversations to the people in the photo (A–C).

1
A Let's keep in touch.
B Yes, sure. Here's my email address.
A Thanks a lot. Here's mine.
B Cheers. See you later, maybe.

2
A It was nice meeting you.
B You too. See you at school, probably.
A Yes, I'm sure we will.

3
A It was nice to see you again.
B You too. I hope we meet again soon.
A Yes, I hope so. Bye.

b) **R2.12** Listen and check.

Real World
Ending conversations

6 Fill in the gaps with the correct words.

See	meeting	later
was	hope	keep

1 It _____ nice to see you again.
2 I _____ we meet again soon.
3 It was nice _____ you.
4 _____ you at school, probably.
5 Let's _____ in touch.
6 See you _____ , maybe.

7 R2.13 P Listen and practise the sentences in **6**.

It was nice to see you again.

8 a) Work in pairs. Write a conversation at a party. Use the phrases in **bold** from **3a)** and the sentences from **6**.

b) Swap your conversation with another pair. Correct any mistakes.

c) Role-play the conversation for a different pair of students.

♪ R2.14 Look at the song *I Got You Babe* on p100. Follow the instructions.

1 a) Write the verbs.

1 **asty**   s_tay_
2 **evale**   l_____
3 **eddice**   d_____
4 **lesl**   s_____
5 **istiv**   v_____
6 **mecboe**   b_____
7 **vhae**   h_____
8 **ratts**   s_____

b) Work in pairs. Write the Past Simple forms of the verbs in **1a)**. Which are irregular? G2.1

2 a) Put the verbs in brackets in the Past Simple. Then complete the sentences for you. G2.1

1 Last weekend I _____ (go) …
Last weekend I went shopping.
2 Last month I _____ (buy) …
3 I _____ (get) this English book … ago.
4 My last holiday _____ (be) in …
5 The day before yesterday I _____ (see) …
6 I first _____ (come) to this school/college … ago.

b) Work in pairs. Take turns to say your sentences. Ask follow-up questions.

3 a) Match a verb in A to a phrase in B. V2.2

A	B
get	someone out
break	out with someone
go	in love
ask	on a date
fall	up with someone
get	married to someone
meet	engaged to someone
go	someone for the first time

b) Use the phrases in **3a)** and write sentences about a relationship (real or imaginary).

c) Work in pairs. Talk about the relationships. Ask follow-up questions. Is your partner's story true?

4 a) Write sentences with the Past Simple or Past Continuous. G2.1 G2.2

a) He / get / out of a taxi and he / not see / me.
He was getting out of a taxi and he didn't see me.
b) We / get / married six years ago.
c) I first / meet / Greg when I / cycle / to work.
d) While we / wait / to see a doctor Greg / ask / me out.
e) When he / open / the taxi door it / hit / me.
f) Greg / take / me to hospital in the taxi.

b) Work in pairs. Put the sentences in order.

5 a) Write endings for these sentences on a piece of paper. Don't write them in order. V2.3

1 I went home because …
2 I couldn't do it so …
3 When I saw him …
4 I stayed there until …
5 While I was watching TV …

b) Work in pairs. Swap papers. Match your partner's endings with 1–5 in **5a)**.

c) Check your answers with your partner. Are you correct?

Progress Portfolio

a) Tick the things you can do in English.

☐ I can describe past events and say when they happened.
☐ I can talk about relationships.
☐ I can understand the main points of a simple story.
☐ I can make sentences with *when, so, because*, etc.
☐ I can start and end social conversations.

b) What do you need to study again? ● 2A–D

3A Getting qualified

Vocabulary employment
Grammar *have to/had to*
Help with Listening *have to* and *have*
Review Present Simple; Past Simple

QUICK REVIEW ● ● ●
Write the letters of the alphabet A–Z. Work in pairs. Try to write one job for each letter. Which pair has the most?

A | Gary

B | Melissa

Vocabulary Employment

1 **a)** Tick the phrases you know. Then do the exercise in **V3.1** p123.

I'd like ...	I'd like a job with ...
a good salary	flexible working hours
friendly colleagues	opportunities for travel
my own office	opportunities for promotion
long holidays	holiday pay
a good boss	on-the-job training
job security	sick pay

b) Choose three things from **1a)** that are important to you and three things that are not important to you.

c) Work in pairs. Compare your ideas. How many are the same?

Listening and Grammar

2 **a)** Work in groups. Look at photos A–C. Choose three phrases from **1a)** that you think are true for each job.

b) Match sentences 1–3 to the photos.

1 I **had to do** 72 weeks' basic training, but I **didn't have to pay** for it – the company did.
2 You **don't have to go** to university, but you probably learn more facts than a university student.
3 You **have to have** a degree and the training takes five years.

c) **R3.1** Listen and check.

Help with Grammar *have to/had to* (1): positive and negative

3 **a)** Match the phrases in **bold** in **2b)** with these meanings.

a) It is necessary to do this.
b) It is not necessary to do this, but you can if you want.
c) It was necessary to do this in the past.
d) It wasn't necessary to do this in the past.

b) Choose the correct verb form in these sentences. Which verb form follows *have to*?

1 I/You/We/They *has to/have to* pay for it.
2 He/She *has to/have to* pay for it.
3 I/You/We/They *don't/doesn't* have to pay for it.
4 He/She *don't/doesn't* have to pay for it.

c) How do you make the Past Simple positive and negative forms of *have to*?

d) Check in **G3.1** p123.

Nigel

 7 **a)** Read about Gary's training again. Answer these questions.

1 What does a London taxi driver have to know?
2 Do taxi drivers have to do oral tests without a map?
3 How many oral tests did Gary have to do?
4 Does Gary have to work very long hours now?
5 Did his son have to buy his own taxi?

b) Work in pairs and compare answers. What do you think is the most surprising thing about a taxi driver's training?

Grammar and Listening

Help with Grammar *have to/had to* (2): questions and short answers

 8 **a)** Look at the questions in 7a). How do we make questions with *have to* in the Present Simple and Past Simple?

b) What are the positive and negative short answers for these questions?
1 Do you have to have a degree?
2 Does he have to work at night?
3 Did they have to pass an oral test?

c) Check in **G3.2** p124.

Help with Listening *have to* and *have*

 4 **a)** **R3.2** Listen and notice the difference between *have to* and *have* in these sentences.

1 You have to /hæftə/ work very hard.
2 You don't have /hæv/ much free time.
3 You have to /hæftə/ have /hæv/ a degree.

b) **R3.3** Listen and put these words/phrases in the order you hear them.

have	have to	had to	has to
didn't have to		don't have to 1	

5 **R3.3** **P** Listen again and practise.

You don't have to /hæftə/ go to university.

6 Read about Gary's training. Fill in the gaps with the correct form of *have to*.

You ¹ *don't have to* go to university, but you probably learn more facts than a university student – at least that's what people say. A London taxi driver ² _____ know 25,000 streets and all the important places in the city. This is called The Knowledge. To get The Knowledge, a taxi driver ³ _____ pass written and oral tests. You ⁴ _____ pass these before you can get a licence. In the oral tests you ⁵ _____ tell the examiner all the streets you drive down to get from one place to another – and you can't use a map. I ⁶ _____ do twelve oral tests before I got my licence. Others do a lot more.

After I got my licence I ⁷ _____ borrow £60,000 from the bank to buy my taxi. Then I ⁸ _____ work day and night to pay the money back. I'm really pleased I ⁹ _____ (not) do that now. My son got his licence last year. Then he got a job in a taxi company, so he ¹⁰ _____ (not) buy his own taxi. He ¹¹ _____ work when the company tells him to – but at least he ¹² _____ (not) pay lots of money back to the bank!

9 **a)** Make questions about Melissa and Nigel with the correct form of *have to* in the Present Simple or Past Simple.

1 What / Melissa / do in the holidays?
What did Melissa have to do in the holidays?
2 How many final exams / a student vet / do?
3 How much / Melissa / pay for her course?
4 How much / pilots / pay for their training now?
5 How many written exams / Nigel / pass?
6 What / he / do when he started work?

b) **R3.4** Listen to Melissa and Nigel and answer the questions.

Get ready ... Get it right!

 10 Work in pairs. Student A → p107. Student B → p115. Follow the instructions.

Vocabulary looking for a job
Grammar Present Continuous and
Present Simple; activity and state verbs
Review employment; question words

QUICK REVIEW ●●●
Think of two people you know with jobs. Work in pairs.
Tell your partner what these people have to do in their jobs.
Which person has the best job, do you think?

Vocabulary Looking for a job

1 **a)** Tick the phrases you know.
Check new words/phrases in
V3.2 p123.

> find a job   write a CV
> go for an interview
> lose your job *1*   look for a job
> fill in an application form
> be unemployed   apply for a job
> get unemployment benefit
> earn a lot of money

b) Put the phrases in **1a)** in order.
There is more than one possible
order.

c) Work in pairs. Compare
answers. Are they the same?

2 Work in groups. Use the
phrases in **1a)** to talk about you
or the people you know.

I went for a job interview last week.
My friend Johann is unemployed.

Reading and Grammar

3 **a)** Look at the photos. What
are the people doing?

b) Read the letters and match
them to the photos.

c) Read the letters again. Are
sentences a)–f) correct? Change
the incorrect sentences.

a) Kevin is looking for his first job.
b) He reads the job adverts twice
   a week.
c) He's working in his mother's
   garden today.
d) George knows a lot about
   computers.
e) He lost his job two months ago.
f) He goes to a lot of interviews.

Ⓐ   Ⓑ

Letters
TO THE EDITOR

A vicious circle

Dear Sir,
My son, Kevin, left school two months
ago and now [1]**he's looking** for his first
job. The problem is that companies
always say they want people with
experience, but how can he get
experience if no one gives him a job?
[2]**He reads** the adverts in the paper
every day, but there's nothing for
people like him. Today [3]**he's doing**
some gardening for our neighbours to
earn a bit of money, but [4]**he needs** a
real job.
Mrs J McKenzie
Wolverhampton

Give me a chance

Dear Sir,
I read your report on
unemployment in yesterday's
paper and [5]**I'm writing** to tell
you how it feels to be
unemployed. I'm 54 years old
and I worked for a computer
company for 17 years until it
closed down four months ago.
[6]**I'm applying** for every job I can,
but [7]**I never get** an interview
because [8]**people think** I'm too
old – it's very frustrating. I've got
a lot of experience and I want to
work. I just need someone to give
me a chance.
George Carter
Tipton

Help with Grammar Present Continuous and Present Simple

4 **a)** Look at the verb forms 1–8 in the letters. Which are in the Present Simple and which are in the Present Continuous?

b) Match the verb forms 1–8 to these meanings. There are two verb forms for each meaning.

- We use the **Present Continuous** for things that:
  a) are happening at the moment of speaking. *he's doing*
  b) are temporary and happening around now, but maybe not at the moment of speaking.

- We use the **Present Simple** for:
  a) daily routines and things we always/sometimes/never do.
  b) verbs that describe states (*be, want, have got, think,* etc.).

c) Do these verbs describe activities (A) or states (S)? Do we usually use state verbs in the Present Continuous?

play *A*	like *S*	work	write	hate	eat	know
remember	run	understand	do	believe		

d) How do we make negatives and questions in the Present Simple and Present Continuous?

e) Check in G3.3 p124.

5 R3.5 P Listen and practise.

He's doing some gardening.

6 **a)** Read George's email. What's his new job? How did he get it?

> Hi Andrew!
>
> Guess what? I ¹*'ve got* (have got) a new job! ² _____ you _____ (remember) that letter I wrote to the paper? Well, the manager of a local computer company read it and offered me a job! The company ³_____ (do) very well at the moment and they really ⁴_____ (need) people with experience. I ⁵_____ (not work) now – it's my lunch break – so I ⁶_____ (write) a few emails to my friends to tell them my news. I'm a technical support engineer and I ⁷_____ (help) customers with their computer problems. It's only my first week, so I ⁸_____ (still learn) about all the products, but I really ⁹_____ (like) it here. I ¹⁰_____ (work) quite long days, but I ¹¹_____ (not work) at the weekends. Anyway, I have to go – the phone ¹²_____ (ring).
>
> George

b) Put the verbs in George's email in the Present Simple or Present Continuous.

c) Work in pairs. Compare answers. Explain why you chose each verb form.

7 Work in pairs. Student A → p107. Student B → p115. Follow the instructions.

8 Work in groups. Discuss these questions.

1. Is it more difficult to be unemployed when you're young or when you're older? Why?
2. Is unemployment a problem in your country?
3. Can people in your country get unemployment benefit?
4. What's the best way to find a job?

Get ready ... Get it right!

9 **a)** Choose the correct answers.

> **Find someone who ...**
>
> 1. ... looks /is looking for a job at the moment.
> 2. ... has/is having an interesting job.
> 3. ... studies/is studying for an exam.
> 4. ... usually gets up/is getting up before seven o'clock.
> 5. ... wants/is wanting to live in a different country.
> 6. ... tries/is trying to stop smoking.
> 7. ... reads/is reading a newspaper every day.
> 8. ... reads/is reading a good book at the moment.

b) Make questions with *you* for each sentence.

Are you looking for a job at the moment?

10 **a)** Ask other students your questions. Find one person who answers yes for each question. Then ask two follow-up questions.

b) Work in groups. Tell the other students six things you know about the class.

3C Strange jobs

Vocabulary word building:
noun endings
Skills Listening: a radio interview;
Reading: a magazine article
Help with Listening linking (1):
consonant-vowel
Review present and past verb forms;
have to; *so* and *because*

QUICK REVIEW ●●●

Write the names of three people you know well. Work in pairs. Ask your partner what these people usually do in their free time and what they're doing at the moment.

Listening and Vocabulary

1 **a)** Think of three jobs that you would like to do and three jobs you would hate to do.

b) Work in groups and compare your ideas. Are there any jobs you would all like to do?

> We'd all like to be writers.

2 **a)** Match these words to pictures A–C.

> cream   C   chewing gum   washing-up liquid
> strawberries   The Statue of Liberty
> rubbish   paint   worms   a sausage

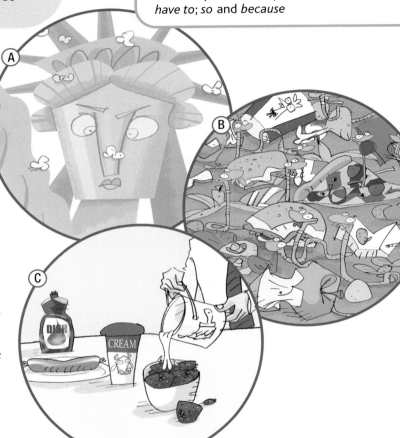

b) **R3.6** Listen to Daniel Ash talking about his new book, *What do you do?*. Put the pictures in order.

c) Listen again. Tick the true sentences. Correct the false sentences.

1 The jobs in the book are from different countries.
2 Brad Fields's company only cleans gum from the Statue of Liberty.
3 Americans chew 56 billion pieces of gum a year.
4 Food stylists take photos of food.
5 They paint sausages with washing-up liquid and coffee.
6 Worm farmers use worms to eat rubbish.

d) Which job do you think is the most unusual?

Help with Listening Linking (1): consonant-vowel

● We usually link words that end in a consonant sound with words that start with a vowel sound.

3 **a)** **R3.6** Listen to the beginning of the interview again. Notice the consonant-vowel linking.

Daniel Ash, your new book is a collection of articles about people with strange jobs.
Yes, I collected stories about unusual jobs from all over the world.

b) Look at R3.6, p147. Listen to the interview again and notice the linking.

Help with Vocabulary
Word building: noun endings

4 **a)** Look at this table. How do we make the nouns? Complete the *ending* column.

verb	noun	ending
collect	collection	*-ion*
act	actor	
assist	assistant	
clean	cleaner	
advertise	advertisement	
paint	paint	

b) Which endings do we use for people's jobs?

TIP! ● We can also make job words by adding *-ist* or *-ian* to nouns: *art* → *artist, music* → *musician*.

c) Check in **V3.3** p123.

5 **a)** Work in pairs. Write all the jobs you know with the endings *-or*, *-ant*, *-er*, *-ist* and *-ian*.

b) Compare lists with another pair. Who has the most?

6 Are these words nouns (N) or verbs (V)? Look at the endings. Which three words can be both a noun and a verb?

decision *N*	examine *V*	cook *N, V*	interviewer
decide	examination	excite	argument	visit
discussion	interview	visitor	guitarist	discuss
excitement	argue	politician	examiner

7 **a)** Choose the correct words.

1 When did you last have an *interview/interviewer* for a job?
2 Have you got a big *collect/collection* of CDs?
3 Do you ever *argue/argument* with your friends?
4 What was the last important *decide/decision* you made?
5 Do you like watching *advertise/advertisements* on TV?
6 What was the last *examine/examination* you took?

b) Work in pairs. Take turns to ask and answer the questions.

Reading

 8 **a)** Do you like circuses? Why?/Why not?

b) Read an interview with Michelle Fossett, a knife thrower's assistant. Fill in gaps a)–f) in the article with questions 1–6.

1 Did you have any accidents in those ten years?
2 How did you meet your knife-throwing partner?
3 Did he say sorry?
4 How did you become a knife thrower's assistant?
5 Which is worse, being the assistant or the thrower?
6 When was your first show together?

c) Read the article again. Complete the sentences.

1 Michelle first assisted her father because her mother ...
2 We know her father was a good knife thrower because he ...
3 Her partner hit her three times because he ...
4 She had to do the next show so she ...
5 Her partner didn't apologise so they ...

d) How many words from 4a) and 6 can you find in the article? Are they nouns or verbs?

9 Work in groups. Student A → p102, Student B → p110, Student C → p118. Follow the instructions.

Report

Someone's got to do it

a) _____

I was born into the circus. My dad was a knife thrower and my mum was his assistant. One day Mum couldn't assist him, so I did. I didn't have to, it was my decision. This was when I was 12. Dad never hit me or my mum – he was very good.

b) _____

I met him at my uncle's circus. He wanted to be a knife thrower and he needed an assistant. We had to practise for hours every day. But it was fantastic to hear our first audience go "Ooh!". The last part of the act was throwing six knives on fire. The audience really loved that.

c) _____

Over ten years ago. And we worked out that, in the first ten years of our act, my partner threw 195,200 knives at me!

d) _____

Yes, when he tried to throw the knives too close together. He hit me three times – in the leg, in the arm and the top of my head! But I couldn't go to the doctor's because I had to do the next show. That's what circus people do – the show must go on.

e) _____

No, he didn't say sorry, but then he never apologises! I got really angry about that and we had a big argument – but after the show, not in front of the audience. That's unprofessional.

f) _____

It's the same. If something goes wrong, we both feel really bad! But I love the excitement. It's wonderful when 500 people are watching me and I'm making them happy.

Adapted from *The Times Magazine* 5/08/00

QUICK REVIEW ● ● ●
Work in pairs. How many nouns can you think of with these endings: *-ion, -or, -ant, -er, -ment, -ist* and *-ian*? Swap lists with another pair. Write verbs for the nouns, if possible.

1 Work in groups. Discuss these questions.

1 Do you prefer working/studying in the morning or the evening? Why?
2 When was the last time you worked/studied late? Why?
3 Do you ever cancel things because you have to work/study?

2 a) **R3.7** Listen and put the pictures in order.

Wayne

Rita

Paul

b) Work in pairs. Who said these sentences?

1 I'm sorry, I couldn't finish it yesterday.
2 I'll do it now and email it to you.
3 I have to take a client out to dinner.
4 I'm really sorry, but I can't see you tonight.
5 I had to help Katie.
6 I'll see you on Friday, I promise.
7 I'll call you at the weekend.

c) Listen again and check.

Real World Apologies, reasons and promises

3 a) Look at the sentences in 2b). Which are: apologies (A), reasons (R), promises (P)?

b) Complete sentences 1–3 with a), b) or c).
a) I'll …
b) I have to/had to …
c) I'm (really) sorry, (but) I can't/couldn't …

1 For apologies we often use ....
2 For reasons we often use ....
3 For promises we often use ....

c) Look again at the sentences in 2b). Which verb form comes after *'ll, can't, couldn't, have to* and *had to*?

d) Fill in the gaps in these responses to apologies.

| time | happened | not |
| worry | right | |

1 Oh, don't .... Another .... , maybe.
2 Oh, dear. What .... ?
3 Oh, ... Why .... ?

e) Check in **RW3.1** p125.

4 Work in pairs. Look at R3.7, p147. Underline all the apologies, reasons and promises.

5 R3.8 P Listen and practise the sentences in 2b).

I'm sorry, I couldn't finish it yesterday.

6 a) Fill in the gaps with 'll, can't, couldn't, have to or had to.

1 Sorry, I _can't_ cook tonight – I .... work late. But I .... cook tomorrow, I promise.
2 I .... phone Anne last night, but I .... call her this evening.
3 I'm sorry I .... come to the meeting yesterday. My son was ill so I .... stay at home.
4 I'm really sorry, but I .... come and see you tomorrow because I .... study for my exam.
5 I .... go to the wedding last weekend because .... I go to a conference.
6 Terry .... come for dinner tonight. He .... fly to Rome on business yesterday evening, but he .... phone you when he gets back.

b) Work in pairs. Compare answers.

7 Work in pairs. Student A → p104. Student B → p112. Follow the instructions.

3 Review
Language Summary 3, p123

1 a) Fill in the missing vowels. V3.1

1 a good s a l a r y
2 f l _ x _ b l _ working hours
3 on-the-job t r _ _ n _ n g
4 job s _ c _ r _ t y
5 s _ c k p _ y
6 l _ n g h _ l _ d _ ys

b) Work in pairs. Think of a job for each phrase in 1a).

2 a) Make these sentences true. Fill in the gaps with the correct form of (not) have to. G3.1

1 Pilots _have to_ pay a lot for their training.
2 London taxi drivers .... have a degree.
3 You .... study for a long time to be a vet.
4 Teachers .... cook lunch for the children.
5 Policemen .... wear special clothes.
6 A waiter .... go to college.

b) Work in pairs. Compare answers.

3 a) Write three true and three false sentences about what you had to do last week.
I had to work on Sunday.

b) Work in pairs. Swap papers. Guess which of your partner's sentences are true. Ask questions to check and then find out more information. G3.2
Did you have to work on Sunday? Yes, I did.
What did you have to do?

4 Match a verb in A to a phrase in B. V3.2

A	B
get	for a job
earn	for a job interview
be	your job
go	lots of money
apply	unemployed
lose	unemployment benefit

5 a) One verb form in each sentence is incorrect. Correct the mistakes. G3.3

'm looking
1 I look for a new job because I need more money.
2 I start work at 8 every day and I'm never finishing before 7.
3 Right now I'm applying for a job and my husband cooks the dinner.
4 He cooks every evening and I'm not thinking that's right!
5 I'm needing to find a job, so I'm writing my CV.

b) Work in pairs. Compare answers. Say why you corrected each verb form.

6 a) Write a noun for each verb. Use an ending if necessary. There is sometimes more than one answer. V3.3

collect	act	advertise
paint	assist	argue	visit
cook	examine	decide

b) Work in pairs. Compare answers. Which of your words are jobs?

Progress Portfolio

a) Tick the things you can do in English.

☐ I can talk about things I like/don't like about jobs.

☐ I can talk about what people have to do in their jobs.

☐ I can say what people are doing now and what they usually do.

☐ I can apologise to people and give reasons.

☐ I can promise to do things.

b) What do you need to study again? ● 3A–D

4 That's entertainment!

 The silver screen

Vocabulary types of film; past participles
Grammar Present Perfect for life experiences (1): positive and negative
Review Past Simple

QUICK REVIEW ●●●

Write three true sentences and three false sentences about what you did last week. Work in pairs. Say your sentences. Your partner guesses which are false.

Vocabulary Types of film

1 Work in groups. Discuss these questions.

1 Who are your favourite film stars?
2 How often do you go to the cinema or rent a video/DVD?
3 Which is better – watching a film in the cinema or on video/DVD? Why?

2 **a)** Work in pairs. Think of an example of these types of film. Check new words in **V4.1** p126.

a love story	a comedy	a cartoon	a war film
a thriller	an action film	a horror film	
a western	a historical drama	a musical	
a science-fiction (sci-fi) film		a romantic comedy	

a love story – 'Casablanca'

b) Work in groups. Compare answers. Then tell the other students what types of film you like and don't like.

3 **a)** Match questions 1–4 with a)–d).

1 What kind of film is it?
2 Who's in it?
3 What's it about?
4 What's it like?

a) the actors
b) the type of film
c) the person's opinion of the film
d) the plot (the story of the film)

b) **R4.1** **P** Listen and practise. Copy the linking.

What kind of film is it?

c) Write the names of the last film you saw: on TV, on video/DVD, in the cinema. Work in pairs. Ask your partner the questions in **3a)**.

> What was the last film you saw on TV?

> *Dawn of the Dead.*

> What kind of film is it?

> It's a horror film.

Reading and Grammar

4 **a)** What do you know about the Star Wars films? Talk about these things.

- type of film
- the director
- human characters
- robots and aliens
- plot
- actors

b) Read the article about Todd Philips. Find four things that tell you he is a big Star Wars fan.

5 Read the article again. Answer these questions.

1 When did Todd first see the movie *Star Wars*?
2 Where did he meet his wife?
3 What was unusual about his wedding?
4 How long did he queue for in order to see *Attack of the Clones*?
5 Why does he like the Star Wars films?
6 When did he meet Ewan McGregor?

FEEL THE FORCE!

On May 25th 1977, seven-year-old Todd Philips went to see the movie *Star Wars* for the first time. Now Todd is the president of the California Star Wars Society and is probably the biggest Star Wars fan in the world. He's written hundreds of newspaper articles about the films and he's been to Star Wars conferences all over the world. Todd met his wife, Holly, at a Star Wars party in 1994 and at their wedding everybody looked like Star Wars characters! And in January 2002 Todd started queuing to see *Star Wars Episode 2: Attack of the Clones* – four months before the film opened!

Help with Grammar Present Perfect for life experiences (1): positive and negative

6 **a)** Look at these sentences. Then choose the correct verb form in the rules.

Present Perfect	He's **been** to Star Wars conferences all over the world.
Past Simple	He **met** his wife, Holly, in 1994.

- We use the *Present Perfect/Past Simple* for experiences that happened some time before now. We don't know or don't say when they happened.

- We use the *Present Perfect/Past Simple* if we say exactly when something happened.

b) Fill in the gaps for the Present Perfect with *'ve*, *haven't*, *'s* or *hasn't*.

POSITIVE
I/you/we/they + ... (= *have*) + past participle
he/she/it + ... (= *has*) + past participle

NEGATIVE
I/you/we/they + ... + past participle
he/she/it + ... + past participle

c) How do we make past participles of regular verbs? Is there a rule for past participles of irregular verbs?

d) Check in G4.1 p127.

7 **a)** Look at the article again. Find four examples of the Present Perfect and four examples of the Past Simple.

b) Compare answers with a partner. When did the Past Simple examples happen?

"I love the films because they're about the battle between good and evil," says Todd. "They have everything – action, comedy, romance and amazing special effects. And you can watch them again and again. I've seen the first film over a hundred times!"

Todd has also met some of the actors. "Last year I met Ewan McGregor and I've also had dinner with Harrison Ford," says Todd. "But I haven't met George Lucas, the director. One day I'd like to buy him a drink and thank him for all the happiness he's given me."

8 **a)** Write the Past Simple and the past participle of these irregular verbs. Check in the Irregular Verb List, p159.

be *was/were, been*	give	go	have	hear
make	meet	read	see	take	win	write

b) R4.2 P Listen and practise.
be, was/were, been

9 Read about the actor, Ewan McGregor. Put the verbs in the correct form of the Present Perfect or Past Simple.

http://www.actorprofiles.co.uk/ewanmcgregor

EWAN McGREGOR

Ewan McGregor [1] _was_ (be) born in Scotland in 1971. He [2] _____ (decide) to be an actor when he was only nine and he [3] _____ (make) his first film in 1992. So far in his career he [4] _____ (appear) in a lot of different types of film, including comedies, musicals, dramas and the Star Wars movies. His uncle, Denis Lawson, [5] _____ (be) in the original *Star Wars* in 1977 and McGregor [6] _____ (star) in his first Star Wars movie 22 years later. In his career Ewan [7] _____ (work) with actresses like Cameron Diaz and Nicole Kidman, and his films [8] _____ (win) lots of awards. He loves acting and when he [9] _____ (finish) filming the musical, *Moulin Rouge*, he said, "I [10] _____ (never be) happier to do anything in my life."

Get ready ... Get it right!

10 On six pieces of paper write three interesting things you have done in your life and three things you haven't done but would like to do. Use verbs from 8a) or your own ideas.

I've been to South Africa.
I haven't seen any Star Wars films.

11 **a)** Work in groups of six. Put all your sentences in a bag. Take turns to choose a sentence and read it to the group. The other students guess who wrote it.

b) Take turns to tell the group when your three interesting things happened and ask follow-up questions to find out more information.

I went to South Africa in 2002.

What did you do there?

4B The rhythm of life

Vocabulary music
Grammar Present Perfect for life experiences (2): questions with *ever*
Help with Listening linking (2): /w/ sounds
Review Present Perfect positive and negative; Past Simple

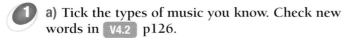

QUICK REVIEW ●●●
Write eight verbs. What is the Past Simple and past participle of each verb? Work in pairs. Test each other on the verbs: A *see*. B *saw, seen*.

Vocabulary Music

1 **a)** Tick the types of music you know. Check new words in **V4.2** p126.

jazz	clássical music	blues	róck music	rap
coúntry music	ópera	póp music	rock'n'róll	
dánce music	traditional fólk music	réggae		

b) Answer these questions.

1 What types of music do/don't you like?
2 Who are your favourite bands/singers/composers?
3 What were the last two CDs you bought?
4 What was the last concert you went to?

c) Work in groups. Compare answers. Do you like the same music?

Listening and Grammar

2 **a)** Look at photos 1–3. Which is: a) a jazz concert? b) a club? c) a rock festival? Which would you like to go to?

b) **R4.3** Scott and Julie are talking about their musical experiences. What types of music do they like?

3 **a)** Work in pairs. Fill in the gaps with *Scott* or *Julie*.

1 .... has been to lots of rock festivals.
2 .... has never seen U2 in concert.
3 .... hasn't been to a classical concert.
4 .... has been to hundreds of jazz concerts.
5 .... has never heard of Miles Davis.
6 .... hasn't heard of Radiohead.

b) **R4.3** Listen again and check.

4 **a)** Look at the beginning of the conversation. Which verb forms did Scott and Julie say?

SCOTT *Did you ever go/Have you ever been* to a rock festival?
JULIE Yes, I *did/have*. I *went/have been* to lots, actually. The last one *was/has been* in Germany.
SCOTT Oh, right. Who *did you see/have you seen* there?
JULIE *I saw/I've seen* David Bowie and U2. They *were/have been* great!

b) **R4.3** Listen again and check.

1

Help with Grammar Present Perfect for life experiences (2): questions with *ever*

5 **a)** Look again at **4a)**. Then complete the rules with *Present Perfect* or *Past Simple*.

● We use the .... to ask about people's experiences. We don't ask when these experiences happened.

● We use the .... to ask for more information about these experiences.

b) Fill in the gaps in the table with *Have, Has, seen* or *ever*.

auxiliary	subject	ever	past participle	
Have	you		been	to a rock festival?
	they	ever		U2 in concert?
	Julie		heard	of Miles Davis?

TIP! ● *ever* + Present Perfect = any time in your life until now.

c) Write the positive and negative short answers for the questions in the table.

d) Check in **G4.2** p127.

(2)

(3)

6 R4.4 **P** Listen and practise.

Have you ever been to a rock festival?

7 **a)** Put the verbs in brackets in the Present Perfect or Past Simple.

1

JULIE .... you ever .... anyone famous? (meet)

SCOTT Yes, I .... , actually. When I .... in Mexico on vacation. (be)

JULIE Really? Who .... you .... ? (meet)

SCOTT Mick Jagger. He .... in the same restaurant as me. (be)

2

SCOTT .... your mother ever .... to a rock concert? (go)

JULIE Yes, she .... She .... to one or two when she was young. (go)

SCOTT Who .... she .... ? (see)

JULIE Well, I know she .... David Bowie before he .... famous. (see, become)

3

SCOTT .... you ever .... to play an instrument? (learn)

JULIE No, I .... What about you?

SCOTT Well, I .... to learn the piano at school. (try)

JULIE .... you any good? (be)

SCOTT No, I .... no idea what I was doing! (have)

b) R4.5 Listen and check.

Help with Listening Linking (2): /w/ sounds

- When a word ends with an /uː/ or /əʊ/ sound and the next word starts with a vowel sound, we often link them with a /w/ sound.

8 **a)** R4.5 Listen again to the conversations in **7a)**. Notice the linking /w/ sounds.

Have you‿/w/‿ever met anyone famous?

Yes, I have, actually. When I was in Mexico‿/w/‿on vacation.

b) Look at R4.5, p148. Listen again and notice the linking /w/ sounds.

9 **a)** Choose three experiences from A and three from B. Then write six *Have you ever ... ?* questions.

A	B
learn to play an instrument	miss a plane
go to a jazz or classical concert	spend more than €1,000 in one day
have dancing or singing lessons	see a film more than five times
be in a band or an orchestra	do yoga, judo or aerobics
go to the opera or the ballet	stay in a five-star hotel

b) Work in pairs, but don't talk to your partner. Guess your partner's answers to your questions.

c) Take turns to ask and answer your questions. Ask follow-up questions if possible. How many of your guesses were correct?

Have you ever ... ?

Yes, I have.

Yes, once/twice/lots of times.

No, I haven't./No, never.

When did you ... ?

Who ... ?

Where were you ... ?

Get ready ... Get it right!

10 Work in pairs. Student A → page 109. Student B → page 117. Follow the instructions.

Vocabulary TV nouns and verbs; *-ed* and *-ing* adjectives
Skills Reading and Listening: a magazine quiz; Reading: a newspaper article
Help with Listening linking (3): /r/ and /j/ sounds
Review Present Perfect; Past Simple

VOCABULARY AND SKILLS

QUICK REVIEW ●●●
Think of four interesting places in the town/city you are in now. Work in pairs. Ask your partner if he/she has ever been there. If yes, ask follow-up questions.

Vocabulary
TV nouns and verbs

1 a) Put these words into three groups.

cable or satellite TV
the news   turn on
chat shows   soap operas
documentaries
reality TV programmes
a DVD player   game shows
record a programme
current affairs programmes
dramas   the remote control
turn off   turn over
sports programmes
a video recorder [US: a VCR]

1 TV equipment
   cable or satellite TV
2 TV programmes
   the news
3 TV verbs
   turn on

b) Check in **V4.3** p126.

2 Work in groups. Ask and answer these questions. Use the words in **1a)** in your answers.

1 What TV equipment have you got in your home?
2 Which types of TV programme are popular in your country? Which aren't very popular?
3 Which types of TV programme do you like? Which don't you like?
4 What did you watch last night/last week?

Are you a telly addict?

	you	your partner	Toby
1 Do you watch TV for more than twenty hours a week?			
2 Have you ever watched TV all night?			
3 Do you ever work or study with the TV on?			
4 Have you got a TV in your bedroom or the kitchen?			
5 Do you always have to have the remote control?			
6 Do you sometimes have dinner in front of the TV?			
7 Do you know exactly when all your favourite programmes are on?			
8 Have you ever missed something important because you wanted to watch TV?			

Reading and Listening

3 a) Do the quiz. Put a tick (✓) or a cross (✗) in the *you* column.

b) Work in pairs. Take turns to ask and answer the questions in the quiz. Put a tick or a cross in the *your partner* column. Look at p158. Are you and your partner telly addicts?

4 **R4.6** Jo and Toby are flatmates. Listen to Toby's answers to the quiz and put a tick or a cross in the *Toby* column. How many ticks did he get?

Help with Listening Linking (3): /r/ and /j/ sounds

● When a word ends with an /ə/, /ɜː/, /ɔː/, or /eə/ sound and the next word starts with a vowel sound, we often link them with a /r/ sound.

● When a word ends with an /i/, /iː/ or /aɪ/ sound and the next word starts with a vowel sound, we often link them with a /j/ sound.

5 a) **R4.6** Listen to the beginning of the conversation again and notice the linking sounds.

Where_/r/_are my glasses?   They're_/r/_over there_/r/_on the table.
Hey, here's a quiz for you. It's about telly_/j/_addicts.

b) Look at R4.6, p148. Listen to the conversation again and notice the linking sounds /r/, /j/ and /w/.

Reading

 6 **a)** Work in pairs. Guess the answers to these questions. Don't read the newspaper article.

1 How much TV does an American family watch every day?
2 Who watches more TV in the UK, men or women?
3 How many murders do American children see on TV before they are 18?
4 How many adverts do they see every year?
5 What is TV Turnoff Week, do you think?

b) Read the article and answer the questions. Were your guesses correct?

Kill your TV!

Could you live without television for a week? That's what millions of people do every April as part of TV Turnoff Week, which is organised by anti-television groups like NoTV.com and White Dot.

"Sure, TV can sometimes be fun and exciting, especially when you're tired at the end of the day," says Rudy Matthews from NoTV.com, "but most of the time it's just boring. We want people to turn off the TV for a week and do something more interesting instead."

You may be surprised how much television we watch. The average American family watches TV for 7 hours and 40 minutes every day and British men watch 27 hours a week (British women watch 'only' 24 hours). This means we spend over ten years of our life watching TV – what a frightening thought!

Many people are worried about how much TV children watch. Every American child sees 16,000 murders on TV before he or she is 18, and 20,000 adverts every year. Teacher Susan Walsh thinks this is a problem. "Children in the USA spend more time watching TV than in school and that's very worrying."

TV Turnoff Week started in the USA in 1995 and now happens every year in the UK, France, Holland and Australia. More than 25 million people have turned off their TV, so why don't you do the same?

 7 Work in groups. Discuss these questions.

1 Is watching too much TV a problem in your country, do you think? Why?/Why not?
2 How much TV do children watch? Who decides what to watch – the child or the parent?
3 Would you like to live without TV for a week? Why?/Why not?

Help with Vocabulary *-ed* and *-ing* adjectives

 8 **a)** Look at these two sentences. Then choose *-ed* or *-ing* in the rules.

*TV can sometimes be fun and excit**ing**.*
*Many people are worri**ed** about how much TV children watch.*

- We use *-ed/-ing* adjectives to describe how people feel.
- We use *-ed/-ing* adjectives to describe the thing, situation, place or person that causes the feeling.

b) Check in V4.4 p127.

 **9** **a)** Find all the *-ed* or *-ing* adjectives in the article.

b) Which of these *-ed* endings are pronounced /ɪd/, do you think?

| excited | worried | surprised | tired |
| frightened | bored | interested |

c) R4.7 Listen and check.

d) R4.8 P Listen and practise the *-ed/-ing* adjectives.

 10 **a)** Choose the correct words.

1 Were you *surprised/surprising* by anything in the article?
2 Which TV programmes do you think are *bored/boring*?
3 What's the most *frightened/frightening* film you've ever seen?
4 When was the last time you were really *tired/tiring*?
5 What's the most *excited/exciting* holiday you've ever had?
6 What are you *interested/interesting* in?

b) Work in pairs. Take turns to ask and answer the questions. Ask follow-up questions if possible.

c) Tell the class two things you found out about your partner.

4D What do you think?

Real World agreeing, disagreeing and asking for opinions
Review TV vocabulary; Present Simple

QUICK REVIEW ● ● ●
Write words/phrases for these headings: TV equipment, TV verbs, TV programmes. Compare lists with a partner. Find three types of programme you both like.

Penny Little Jackie Nash Stuart Downs Mr Davis

1 Work in groups. Discuss these questions.

1 Did you have to pay for your school/university education? If yes, who paid?
2 Do you think people should pay for education? Why?/Why not?

2 a) **R4.9** Look at the picture and listen to the beginning of the TV programme. Then answer the questions.

1 Who is a student?
2 Who is a politician?
3 Who works in a university?
4 What question does Mr Davis ask?
5 What kind of programme is it?

b) R4.10 Listen to the TV programme. Which people in the picture think that university education should be free?

c) Listen again. Are these sentences true or false?

1 Stuart thinks universities need more money.
2 Stuart and Penny had to pay to go to university.
3 There were more university students 20 years ago.
4 Jackie thinks the government spends money on the wrong things.
5 Mr Davis went to university.

Real World Agreeing, disagreeing and asking for opinions

3 a) Look at these phrases. Are they ways of: a) agreeing? b) disagreeing? c) asking for opinions?

1 What do you think? c)
2 I'm sorry, I don't agree.
3 I'm not sure about that.
4 Yes, maybe you're right.
5 What about you, (Jackie)?
6 Do you think ... ?
7 No, definitely not.
8 Yes, definitely.
9 I agree (with Jackie).
10 Do you agree (with that)?
11 Yes, I think so.
12 No, I don't think so.

b) Check in **RW4.1** p127.

4 Look at R4.10, p148. Find all the phrases for agreeing, disagreeing and asking for opinions.

5 R4.11 P Listen and practise the phrases in 3a).

What do you think?

6 a) Look at these sentences. Think of reasons why you agree or disagree with them.

1 School holidays are too long.
2 All children should do sport at school.
3 Schools only for boys or only for girls are a bad idea.
4 Boys should learn to cook at school.
5 Exams are the best way to find out what students know.
6 All children should stay at school until they are 18.

b) Work in pairs. Take turns to ask your partner for his/her opinion on the sentences in 6a). Respond with phrases from 3a). Continue the conversation if possible.

> Do you think school holidays are too long?

> Yes, definitely. They should be much shorter. What do you think?

> I'm not sure about that. I think …

7 Work in groups. Student A → p105. Student B → p113. Student C → p118. Follow the instructions.

4 Review Language Summary 4, p126

1 a) Find ten types of film. V4.1

```
L O V E S T O R Y H
J U T R C B O N W O
C M U S I C A L E R
A F V E F W Q U S R
R O P G I B L S T O
T W A R F I L M E R
O T H R I L L E R F
O G M O L H U I N I
N Z C O M E D Y R L
A C T I O N F I L M
```

b) Tell your partner about your favourite film of all time. Ask follow-up questions.

A *My favourite film is 'Twins'.*
B *What kind of film is it?*

2 a) Use these verbs in the Present Perfect to make the sentences true for you. G4.1

go climb act
cook see go

1 I *haven't been* to a lot of countries.
2 I _____ a lot of films in English.
3 I _____ on a boat or a ship.
4 I _____ a mountain.
5 I _____ dinner for more than ten people.
6 I _____ in a play.

b) Work in pairs. Compare sentences. Ask follow-up questions if possible.

c) Work with a different student. Tell him/her about your first partner.

3 a) Join these pieces of paper to make six types of music. V4.2

ro ck
class nce ues ja
p reg bl gae op
da zz ical

b) Work in pairs. Talk about the music/musicians your family and friends like and don't like.

4 a) Write the name of your favourite: sport, city, food, free time activity, TV programme, restaurant.

b) Make questions with *Have you ever … ?* about the things on your list. G4.2

Have you ever played golf?

c) Work in pairs. Take turns to ask and answer the questions. Ask follow-up questions if possible.

5 a) Complete the adjectives with *-ed, -ied,* or *-ing*. Then tick the sentences that are true for you. V4.4

1 Most TV programmes are very interest_____ .
2 I'm worr_____ about children watching too much TV.
3 I think listening to the radio is bor_____ .
4 I've never been frighten_____ at the cinema.
5 I'm really interest_____ in art.

b) Work in pairs. Did you tick the same sentences?

Progress Portfolio

a) Tick the things you can do in English.

☐ I can talk about different types of film, music and TV programme.

☐ I can talk about my experiences and give more details about when they happened.

☐ I can ask other people about their experiences.

☐ I can ask for opinions and agree or disagree with other people.

b) What do you need to study again? 4A–D

5 Into the future

5A Man or machine?

Vocabulary verb-noun collocations (1)
Grammar *will* for prediction; *might*;
will be able to
Help with Listening *'ll* and *won't*
Review *Have you ever ... ?*

QUICK REVIEW ●●●
Work in pairs. Ask *Have you ever ... ?*
questions and find five things
you've done in your life that your
partner hasn't done.

Vocabulary
Verb-noun collocations (1)

1 Work in groups. Discuss
these questions.

1 Which invention was the
most important, do you think:
TV, cars or computers? Why?
2 Have you seen any films with
robots in? What were they
about? Did you like them?
3 Would you like to have
a robot? Why?/Why not?

2 **a)** Match the verbs in A to the
words/phrases in B. Check in
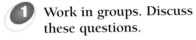 p128.

A	B
look after	someone's face
build	old people
recognise	cars
take over	someone
look like	easily
move around	the world
do	the carpets
feed	the cat
clean	the housework

b) Write another word/phrase
for each verb in A in **2a)**.

look after a pet

c) Work in pairs. Which of the
things in **2a)** can robots do
now, do you think?

Listening and Grammar

3 **a)**  Listen to an interview with
Dr Dylan Evans, a robotics expert.
Tick the things he talks about.

- things robots can do now
- robots and sport
- intelligent robots
- his own robots
- robots in the home
- robots in 2020
- robot toys for children
- robot animals
- robots on TV

b) Listen again. Which of these
sentences does Dr Evans think
are true?

1 At the moment robots can
move around easily.
2 By 2020 robots will be able
to walk and run.
3 By 2050 robots might win the
football World Cup.
4 Not many people will have
robots in their homes.
5 Domestic robots won't
look like humans.
6 Robots will take over
the world.

c) Work in pairs. Were your
guesses in **2c)** correct?

Dr Dylan Evans

Help with Grammar *will* for prediction; *might*; *will be able to*

4 **a)** Look at sentences 3–6 in **3b**). Then answer the questions.

1 Do we use *will* to predict the future or talk about personal plans?
2 Which verb form comes after *will*?
3 What's the negative form of *will*?
4 Which verb do we use to say *will possibly*?

b) Make questions with these words. What are the positive and negative short answers to these questions?

1 humans / domestic robots / Will / look like ?
2 robots / the world / take over / will / Do you think ?

c) Look at sentences 1 and 2 in **3b**). Then answer the questions.

1 How do we talk about ability in: a) the present? b) the future?
2 Which verb form comes after *will be able to*?

d) Check in **G5.1** p128.

5 **a)** Look at these ideas about the year 2020. Write sentences you think are true.

b) Work in groups. Compare sentences. Give reasons for your ideas if possible.

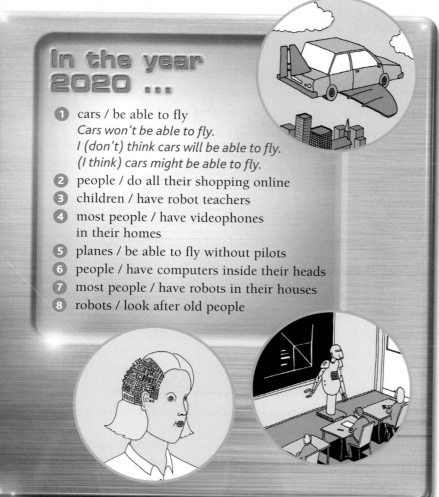

In the year 2020 …

1 cars / be able to fly
Cars won't be able to fly.
I (don't) think cars will be able to fly.
(I think) cars might be able to fly.
2 people / do all their shopping online
3 children / have robot teachers
4 most people / have videophones in their homes
5 planes / be able to fly without pilots
6 people / have computers inside their heads
7 most people / have robots in their houses
8 robots / look after old people

Help with Listening *'ll* and *won't*

6 **a)** **R5.2** Listen to how we say these phrases. Notice the difference.

1	I stay	I'll stay
2	you have	you'll have
3	we go	we'll go
4	they have	they'll have
5	I want	I won't

b) **R5.3** Listen to these sentences. Circle the words you hear.

1 *I/I'll* stay at home all day.
2 *They/They'll* have their own lives.
3 *We/We'll* have two children.
4 *I/I'll* speak English fluently.
5 *We want to/We won't* be in England.
6 *I want to/I won't* have children.

7 **a)** **R5.4** Listen to four conversations about life in the year 2020. Match conversations 1–4 to the things they talk about a)–d).

a) work and studies
b) living abroad
c) his/her future family
d) age and appearance

b) Listen again. Make notes on what each person says.

c) Work in pairs. Compare notes.

d) Look at R5.4, p149. Listen again and find all the examples of *will*, *won't*, *might* and *be able to*.

8 **R5.5** **P** Listen and practise.

I'll /aɪl/ stay at home all day.

9 **a)** Make five sentences with *will*, *won't* or *might* about you or your family's life in 2020.

b) Work in groups. Compare sentences. Are any the same?

Get ready …
Get it right!

10 Work in pairs. Student A → p105. Student B → p113. Follow the instructions.

5B Never too old

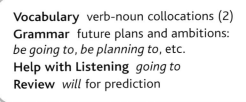

Vocabulary verb-noun collocations (2)
Grammar future plans and ambitions:
be going to, be planning to, etc.
Help with Listening *going to*
Review *will* for prediction

QUICK REVIEW ●●●
Make five sentences with *will, won't* or *might*
about your life in three years' time. Work in threes.
Compare sentences. Are any the same?

Vocabulary and Grammar

1 Work in groups. Answer the
questions.

1 At what age do people usually
retire in your country?
2 Do you know anyone who
is retired? How do they spend
their time?
3 What's the best and worst
thing about being retired, do
you think?

2 Choose the correct verbs in these
phrases. Check in V5.2 p128.

1 (have)/*spend* a great time
2 *spend/give* time doing (something)
3 *make/do* a degree (in biology)
4 *take/spend* time with (someone)
5 *live/leave* abroad
6 *take/make* photos
7 *learn/want* how to do (something)
8 *get/do* a suntan

3 a) Read these people's plans for
when they retire. Match them to
photos A–C.

1 I'm going to retire next year.
I'm looking forward to spending
more time doing the things
I enjoy. And I'm thinking of
doing a degree in history of art.

2 I'm planning to retire early,
before I'm 50. I'm not going to
work after that. Then I'd like
to live abroad.

3 We're going to drive around
Australia. We're hoping to spend
about a year travelling and we're
really looking forward to it.
I'm sure we'll have a great time.

b) R5.6 Listen and check.

Rick

Kelly and Greg

Help with Grammar Future plans and ambitions

4 **a)** Look at these sentences. Then answer questions 1–4.

We're going to drive around Australia.
I'm sure we'll have a great time.

1 Do both sentences talk about the future?
2 Which is a prediction?
3 Which is a plan?
4 Which verb form comes after *be going to*?

b) How do we make negatives and questions with *be going to*?

c) Check in G5.2 p129.

5 **a)** Find these phrases in 3a). Which verb form comes after each
phrase: the *infinitive with to* or *verb+ing*?

1 I'm planning ... *infinitive with to*
2 We're hoping ...
3 I'm looking forward to ...
4 I'd like ...
5 I'm thinking of ...

b) Answer these questions.

1 Which phrase in **5a)** means: *I'm excited about this and I'm going to
enjoy it when it happens*?
2 Which is more certain: *I'm planning to ...* or *I'm thinking of ...* ?
3 Which is less certain: *I'm going to ...* or *I'm hoping to ...* ?

c) Check in G5.3 p129.

C

Joyce

6 **a)** Complete paragraphs 1–3 with the correct form of the verbs in the boxes. Which people in photos A–C said them, do you think?

~~buy~~ write take drive

1 We're going to a) *buy* a camper van and b)_____ across the desert. Kelly's thinking of c)_____ a book about our journey and I'm going to d)_____ lots of photographs.

go spend learn visit

2 I'm also hoping to a)_____ Italian. I'd like to b)_____ to Italy one day and c)_____ all their wonderful art galleries. And I'm looking forward to d)_____ more time with my grandchildren.

spend learn get go

3 I'm planning to a)_____ and live somewhere hot, like the Caribbean. I'm really looking forward to b)_____ every day at the beach and c)_____ a suntan, and I'd like to d)_____ how to dive.

b) R5.7 Listen and check.

7 R5.8 P Listen and practise.
bŭy a cǎmper vǎn → We're gŏing to /ɡəʊɪŋtə/ bŭy a cǎmper vǎn.

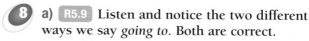

Help with Listening *going to*

8 **a)** R5.9 Listen and notice the two different ways we say *going to*. Both are correct.

a) I'm going to /ɡəʊɪŋtə/ retire next year.
b) We're going to /ɡʌnə/ drive around Australia.

b) R5.10 Listen to these people's sentences. Do you hear: a) /ɡəʊɪŋtə/ or b) /ɡʌnə/?

1 I'm not going to work after that. *b)*
2 We're going to buy a camper van.
3 I'm going to write a book.
4 When are you going to retire?
5 He's going to live abroad.
6 We're going to have a great time.

9 **a)** Write six sentences about your plans and ambitions. Use *be going to* and phrases from 5a).
I'm going to study history next year.
I'm thinking of buying a car in the next few weeks.

b) Work in groups. Talk about your plans and ambitions. Which are the most unusual?

Get ready ... Get it right!

10 Look at these possible plans and ambitions. Make *yes/no* questions with *you*.

Find someone who ...

... is going to visit friends next month.
Are you going to visit friends next month?
... would like to live in a different country.
... is planning to move house.
... is looking forward to something special.
... is thinking of changing their job or course.
... is going to take an exam this year.
... would like to write a book.
... is hoping to retire early.

January 24

11 **a)** Ask other students your questions. Find one person who is going to do each thing. Then ask two follow-up questions.

b) Work in groups. Tell the group about three people who have similar plans and ambitions to you.

5C Out of this world

Vocabulary verbs and prepositions
Skills Reading: a magazine article;
Listening: a radio interview
Help with Listening linking: review (1)
Review *will* for prediction; past verb forms

QUICK REVIEW ●●●
Write one thing you are: looking forward to, going to do next week, hoping to do next year, thinking of doing tonight, planning to do next month. Compare answers in pairs. Which is the most interesting?

Reading and Vocabulary

1 Work in groups. Discuss these questions.

1 Would you like to go on holiday in space? Why?/Why not?
2 What are the two best and the two worst things about a space holiday, do you think?

2 **a)** You are going to read about space holidays. Check these words with your teacher or in a dictionary.

a rocket	a spaceship	Earth	tourism
a trip	circular	a screen	revolve

b) Read the article about space holidays. Match headings a)–d) to paragraphs 1–4.

a) Space hotels
b) Going to the moon
c) The future of tourism
d) The first space tourists

3 **a)** Read the article again. Then answer these questions.

1 Who are these people?
   a) Dennis Tito
   b) Mark Shuttleworth
   c) Eric Anderson
   d) Gene Meyers

2 Which company is thinking of doing these things?
   a) building a hotel in space
   b) flying tourists to the moon
   c) building a hotel on the moon
   d) taking tourists on rocket trips

3 Find these numbers in the article. What do they describe?
   a) $20 million
   b) $100,000
   c) $25,000
   d) $500 million

b) Which facts in the article do you think are surprising?

Get away from it all!

1 _____

In 2001 an American, Dennis Tito, became the world's first space tourist. He **travelled** to the International Space Station by rocket and stayed there for ten days. A year later South African millionaire, Mark Shuttleworth, **went** on the same trip. When he **returned** to Earth he said, "Every second will be with me for the rest of my life." Both men **paid** $20 million for their holidays.

2 _____

The company that organised their trips is called Space Adventures. Its president, Eric Anderson, thinks space tourism will be the next big thing. "Everyone's **looking** for a new experience," he says. In a few years he's going to start **selling** rocket trips to the public for about $100,000.

Help with Vocabulary Verbs and prepositions

4 **a)** Verbs and prepositions often go together. Find these verbs in the article. Then fill in the gaps with the correct prepositions.

1 **travel** _to_ a place _by_ a method of transport
2 **go** _____ a trip
3 **return** _____ the place you started
4 **pay** an amount of money _____ something
5 **look** _____ something you want to find
6 **sell** something _____ people _____ an amount of money
7 **look** _____ _____ a window
8 **spend** an amount of money _____ something
9 **fly** _____ a place
10 **talk** _____ a topic

b) Check in **V5.3** p128.

Listening

 a) How many planets are there in our solar system? Do you know their names in English?

b) Work in pairs. Do the quiz.

Mars: The Red Planet

1 What's the temperature like on Mars?
a) Very hot.
b) The same as on Earth.
c) Very cold.

2 Which planet is nearer to the Sun?
a) Mars.
b) Earth.

3 Is Mars bigger than Earth?
a) Yes, it is.
b) It's the same size.
c) No, it's smaller.

4 Is there oxygen on Mars?
a) Yes, there is.
b) No, there isn't.
c) We don't know.

5 Is there water on Mars?
a) Yes, definitely.
b) Maybe.
c) No, definitely not.

6 Is there life on Mars?
a) Yes, definitely.
b) Maybe.
c) No, definitely not.

3 _____

Another company, The Space Island Group, is planning to build a circular hotel in space, like the spaceship in the film *2001: A Space Odyssey*. It will have everything a normal hotel has, except that the bedrooms won't have windows. This is because the hotel will revolve and people will feel sick if they **look** out of a window. Instead there will be screens showing pictures from space. Gene Meyers, the company's president, thinks that in 2020 a five-day holiday at the hotel might cost only $25,000.

4 _____

Other companies have even bigger plans. Bigelow Aerospace is **spending** $500 million on a plan to build a 700-metre spaceship to **fly** tourists to the moon. There will be 100 tourists on each trip and each person will have a private room with a view of the Earth's sunset. The Hilton Hotel Group have even **talked** about building a hotel on the moon.

At the moment only millionaires can go on holiday in space. But one day you might be able to go there yourself – and it could be sooner than you think!

 a) R5.11 Listen to an interview with Mars expert, Anthony Shuster. Check your answers to the quiz.

b) Listen again. Are these sentences true or false?

1 Anthony has written a book about Mars.
2 Mars is 78 million kilometres from the Sun.
3 In the 1970s scientists thought there was life on Mars.
4 Photographs show that there is water on Mars.
5 Anthony thinks we will see men on Mars in the future.

Help with Listening Linking: review (1)

 a) Look at this sentence. Why do we link these words?

Now joining Martina ~/r/~ and me ~/j/~ in the studio ~/w/~ is Anthony Shuster, who's written a new book on Mars called The Red Planet.

b) R5.11 Look at R5.11, p149. Listen again and notice the linking.

9 Work in groups. Discuss these questions.

1 Do you think it's a good idea to spend money on a space programme? Why?/Why not?
2 Imagine you're going on a space holiday. You can take three personal possessions. What are they?

10 Look at p118. Follow the instructions.

5 **a)** Fill in the gaps with the correct form of the verbs in brackets and the correct prepositions.

1 What was the last place you *flew* (fly) *to* ?
2 What do you and your friends usually _____ (talk) _____ ?
3 How much do you usually _____ (spend) _____ food a week?
4 Have you ever _____ (sell) anything _____ a friend?
5 Do you know anyone who _____ (look) _____ a place to live at the moment?
6 How do you normally _____ (pay) _____ meals in a restaurant?
7 What do you see when you _____ (look) _____ your bedroom window?

b) Work in pairs. Take turns to ask and answer the questions. Continue the conversation if possible.

5D It's for charity

Real World offers,
suggestions and requests
Review *be going to*

QUICK REVIEW ●●●

Work in pairs. Take turns to ask and answer *yes/no* questions with *be going to* about next weekend: *Are you going to eat out?* Find five things you're both going to do.

1 Work in groups. Discuss these questions.

1 Which is the biggest charity organisation in your country?
2 Have you (or someone you know) ever raised money for a charity? If yes, what did you/they do?
3 What do you think the British charity, Children in Need, does?

2 **a)** R5.12 Listen to some people planning an event for Children in Need. Which of these events are they planning?

> a concert   a disco   a quiz night   a karaoke night

b) Listen again. Tick the things they plan to do.

- make tickets
- make posters
- put up posters
- have a live band
- put an advert in the paper
- buy food and drink
- write quiz questions
- hire a karaoke machine

Real World Offers, suggestions and requests

3 **a)** Write these headings in the correct places a)–d) in the table.

> making suggestions   making requests
> making offers   responding to offers

a) _____	b) _____
Shall I make some posters? **Can I** give you a hand? **I'll** help you, if you like.	Yes, that'd be great. Great, thanks a lot. Yes, why not? No, don't worry. Thanks anyway.
c) _____	d) _____
Will you organise that? **Could you** give me a hand? **Can you** do that?	**Shall we** start? **Let's** decide who does what. **Why don't we** ask Steve?

b) Which verb form comes after the phrases in **bold**?

c) Check in RW5.1 p129.

4 Look at R5.12, p149. Read the conversation and find all the suggestions, requests, offers and responses.

5 R5.13 P Listen and practise the sentences in 3a). Copy the intonation.

Shall I make some posters?

6 **a)** Fill in the gaps with the phrases in the boxes.

> ~~Shall we~~   thanks   Could you
> why don't   why not   I'll

JANET   ¹ *Shall we* put some posters up in the library?
KIM   Yes, ² _____ ?
JANET   And ³ _____ we tell the local paper about the event?
KIM   That's a good idea. ⁴ _____ organise that?
JANET   Yes, of course. ⁵ _____ call them tomorrow.
KIM   Great, ⁶ _____ a lot.

> ~~can you~~   don't worry   that'd be
> Shall I   Let's   Can I

RAY   Steve, ⁷ *can you* play at our charity event?
STEVE   Yes, of course. ⁸ _____ bring some CDs too?
RAY   Yes, ⁹ _____ great. Thanks.
STEVE   ¹⁰ _____ give you a hand with anything else?
RAY   No, ¹¹ _____ . Thanks anyway.
STEVE   Right. ¹² _____ choose some CDs.

b) R5.14 Listen and check. Then work in pairs. Practise the conversations.

5 Review

Language Summary 5, p128

1 **a)** Write two things that go with these verbs: *do, recognise, look after, clean, feed, build.* V5.1

do the housework
do your homework

b) Work in pairs. Compare answers.

2 **a)** Write one thing you think: <u>will</u> happen, <u>might</u> happen and <u>won't</u> happen before the year 3000. G5.1

b) Work in groups. Take turns to say your predictions.

3 **a)** Fill in the gaps with the correct form of these verbs. V5.2

~~do~~   spend (x2)   get
have   take   live   know

1 I want to __do__ a degree in English.
2 I'd like to _____ abroad when I retire.
3 I _____ a great time last weekend.
4 I usually _____ lots of photos on holiday.
5 I _____ a suntan very easily.
6 I _____ a lot of time with my family.
7 I _____ how to use a computer.
8 I _____ a lot of time talking on the phone.

b) Make questions with *you* from the sentences in **3a)**.

Do you want to do a degree in English?

c) Work in pairs. Take turns to ask four of your questions. Ask follow-up questions if possible.

4 **a)** Put the verbs in brackets in the correct form and complete the sentences for you. G5.3

1 I'm planning to (go) …
2 Next weekend I'm going to (see) …
3 I'm hoping to (have) …
4 I'm thinking of (learn) …
5 I'd like to (visit) …
6 I'm looking forward to (spend) …

b) Work in groups. Compare sentences.

5 **a)** Four of the <u>underlined</u> prepositions are incorrect. Correct the mistakes. V5.3 G5.2

1 When did you last go <u>by</u> a trip?
2 Do you usually pay <u>with</u> things by credit card?
3 How much do you spend <u>for</u> books a year?
4 What do your family usually talk <u>about</u>?
5 Are any of your friends looking <u>on</u> a job?

b) Work in pairs. Take turns to ask and answer the questions.

Progress Portfolio

a) Tick the things you can do in English.

☐ I can make predictions about the future.

☐ I can understand the main points of a radio interview.

☐ I can ask and answer questions about personal future plans.

☐ I can understand the main points of a newspaper article.

☐ I can ask for and offer help.

☐ I can make suggestions.

b) What do you need to study again? ● 5A–D

7 **a)** Work in groups of four. Choose a chairperson. Imagine you are going to organise a charity event. Decide on the type of event you want to have, and when and where the event will be.

Let's have a disco.

Good idea. Where shall we have it?

b) Make a list of things you need to do. Use the ideas in **2b)** and your own.

c) Discuss who is going to do the things on the list. Use the phrases from **3a)**. Make notes on who is going to do each thing.

8 Work with people from different groups. Tell them about the event you have planned. Which event will be the best, do you think?

We're going to have a disco.

♪ R5.15 Look at the song *Space Oddity* on p100. Follow the instructions.

6 Family and friends

6A Life with teenagers

Vocabulary character adjectives
Grammar making comparisons: comparatives, *a lot, much, a bit,* *(not) as … as*
Review describing appearance

QUICK REVIEW ● ● ●
Write all the adjectives you know to describe people's appearance (*tall,* etc.) and character (*friendly,* etc.). Work in groups and compare words. Who has the most?

Vocabulary Character adjectives

1 Tick the adjectives you know. Check new words in V6.1 p130.

> shy   bright   noisy   stubborn   helpful
> moody   patient   lazy   honest   selfish
> mature   polite   aggressive   ambitious
> organised   considerate   easy-going

2 a) Choose four adjectives from **1** that describe your character and four that don't. Write them on a piece of paper. Don't write them in order.

b) Work in pairs. Swap lists. Take turns to guess which four adjectives describe your partner.

Reading and Grammar

3 Work in groups. Discuss these questions.

1 Which is the most difficult to be: a child, a teenager, a middle-aged person, an elderly person? Why?
2 Which is the most difficult to live with? Why?

4 a) Look at the headline in the article. Who is 'the enemy', do you think? Read the first paragraph only and find out.

b) Read about Marilyn Scott's family. Who is easier to live with, Tom or Harry? Why?

c) Read the article again. Tick the true sentences. Correct the false ones.

1 Marilyn's two sons are quite similar.
2 Harry is doing badly at school.
3 Harry knows which job he wants to do.
4 Tom doesn't study very hard.
5 Tom isn't very ambitious.
6 Marilyn is only worried about Harry.

LIVING WITH THE ENEMY

PEOPLE often say that living with teenagers is worse than living with any other age group. But is this true? We talked to two parents with teenage children to find out.

Marilyn Scott

Yes, sometimes it's really difficult living with teenagers. But it isn't only their age, it's also the type of people they are. My two sons are completely different. Tom's easier to live with than Harry. Harry's a typical moody fifteen-year-old. He's a lot noisier and more aggressive than Tom, and he isn't as considerate. So he's much harder to live with. But Harry's got his good side too. He's very bright and his exam results are always better than Tom's.

Tom's two years older than Harry, so he's more mature and less stubborn than his brother.

He's also a bit more patient and can be very helpful when he wants to be. But he's got bigger problems at school. He's as intelligent as Harry, but he's much lazier and his exam results are always worse than his brother's. Harry wants to be a pilot when he leaves school, but Tom doesn't know what he wants to do.

In some ways I'm a bit more worried about Harry because he isn't as happy as Tom. But I also worry about Tom because he hasn't got any plans for his future. Yes, life is hard living with teenagers, but I'll miss them when they leave home.

Help with Grammar
Making comparisons

 5 **a)** Find the comparative forms of these adjectives in the article about Marilyn Scott's family. Then answer questions 1–5.

| easy | aggressive | good |
| old | mature | big | bad |

1 When do we use *-er*?
2 When do we use *more*?
3 What are the spelling rules for adjectives like *noisy* and *big*?
4 Which adjectives are irregular?
5 What is the opposite of *more*? Find an example in the article.

b) Which word is missing in this sentence?

Tom's two years older .... Harry.

c) Which of these words in **bold** mean: a big difference? a small difference?

| **a lot** noisier | **much** lazier |
| **a bit** more worried | |

d) Look at these sentences. Then answer questions 1–3.

Tom's as intelligent as Harry.
Harry isn't as happy as Tom.

1 Which sentence means the boys are different?
2 Which sentence means they are the same?
3 Do we use the adjective or its comparative form with *(not) as … as*?

e) Check in G6.1 p131.

6 R6.1   P Listen and practise. Copy the stress.

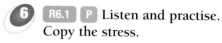
Tȯm's eȧsier to lȋve with than Hȧrry.

7 Read about Robert Macey's family. Complete the article with the adjective or its comparative form. Who is easier to live with, Carol or Beth?

Robert Macey
We've got two girls – Carol is eight and Beth is sixteen. Carol's a lot ¹.............. (difficult) to live with than her sister, so I think teenagers are ².............. (easy) to live with than young children. Beth's much ³.............. (easy-going) and she isn't as ⁴.............. (selfish) as Carol – but sometimes they're both as ⁵.............. (moody) as each other! Also Carol is less ⁶.............. (polite) and much ⁷.............. (noisy), but I think that's just because she's ⁸.............. (young). They're both doing OK at school, but Carol's a bit ⁹.............. (bright) than Beth was at her age and her reports are always ¹⁰.............. (good) than Beth's. But perhaps Beth's reports aren't as ¹¹.............. (good) as Carol's because these days she's ¹².............. (interested) in boys than her school work!

8 **a)** Write six sentences to compare yourself and a friend. Use *a lot, much, a bit, (not) as … as,* and the adjectives from **1** and the Quick Review.

Olivia's a bit taller than me.
I'm not as organised as she is.

b) Work in pairs. Take turns to tell your partner about your friend.

Get ready … Get it right!

9 **a)** Think about your life now and your life when you were a teenager. (If you are a teenager now, think about your life now and your life five years ago.) For both of these times in your life write two adjectives each for your: a) personality, b) appearance, c) day-to-day life.

b) Plan how you can compare your life now to when you were a teenager/five years ago.

I'm much less shy now than I was then.
I was a bit thinner when I was a teenager.
My life isn't as stressful as it was five years ago.

10 Work in groups. Tell the other students about the differences between now and then. Give reasons if possible.

Vocabulary relationships (2)
Grammar superlatives
Review comparatives; Present Continuous

QUICK REVIEW ●●●
Write eight character adjectives. Then think of one person you know for each adjective. Work in pairs. Tell your partner about the people.

Patrick
Harriet
Eric
Naomi
Diana
Jake
Rupert
Charlie
Dom

Vocabulary Relationships (2)

1 **a)** Put these words into two groups: *family relationships* and *other relationships*. Check new words in **V6.2** p130.

uncle	aunt	boss	niece	nephew	flatmate	cousin
close friend	ex-girlfriend	neighbour	stepfather	grandmother
colleague	sister-in-law	employer	employee	relative

b) How many other words can you make with *ex-, step- grand-* and *-in-law*?

2 **a)** Make a list of all the roles you play in life.

I'm a mother, a boss, a sister …

b) Work in pairs. Discuss these questions.

1 Which of your roles do you like? Which don't you like?
2 How many of the same roles do you have?

I really like being a mother.

Me too, but I don't like being a boss.

Listening and Grammar

 3 **a)** Work in pairs. Take turns to describe a person in the picture. Don't say his/her name. Your partner says who it is.

> This person is wearing a long white dress. She looks very happy!

b) Guess the names of these people.

1 Jake's twin brother *Dom*
2 Jake's great-uncle
3 Jake's best friend
4 Jake's colleague
5 Jake's aunt
6 Eric's wife

4 **a)** R6.2 Listen to Dom and Charlie talking at the wedding. Check your answers to **3b)**.

b) Listen again and fill in the gaps.

Diana's best ¹*friend* is Naomi. She's also the happiest person Dom knows. Her ²_____ , Eric, is the most boring man Dom's ever ³_____ and Charlie thinks he's got the worst ⁴_____ ever. Dom's richest relative is his ⁵_____ , Harriet. She's also got the biggest ⁶_____ . The owner of the most popular ⁷_____ in town is Rupert. Patrick is Dom's least favourite ⁸_____ . He's ⁹_____ next birthday and his ¹⁰_____ is only 76!

Help with Grammar Superlatives

 5 **a)** Look at **4b)** again. Find the superlatives of these adjectives. Then answer questions 1–5.

good	happy	boring	bad
rich	big	popular	

1 When do we use *-est*?
2 When do we use *most*?
3 What are the spelling rules for adjectives like *big* and *funny*?
4 Which adjectives are irregular?
5 What is the superlative form of *less*?

b) Which word is missing in this sentence?

She's _____ happiest person Dom knows.

c) Look at these sentences. Why don't we use *the* before the superlatives?

He's Jake's best friend.
She's our richest relative.

d) Check in G6.2 p131.

 6 R6.3 **P** Listen and practise.

She's the happiest person I know.

7 **a)** Write the comparative and superlative forms of these adjectives.

intelligent	busy	fat	popular	good	helpful
bad	stubborn	bright	thin	lazy	far

b) Work in pairs. Check your partner's answers and spelling.

8 Fill in the gaps in Dom's sentences with the superlative form of the adjective in brackets. Use *the* if necessary.

1 Diana's _the youngest_ (young) company director in the UK.
2 Her parents are _____ (happy) married couple I know.
3 Diana's _____ (organised) person I've ever met.
4 She's also my boss's _____ (good) friend.
5 Jake is _____ (helpful) person in the world.
6 He's also the world's _____ (bad) driver.
7 This is _____ (important) day of his life.
8 And he's wearing my _____ (expensive) shirt!

Get ready ... Get it right!

9 Draw your family tree. Then think of one superlative to describe each person on your family tree.

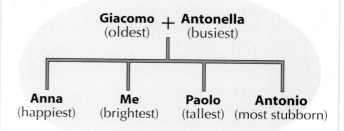

Giacomo + **Antonella**
(oldest)   (busiest)

Anna · **Me** · **Paolo** · **Antonio**
(happiest) (brightest) (tallest) (most stubborn)

 10 **a)** Work in pairs. Take turns to tell your partner about your family tree. Use at least one superlative for each person. Ask questions to find out more information.

b) Which person/people in your partner's family would you like to meet?

6C Family Business

Vocabulary prefixes and opposites of adjectives: *un-, in-, im-, dis-*
Skills Reading: a TV guide; Listening: a radio drama
Help with Listening missing words
Review character adjectives; past tenses; *will* and *might*

QUICK REVIEW ●●●
Work in groups. Swap information about your lives and make at least six sentences about the group using superlatives. Tell the class three of your sentences: *Petra's got the biggest family*.

Reading and Vocabulary

1 Work in groups. Discuss these questions.

1 Do you watch or listen to dramas or soap operas on TV or the radio? If yes, which ones?
2 Which soap operas are popular in your country? Why are they popular, do you think?
3 What are typical stories in soap operas?

2 a) Read the first paragraph of the article only. Complete these sentences.

1 *Family Business* is a …
2 The … family own a restaurant called …
3 There's also another restaurant called …
4 The family's main problems are …

b) Read the rest of the article. Then answer these questions.

1 Is The Full Moon restaurant successful?
2 Do Lydia and Clive have a good relationship?
3 How many children have they got?
4 Has Trudy got a job at the moment?
5 Which of their children is a criminal?
6 When did Nick leave the programme?
7 Who are Elizabeth's parents?
8 Where is The Angel restaurant?

c) Work in pairs. Draw a family tree of the Blake family.

Soap update: *Family Business*

In the popular radio drama *Family Business*, things aren't looking good for the Blake family. They own The Full Moon restaurant, but a new restaurant called The Angel is taking all their customers. The Full Moon also has serious money problems and relationships between the family members are getting worse every week. For new listeners here's our guide to the main characters in radio's most popular drama.

Lydia Blake and her husband Clive own The Full Moon restaurant. Lydia is bright and extremely stubborn, and she's very worried about the restaurant. She wants to borrow some money from the bank – if she can't, The Full Moon might have to close.

Clive Blake is the chef at The Full Moon – but being married to Lydia isn't easy. He thinks she's impatient and inconsiderate and would like to ask her for a divorce. But if he does, what will happen to the restaurant he loves?

Darren is the oldest of Lydia and Clive's three children (their other son, Nick, left the programme a year ago). Darren works as a waiter in his parents' restaurant – when he's not stealing cars or staying out all night. The most dishonest and unreliable member of the family, he's the one we love to hate!

Trudy is Lydia and Clive's youngest child. Nineteen-year-old Trudy is unemployed and she can't keep a job for more than two weeks. Is this because she's immature, moody and unhelpful, perhaps?

Kathy is Darren's lovely wife and mother of three-month-old Elizabeth. Kathy is quiet, easy-going and unselfish – but does she have a secret past?

Eve King is the owner of The Angel restaurant, which opened in the same street as The Full Moon last month. Eve is attractive, ambitious – and single!

Help with Vocabulary Prefixes and opposites of adjectives: *un-, in-, im-, dis-*

 3 **a)** Find the opposites of these adjectives in the article. Write them in the table.

| patient | considerate | employed | mature |
| helpful | honest | reliable | selfish |

un-	
in-	
im-	impatient
dis-	

b) Do you know the opposites of these adjectives? Write them in the table.

happy	intelligent	polite	ambitious
friendly	possible	attractive	correct
sure	organised	healthy	

c) Check in V6.3 p130.

4 **a)** R6.4 P Listen and practise. Notice that prefixes (*un-, in-,* etc.) aren't usually stressed.

employed, unemployed

b) Work in pairs. Take turns to say adjectives from 3a) and 3b). Your partner says the opposite adjective.

Listening

5 **a)** R6.5 Listen to the beginning of this week's episode of *Family Business*. Answer these questions.

1 Where are the people?
2 Which characters are talking?
3 What do they talk about?

b) Listen again. Are these sentences true or false?

1 Lydia borrowed some money from the bank this afternoon.
2 The bank wants to close the restaurant.
3 The Full Moon has only got eight customers.
4 The Angel restaurant is full.
5 Trudy has got a new job.
6 She's going to work in a bank.
7 Lydia is very angry with Eve King.

6 **a)** Work in groups. What do you think will happen next? Use the characters from the article and make a list of ideas.

Trudy might leave home.

Maybe Lydia will talk to Eve.

b) Compare ideas with another group or the whole class.

7 **a)** R6.6 Listen to the end of the episode. Were any of your ideas correct?

b) Listen again. Answer these questions.

1 Why is Kathy worried?
2 What is Darren looking for?
3 Does Darren stay at home with his wife and daughter?
4 How much money did the restaurant make this evening?
5 Where did Lydia go?
6 Who's the last person to arrive at the restaurant?
7 Why did he come back?
8 What's happening outside?

Help with Listening Missing words

• In spoken English sometimes we miss out words if the meaning is clear.

 8 **a)** Look at these sentences from the radio drama. Notice the missing words.

KATHY Shouldn't you be at work?
DARREN Having a break. (= **I'm** having a break.)
KATHY You going out? (= **Are** you going out?)
DARREN Yeah. Seen my cigarettes? (= **Have you** seen my cigarettes?)

b) R6.6 Look at R6.6, p151. Listen again and notice the missing words. What kind of words do we miss out?

9 **a)** Work in groups of four. You are going to write the beginning of the next episode of *Family Business*. Before you write, plan what is going to happen. Include at least four characters.

b) Write the beginning of the next episode.

c) Practise the episode in your groups until you can remember it.

d) Role-play your episode for other students. Which episode is the best, do you think?

6D Call me back

Real World leaving phone messages
Help with Listening on the phone
Review requests and offers

Jim Moore

QUICK REVIEW ●●●

Work in pairs. Take turns to describe these characters from the radio drama *Family Business*: Lydia, Clive, Trudy, Darren, Kathy, Elizabeth, Eve King and Nick. What happened in the episode you listened to?

1 Work in pairs. Discuss these questions.

1 Do you use the phone a lot? If yes, which three people do you phone or text the most?
2 Do you ever need to speak English on the phone? If yes, who to?

Help with Listening On the phone

2 **a)** Fill in the gaps with these words.

called	meeting	off	line	leave	message

1 I'm afraid he's taken the afternoon ....
2 Can I take a .... ?
3 Shall I tell him you .... ?
4 Hold the .... , please. I'll put you through.
5 I'm sorry, he's in a ....
6 Would you like to .... a message?

b) R6.7 Listen and check.

c) Match sentences 1–6 in **2a)** to headings a)–c).

a) asking someone to wait
b) saying someone isn't available
c) offering to take a message

3 R6.7 P Listen again and practise. Copy the intonation.

I'm afraid he's taken the afternoon off.

4 **a)** R6.8 Jim is trying to talk to his friend, Peter. Listen and put phone conversations a)–c) in order.

a) Peter phones Jim's office.
b) Jim phones Peter's office.
c) Jim phones Peter's wife.

b) Listen again and answer the questions.

1 Why isn't Peter in his office?
2 Has Jim called Peter's mobile?
3 Why does Jim want to talk to him?
4 Where is Jim when Peter phones him back?

Real World Leaving phone messages

5 **a)** Match these headings to the sentences from the phone conversations.

> saying where people can contact you
> leaving a message
> asking to speak to someone

a) ....

Can I speak to Peter Parker, please?
Is Peter there, please?
Could I speak to Jim Moore, please?

b) ....

Could you ask him/her to phone me tomorrow?
Can you ask him/her to call me back?
Just tell him/her Peter Parker called.

c) ....

He/She can ring me at the office.
He/She can get me on my mobile.
He/She can call me at home this evening.

b) Check in RW6.1 p131.

TIP! ● When we tell people who we are on the phone, we say *This is Jim.* or *It's Jim.* not ~~I'm Jim~~. *This is ...* is more formal than *It's ...* .

6 R6.9 P Listen and practise the sentences in **5a)**. Copy the intonation.

Can I speak to Peter Parker, please?

6 Review

Language Summary 6, p130

Peter Parker

7 **R6.10** Listen to Jim and Peter's conversation. Answer these questions.

1 What is Peter doing?
2 Why is he there?
3 Why does Jim want to talk to him?

8 **a)** Work in pairs. Write a phone conversation between A and B. A is phoning a friend at work. B is a receptionist at the friend's workplace. Use sentences from 5a) and your own ideas.

A *Hello, can I speak to ...*
B *I'm sorry ...*

b) Practise the conversation in pairs until you can remember it.

c) Role-play the conversation for other students.

9 Work in pairs. Student A → p105. Student B → p113. Follow the instructions.

1 **a)** Find 12 adjectives. **V6.1**

bright moody polite good big patient mature ambitious stubborn aggressive easy-going honest

b) Work in pairs. Write six more character adjectives.

c) Which adjectives from 1a) and 1b) have a negative meaning?

2 **a)** Write the comparative form of the adjectives in 1a). **G6.1**

bright → brighter

b) Choose two people in your family. Write six sentences comparing them.

c) Work in pairs. Tell your partner about the people you chose in 2b).

3 **a)** Fill in the gaps with *as* or *than*. **G6.1**

1 I'm taller _____ him/her.
2 He/She isn't _____ patient as me.
3 He/She isn't as good at English _____ me.
4 He/She's less interested in music _____ me.
5 I'm not as ambitious _____ him/her.
6 I'm more organised _____ him/her.

b) Think of someone you know well. Make the sentences in 3a) true for him/her.

c) Work in pairs. Tell your partner about the person you chose.

4 **a)** Write six words for *family relationships* and six words for *other relationships*. **V6.2**

b) Work in pairs. Compare lists. Check your partner's spelling.

5 **a)** Write the superlative form of the adjectives in brackets. Use *the* if necessary. Then complete the sentences about your school days. **G6.2**

1 *The brightest* (bright) student in our class is/was ...
2 My _____ (good) subject is/was ...
3 My _____ (bad) subject at school is/was ...
4 The school's _____ (friendly) teacher is/was ...
5 _____ (popular) sport at school is/was ...
6 _____ (big) class has/had ... students in it.

b) Work in groups. Compare sentences.

6 Work in pairs. Tick the correct adjectives. Correct the prefixes (*un-*, etc.) that are wrong. **V6.3**

unpatient	disimportant
unhealthy	imconsiderate
inorganised	inpossible
unhonest	unmature
imfriendly	unreliable

Progress Portfolio

a) Tick the things you can do in English.

☐ I can describe people's character.

☐ I can compare two or more people or things.

☐ I can talk about different relationships.

☐ I can follow the story of a simple soap opera.

☐ I can leave phone messages.

b) What do you need to study again? **● 6A–D**

7 You need a holiday!

7A 50 places to go

Vocabulary travel
Grammar Present Continuous for future arrangements
Review Present Perfect; superlatives

QUICK REVIEW ●●●

Think of the three most interesting places you have been to. Work in pairs. Take turns to tell your partner about these places: *I've been to Cairo.* Ask questions to find out more information: *What did you do there?*

Vocabulary Travel

 a) Look at these words. What is the difference in meaning? Check in **V7.1** p132.

| a trip   a tour   travel   a journey |

b) Choose the correct words.

1 How long is your *travel/journey* to school?
2 Have you ever been on a business *trip/journey* abroad?
3 Did you *trip/travel* a lot last year?
4 Have you ever been on a bus *trip/tour* of a famous city?
5 What's the longest *journey/travel* you've ever been on?
6 Have you ever been on a package *travel/tour*?

c) Work in pairs. Take turns to ask and answer the questions.

Reading

 Read about a TV programme and answer the questions.

1 What is the programme about?
2 When is it on?
3 How did the BBC choose the places?

50 places to go before you die

Thursday 9 p.m. BBC1 ★★★★

Last month the BBC asked viewers to send in their top five holiday destinations and tonight we find out the results. So sit back and enjoy this tour of the world's greatest beauty spots.

 a) Work in groups. Which of these places are in photos A–C? Which place would you most like to go to? Why?

- The Great Barrier Reef, Australia
- The Grand Canyon, USA
- Cape Town, South Africa
- The South Island, New Zealand
- Disney World, Florida, USA

b) The places in **3a)** were the top five holiday destinations that people chose for the TV programme. Guess which order they were in.

c) Check your answers on p118. Then follow the instructions.

Listening and Grammar

4 **a)** R7.1 Keith and Sophie are neighbours. Listen to their conversation. Where is Sophie going on holiday this year? Who is she going with?

b) Listen again. Tick the true sentences. Correct the false ones.

1 They're leaving on Saturday.
2 They're going on holiday for two weeks.
3 They're staying with friends for a week.
4 They're going on a cycling tour for five days.
5 They're going to some places on a tour bus.
6 Keith's having a holiday this year.

Help with Grammar Present Continuous for future arrangements

5 **a)** Look at sentences 1–3 in **4b**). Then answer questions a)–d).

a) Do these sentences talk about the past, present or future?
b) Do they talk about definite arrangements or something that might happen?
c) Does Sophie know exactly when these things are happening?
d) Has she booked the holiday and the flight?

b) How do you make negatives and questions in the Present Continuous?

c) Check in G7.1 p133.

6 R7.2 P Listen and practise.

We're leaving on Saturday.
How long are you going for?

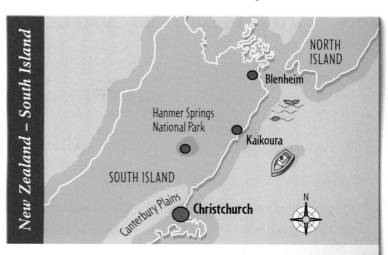

New Zealand – South Island

NORTH ISLAND
Blenheim
Hanmer Springs National Park
Kaikoura
SOUTH ISLAND
Canterbury Plains
Christchurch

Day 1 Monday 11ᵗʰ February
Christchurch to Hanmer Springs

Morning
• Meet at the Plaza Hotel
• Cycle along the coast

Lunch
• Have a picnic lunch on the Canterbury Plains

Afternoon
• Go to the hot pools in Hanmer Springs
• Visit the National Park

Night
• Camp overnight by the river

7 **a)** Read about Day 1 of Sophie and Rob's cycling tour. Write sentences about their first day.

On Monday they're travelling from Christchurch to Hanmer Springs.

b) Work in pairs. Student A → p104. Student B → p112. Follow the instructions.

Get ready ... Get it right!

8 Look at these possible plans. Make *yes/no* questions with *you.*

Find someone who is ...

... going on holiday next month.
Are you going on holiday next month?
... meeting friends after class.
... going out with friends tomorrow evening.
... doing something interesting next week.
... spending next weekend in another town/city.
... taking an exam next month.
... going to a wedding soon.
... travelling abroad in the next two months.

9 Ask other students your questions. Find one person who is doing each thing. Ask follow-up questions.

What are you taking?

Vocabulary things we take on holiday; quantity phrases
Grammar quantifiers; possessive pronouns
Review countable, uncountable and plural nouns

QUICK REVIEW ● ● ●
Write four things you are doing next week or next weekend: *On Saturday I'm going to a party.* Work in groups. Tell other students your sentences. Is anyone doing the same things as you?

Vocabulary Things we take on holiday

1 **a)** Make a list of ten things you always take on holiday.

b) Work in pairs. Compare lists. How many of the things are the same?

2 Sophie and Rob are packing to go to New Zealand. Find these things in the picture. Check new words in **V7.2** p132.

a suitcase *13*	sun cream	shorts	a T-shirt	soap	a swimsuit
film	make-up	chewing gum	shaving foam	a towel	
toothpaste	perfume	sandals	a razor	sunglasses	shampoo
swimming trunks	tea	walking boots	a camera		

Grammar and Listening

3 **a)** Work in pairs. Which of the words in **2** are: countable (C)? uncountable (U)? plural (P)?

a suitcase *C*
sun cream *U*
shorts *P*

b) Which of the plural words are: usually plural? always plural?

shorts – always plural

4 a) Look again at the picture. Choose the correct words.

1 There are **a lot of** CDs/T-shirts.
2 There are **a few** CDs/T-shirts.
3 There are**n't many** CDs/T-shirts.
4 There's **lots of** toothpaste/make-up.
5 There's **a bit of** toothpaste/make-up.
6 There's **a little** toothpaste/make-up.
7 There is**n't much** toothpaste/make-up.

b) Look at the phrases in **bold** in **4a)**. Which mean a large quantity? Which mean a small quantity?

Help with Grammar Quantifiers

5 a) Look at the sentences 1–6. Then complete the rules with *some* or *any*.

1 There's some tea.
2 There are some towels.
3 Is there any sun cream?
4 Are there any T-shirts?
5 There isn't any coffee.
6 There aren't any jackets.

- We usually use _____ in positive sentences.
- We usually use _____ in questions.
- We usually use _____ in negative sentences.

b) Look again at the sentences in **4a)** and **5a)**. Do we use these quantifiers with countable nouns (C), uncountable nouns (U) or both (B)?

1 a lot of/lots of *B*	4 a bit of	7 some
2 a few	5 a little	8 any
3 not many	6 not much	

c) Check in G7.2 p133.

6 R7.3 P Listen and practise the sentences from **4a)** and **5a)**.

There are a lot of T-shirts.

7 a) Match the quantity phrases 1–7 with a)–g).

1 a piece of — a) film
2 a bottle of — b) perfume
3 a packet of — c) chewing gum
4 a roll of — d) shorts
5 a bar of — e) toothpaste
6 a pair of — f) soap
7 a tube of — g) tea

b) R7.4 P Listen and practise the phrases in **7a)**. Copy the linking.

a piece of chewing gum

c) Work in pairs. Think of other things for the quantity phrases in **7a)**.

a piece of paper

8 a) Write three correct sentences and three incorrect sentences about the picture. Use the quantifiers from **5b)** and the quantity phrases from **7a)**.

There are a lot of books.

b) Work in pairs. Swap papers. Find and correct the mistakes.

9 a) R7.5 Listen to Sophie and Rob. Find four mistakes in the picture.

b) Look at R7.5, p151. Listen again and underline all the quantifiers (*a lot of*, etc.).

Grammar and Listening

Help with Grammar Possessive pronouns

10 a) Look at these sentences. Notice the possessive pronouns in **bold**.

*I don't want to take any of **yours**.* (= your things)
*There are a few things I can't get in **mine**.* (= my bag)

b) What are the possessive pronouns for *I, you, he, she, we, they*?

c) Check in G7.3 p133.

11 a) Choose the correct words.

1 A Are these *your/yours* sunglasses?
  B No, those are *my/mine*.

2 A Is that *her/hers* towel?
  B Yes, that one's *her/hers*.

3 A Is that *their/theirs* suitcase?
  B No, it's *our/ours*.

4 A Excuse me. Are these *your/yours*?
  B This one's *my/mine*, but that one's *him/his*, I think.

b) Work in pairs. Take turns to ask and answer questions about the things in the picture and in the classroom.

Whose T-shirts are these?
They're hers.
Whose bag is this?
It's mine.

Get ready ... Get it right!

12 Work in two groups. Group A → p106.
Group B → p114. Follow the instructions.

Vocabulary expressions with *go*
Skills Reading and Listening:
a magazine article
Help with Listening weak forms: review
Review comparatives; Past Simple

VOCABULARY AND SKILLS

QUICK REVIEW ●●●
Work in pairs. Tell your partner what you usually have in your: fridge, kitchen cupboards, bag, wallet. *In my fridge there's usually some cheese, a few eggs and a lot of milk.* Do you have similar things?

Reading and Listening

1 Work in groups. Discuss these questions.

1 When was the last time you stayed in a hotel?
2 Where was the hotel? Why were you there?
3 Did you enjoy staying at this hotel? Why?/Why not?

2 **a)** Check these words with your teacher or in a dictionary.

a rainforest	a shipwreck
a monkey	go snorkelling
tropical fish	go diving	a guide
a piranha	a swimming pool
a suite	staff	room service

b) Read the first paragraph of the article and look at the photos. Are the words in **2a)** in the text about Ariau Amazon Towers or Jules' Undersea Lodge, do you think?

3 Work in two groups. Group A, read about Ariau Amazon Towers. Group B, read about Jules' Undersea Lodge. Find the answers to these questions.

1 What is unusual about the hotel?
2 What facilities are there (restaurants, bars, etc.)?
3 What can you do near the hotel?
4 How many rooms are there?
5 How much does it cost per night?
6 When is a good time to go there?

4 **a)** Work with a student from the other group. Take turns to ask and answer the questions in **3**.

b) R7.6 Read and listen to the texts about the two hotels. Check your partner's answers.

The world's most amazing hotels

In our search for the world's most amazing hotels, we sent Seth Hammond to visit Ariau Amazon Towers in Brazil, while Stephanie Nichols spent the night in Jules' Undersea Lodge in the Florida Keys, USA. Here are their reports.

Ariau Amazon Towers is one of the most incredible hotels I've ever stayed in. It's in the middle of the Amazon rainforest in Brazil, about 60 kilometres from Manaus, the nearest city. What makes it so special is that most of the hotel is up in the trees – 30 metres above the ground! There are two excellent restaurants and after dinner you can go for a drink in one of four treetop bars. Or you can go swimming in one of the hotel's beautiful pools and watch the monkeys and birds in the trees above you.

There are also lots of things to do nearby. **I went for a long walk in the rainforest with an excellent local guide** and saw plants, trees, birds and animals of every description. **You can also go to local villages for the day**, or go on a boat trip along the River Amazon and go fishing for piranhas. Every day is an adventure – I was never bored in the three days I was there.

Ariau Amazon Towers has 278 rooms and suites – including a Tarzan Suite – and it costs around $120 a night. It rains a lot from December to June, so the best time to visit is from July to November.

5 **a)** Work in the same pairs and answer these questions. Which hotel:

1 is smaller?
2 is more expensive?
3 is more comfortable?
4 has more things to do?
5 is more beautiful?
6 is more unusual?

b) Which hotel is better for a holiday, do you think? Why?

I was worried when I arrived in Florida because the hotel I was staying in was underwater – and I couldn't dive. But after a three-hour class I was able to dive down to the hotel with an instructor. (You can get a full diving certificate in three days.)

Jules' Undersea Lodge began as a research laboratory in the 1970s and it's unusual for many reasons. Firstly, it's very small – just two bedrooms, a kitchen and a shared living room. Also there aren't any staff in the Lodge, they're on land. But they monitor the hotel 24 hours a day and you can get room service any time you want. The first evening I was there I ordered a pizza and half an hour later a diver delivered it to me at the hotel!

During the day you can go diving or snorkelling, or go for an underwater walk. **And you should definitely go on a tour of the nearby shipwreck,** an experience you'll never forget. But the best moment was waking up and seeing hundreds of tropical fish watching me through my bedroom window! The Lodge isn't cheap (one night costs $499 per person) but it doesn't matter when you go – it's always wet!

Help with Listening Weak forms: review

• Remember: in sentences we say many small words with a schwa /ə/ sound.

6 a) [R7.7] Listen to the weak and strong forms of these words.

	strong	weak		strong	weak
of	/ɒv/	/əv/	can	/kæn/	/kən/
from	/frɒm/	/frəm/	for	/fɔː/	/fə/
are	/ɑː/	/ə/	to	/tuː/	/tə/
and	/ænd/	/ən/	was	/wɒz/	/wəz/

b) Underline all the words in 6a) in the text about Ariau Amazon Towers.

c) [R7.6] Listen to this text again. Notice the weak forms of the words in 6a).

Help with Vocabulary Expressions with *go*

7 a) Look at the sentences in **bold** in the article. Then complete the rules with *for, with, to, on* or – .

• We use *go* _____ + place.
• We use *go* _____ + person.
• We use *go* _____ + activity (verb+*ing*).
• We use *go* _____ + activity (noun).
• We use *go* _____ + travel words (*a tour, holiday,* etc.).

b) Check in [V7.4] p132.

8 a) Read the article again and find all the other phrases with *go* or *went*.

b) Which expression with *go* from 7a) do we use with these words/phrases? There are three words/phrases for each expression.

the mountains	my family	a business trip
sightseeing	an art gallery	holiday some friends
a drink a journey	sailing	the beach a run
camping a walk	my father-in-law	

go to the mountains   go with my family

9 a) Fill in the gaps with the correct form of *go* and a preposition if necessary.

1 When was the last time you __*went*__ camping?
2 Have you ever _____ an art gallery?
3 How often do you _____ a drink after work/class?
4 When was the last time you _____ the beach?
5 Do you sometimes _____ long walks at the weekends?
6 What was the last long journey you _____ ?
7 Have you ever _____ sailing?
8 Did you _____ holiday last year? If yes, who did you _____ ?

b) Work in pairs. Take turns to ask and answer the questions.

7D I've got a problem

Real World complaints and requests
Vocabulary hotel problems
Help with Listening intonation (1)
Review expressions with *go*

QUICK REVIEW ●●●
Write eight free time activities with *go*: four you often do and four you never do. Don't write them in order. Work in pairs. Swap papers and guess which four activities your partner never does.

1 Work in groups. Have you ever complained about a hotel room, food in a restaurant or something you bought? If yes, tell the other students what happened.

2 a) Look at these complaints. Cross out the incorrect words/phrases.

1 The *window/room/chair* is broken.
2 The *food/TV/shower* isn't hot enough.
3 The *room/chair/lift* is too noisy.
4 My *breakfast/newspaper/bed* hasn't arrived.
5 The *air conditioning/window/remote control* doesn't work.
6 There's something wrong with the *shower/light/room number*.

b) Work in pairs. Think of one more word/phrase you can use in sentences 1–6 in **2a**).

3 a) R7.8 Listen to three guests making complaints to Reception. What problems do they have?

b) Listen again. What are the receptionist's solutions to the problems?

Real World Complaints and requests

4 a) Look at these sentences. Are they complaints (C) or requests (R)?

1 **I'm sorry, but** I've got a bit of a problem. *C*
2 **I wonder if you could** <u>check</u> for me.
3 **I wonder if I could** <u>have</u> some more towels, please.
4 **I'm afraid** I've got a complaint.
5 **Could I** <u>speak</u> to the manager, please?
6 **Could you** <u>help</u> me?
7 **I'm sorry, but** I think there's something wrong with the TV.
8 **Would you mind** <u>sending</u> someone to look at it?

b) Look at the <u>underlined</u> verb forms in **4a**). Then complete these phrases with *infinitive* or *verb+ing*.

1 I wonder if I/you could + ...
2 Could I/you + ...
3 Would you mind + ...

c) Which two phrases in **4b**) are more polite, do you think?

d) Check in RW7.1 p133.

Help with Listening Intonation (1)

● We know if people are being polite by how much their voices go up and down. If their voices are flat, they often sound rude or impatient.

5 R7.9 Listen to the same sentences said twice. Which is polite, a) or b)?

1 (a) b)   4 a) b)
2 a) b)   5 a) b)
3 a) b)   6 a) b)

6 R7.10 P Listen and practise sentences 1–6 in **4a**). Copy the polite intonation.

I'm sorry, but I've got a bit of a problem.

7 Review

Language Summary 7, p132

1 **a)** Correct the <u>underlined</u> words. **V7.1**

1 How often do you <u>trip</u> outside your town/city?
2 What's the longest <u>travel</u> you've ever been on?
3 Do you have to go on business <u>tours</u> for work?
4 Are you planning to go on a package <u>travel</u> this year?
5 Have you ever been on a sightseeing <u>journey</u> of your capital city?

b) Work in pairs. Take turns to ask and answer the questions.

2 **a)** Write two of these arrangements for each day. Don't write them in order.

> ~~gym~~ dentist tennis with Mark
> lunch with Bonny cinema
> Tom's party English exam
> meeting with bank manager

> Thursday __gym__ ____
> Friday ____ ____
> Saturday ____ ____
> Sunday ____ ____

b) Write a verb for each arrangement in 2a).

go to the gym

c) Work in pairs. Guess where the arrangements are in your partner's diary. **G7.1**

Are you going to the gym on Thursday?
Yes, I am./No, I'm not.

3 **a)** Work in pairs. What are Sophie and Rob taking on holiday to New Zealand? Make a list.

b) Compare your list with another partner.

c) Check on p54.

4 **a)** Make sentences about things you have/haven't got in your home. Use these words/phrases. **G7.2**

> a lot of a few a bit of
> bottles of packets of
> any many much some

I've got a lot of books.

b) Work in pairs. Compare your lists. How many things are the same?

5 **a)** Choose the correct word or – . **V7.4**

1 go *by/to* + a place
2 go *with/on* + a person
3 go *–/to* + activity (verb+*ing*)
4 go *for/–* + activity (noun)
5 go *to/on* + travel words

b) Work in pairs. Write three phrases for each expression with *go* in 5a).

go to the beach

c) Use these ideas to plan your perfect weekend.

- place
- people
- transport
- activities

d) Work in pairs. Tell your partner about your weekend.

Progress Portfolio

a) Tick the things you can do in English.

- ☐ I can ask and answer questions about travelling.
- ☐ I can talk about future arrangements.
- ☐ I can talk about quantity (*a bit*, etc.).
- ☐ I can talk about holiday activities.
- ☐ I can make simple complaints and requests in a hotel.

b) What do you need to study again? **● 7A–D**

7 **a)** Work in pairs. Write an eight-line conversation between a receptionist and a hotel guest. Use phrases from 2a) and 4a).

b) Swap papers with another pair of students. Read their conversation and correct any mistakes.

c) Role-play the conversation for the students who wrote it.

8 Work in pairs. Student A → p108. Student B → p116. Follow the instructions.

8 Different cultures

8A Home sweet home

Vocabulary describing your home
Grammar Present Perfect for unfinished past with *for*, *since* and *How long … ?*
Review Past Simple

QUICK REVIEW ●●●
Write the infinitive, Past Simple and past participle of eight irregular verbs. Work in pairs. Take turns to test your partner on your verbs: A *write*. B *wrote, written*.

Vocabulary Describing your home

1 Work in groups. Discuss these questions.

1 Do you live in a house or flat?
2 Do you like living there? Why?/ Why not?

2 **a)** Tick the words in **bold** you know. Check new words in **V8.1** p134.

1 It's **unusual/typical** for the area.
2 It's very **spacious/small**.
3 It's got **air conditioning/central heating**.
4 It's got a **balcony/garden**.
5 It's on a **busy/quiet** road.
6 It's **close to/a long way from** a park.
7 It's in a **nice/fashionable** part of town.
8 It's on the **ground/third/top** floor.

b) Choose five sentences from **2a)** that describe your home.

c) Work in groups. Take turns to tell the other students about your home.

Reading and Grammar

3 **a)** Look at the photos. What is the best thing about each home, do you think?

b) **R8.1** Read and listen to Luke and Bridget. What do they think is the best thing about their homes?

c) Read the texts again. Answer these questions.

1 Where is Coober Pedy?
2 Does Luke like living there?
3 Why do people live underground?
4 When did Bridget and Alain meet?
5 How many rooms has the boat got?

LUKE I live in an opal mining town called Coober Pedy, in Australia. It's in the desert, about 850 km north of Adelaide, the nearest city. ¹**I lived in Adelaide for seven years before I moved to Coober Pedy**, but I prefer living here. The strange thing about this town is that 80% of the people live underground. This is because it's usually over 50° in the summer and below freezing in winter. But the best thing about these underground houses is that it's always about 25°, so we don't need air conditioning or central heating. ²**My family and I have lived in this house for five years**. It's just like a normal house – but without any windows!

Help with Grammar Present Perfect for unfinished past with *for* and *since*

4 **a)** Look at sentences 1 and 2 in Luke's text. Then answer questions a)–c).

a) Does Luke live in Adelaide now?
b) Do Luke and his family live in an underground house now?
c) Which verb forms are in sentences 1 and 2?

b) Complete these rules with *Past Simple* or *Present Perfect*.

● We use the _____ to talk about something that happened in the past but doesn't continue in the present.
● We use the _____ to talk about something that started in the past and continues in the present.

c) How do we make positive and negative sentences with the Present Perfect?

d) Look at sentences 3 and 4 in Bridget's text. Then fill in the gaps in the rules with *for* or *since*.

● We use _____ with a period of time (how long).
● We use _____ with a point in time (when something started).

e) Check in **G8.1** p135.

BRIDGET I live on a houseboat on the River Seine with my husband, Alain, and our daughter, Isabel. I met Alain eight years ago when I was on holiday here in Paris – I'm from Ireland originally, you see. ³**We've been married for six years** and I've lived here since our wedding day. The boat has got everything we want – a kitchen, a big living room, two bedrooms, a bathroom, central heating and a small garden. ⁴**Alain's lived on this boat since 1995** – he never wants to live anywhere else and neither do I. The best thing about our home is that it moves. We can leave tomorrow and go anywhere we want.

5 Look at these words/phrases. Which go with *for*? Which go with *since*?

~~I was born~~	~~an hour~~	a long time	ten o'clock	2002
ten years	three weeks	I was a child	Saturday	ages

since I was born   *for an hour*

6 **a)** Put the verbs in brackets in the Present Perfect or Past Simple. Then complete the sentences for you.

1 I *'ve lived* (live) in my house/flat for .... months/years.
2 I .... (be) in this town/city since ....
3 When I was a child I .... (live) in ....
4 I .... (have) my computer/mobile phone for ....
5 I .... (be) in this English class since ....
6 I .... (start) learning English .... ago.

b) Work in pairs. Compare sentences.

Help with Grammar *How long ... ?*

7 **a)** Look at the text about Luke again. Then answer these questions.

1 How long did Luke live in Adelaide?
2 How long has he lived in his underground house?

b) Answer questions 1–3.

1 Which question in **7a)** is in the:
   a) Past Simple? b) Present Perfect?
2 Which question asks about: a) where Luke lives now? b) where Luke lived before now?
3 Can you answer both questions with: a) *for*? b) *since*?

c) How do we make questions in the Past Simple and Present Perfect with *How long ... ?*

d) Check in **G8.2** p136.

8 **a)** Think of a man you know. Fill the gaps with the verbs in brackets in the Present Perfect or the Past Simple.

1 What's his name?
2 How long .... you .... him? (know)
3 Where .... you first .... him? (meet)
4 Where does he live?
5 How long .... he .... there? (live)
6 Where .... he .... before that? (live)
7 Where does he work or study?
8 How long .... he .... there? (be)
9 When .... you last .... him? (see)

b) **R8.2** **P** Listen and practise the sentences in 8a).

What's his name?
How long have /həv/ you known him?

9 **a)** Work in pairs. Take turns to ask your partner the questions in 8a) about the man he/she knows.

b) Work in different pairs. Take turns to ask your partner about a woman he/she knows.

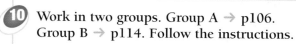

10 Work in two groups. Group A → p106. Group B → p114. Follow the instructions.

Vocabulary going to dinner
Grammar *should, shouldn't, must*; infinitive of purpose
Help with Listening /t/ at the end of words (1)
Review Present Perfect with *How long … ?*

QUICK REVIEW ● ● ●
Work in groups of four. Ask questions with *How long have you … ?* and find out who has: lived in their house/flat the longest, known their best friend the longest, been in this school the longest, had their watch the longest.

Vocabulary Going to dinner

 1 a) Tick the words you know. Then do the exercise in **V8.2** p134.

> the host   the hostess   a guest
> invite someone to dinner
> arrive on time   shake hands   kiss
> a starter   a main course   a dessert

b) Work in groups. Discuss these questions.

1 When was the last time you went for a meal with friends?
2 Who was the host or hostess? How do you know him/her?
3 How many guests were there? Who were they?
4 What did you have for your starter, main course and dessert?

2 Imagine you are invited to someone's house for dinner in the UK. Are these sentences true or false, do you think? Compare answers in groups.

1 It's rude to arrive on time.
2 It's polite to take some food, like cake or ice cream.
3 It's rude to shake hands with people you don't know.
4 It's OK to kiss people you don't know.
5 It's OK to smoke without asking.
6 It's rude to start eating before the host or hostess.
7 It's OK to leave ten minutes after the meal.
8 It's polite to ask people how much they earn.

Listening and Grammar

 3 a) R8.3 Antonia is from Italy. She is asking her friend, Polly, for advice. Listen and tick the sentences in **2** that Polly says are true.

b) Listen again. Answer these questions.

1 Who is Antonia going to dinner with?
2 What are good presents to take for the hostess?
3 Who usually starts eating first?
4 What do they usually do after the meal?
5 What topics can you talk about at dinner?

Help with Grammar *should, shouldn't, must*

 4 a) Look at sentences 1–3. Then choose the correct words in the rules.

1 You **should** wait for the hostess to start eating first.
2 You **shouldn't** ask people how much they earn.
3 You **must** ask the hostess if you can smoke.

● We use *should* to say we think something is a *good/bad* thing to do.
● We use *shouldn't* to say we think something is a *good/bad* thing to do.
● We use *must/should* to give very strong advice.
● After *should, shouldn't* and *must* we use the *infinitive/infinitive with to*.

b) Make questions with these words. What are the positive and negative short answers for question 2?

1 should / arrive / I / What time ?
2 take / I / to eat / Should / something ?

c) Check in G8.3 p136.

Help with Listening /t/ at the end of words (1)

- In spoken English sometimes you don't hear /t/ at the end of words.

5 **a)** **R8.4** **Listen to these sentences. In which sentences do you hear the *t* in bold?**

1 a) You shouldn'**t** arrive late.
   b) You shouldn'**t** leave immediately.

2 a) You mus**t** ask the hostess.
   b) And you mus**t** say you like the food.

3 a) We don'**t** often take food.
   b) Most British people don'**t** smoke.

b) Choose the correct word in these rules.

- We usually hear /t/ before a *vowel/consonant* sound.
- We don't usually hear /t/ before a *vowel/ consonant* sound.

c) **R8.3** Look at R8.3, p152. Listen to Antonia and Polly's conversation again. Notice when we don't say /t/ and the linking between /t/ and a vowel sound.

6 **R8.4** **P** Listen again and practise the sentences in 5a).

You shouldn't arrive late.

7 **a)** A visitor to your country is going to have dinner at someone's house. Write some advice.

b) Compare your advice with other students. Is it the same?

Listening and Grammar

8 **R8.5** Antonia is having dinner with Richard's parents. Listen to their conversation. What advice do his parents give her?

9 Listen again and complete these sentences.

1 I came here to study _____ .
2 I went back to Bath to visit some _____ .
3 You should go to Cambridge to see the _____ .
4 Richard should take you to _____ to see the sights.
5 I want to go to Oxford Street to do some _____ .

Help with Grammar Infinitive of purpose

10 **a)** **Look at these sentences. Do they have the same meaning?**

I came here to study English.
I came here because I wanted to study English.

b) Choose the correct word in the rule.

- To say why we do something, we often use the *infinitive/infinitive with to.*

c) Check in **G8.4** p136.

11 **a)** <u>Underline</u> the infinitives of purpose in the sentences in **9**.

b) Write the names of six places you have been to.

c) Work in pairs. Take turns to ask your partner why he/she went to these places. Continue the conversation if possible.

> Why did you go to Munich?
> To visit my sister.

Get ready ... Get it right!

12 Imagine some friends are coming to visit your city/country. Make notes on six unusual places they should go, and why they should go there.

Istanbul – visit the Blue Mosque
Ephesus – see the Roman city

13 Work in groups. If you are from different places, give your partners advice on where to go in your city/country. If you are from the same place, compare the advice you are going to give your friends. Then decide on the best six places to go.

> You/They should go to Istanbul to visit the Blue Mosque.

> You/They must go to Ephesus to see the Roman city.

Vocabulary travellers' tips; verb patterns
Skills Reading: a magazine article; Listening: a radio interview
Help with Listening understanding fast speech
Review *should*, *shouldn't*, *must*

VOCABULARY AND SKILLS

QUICK REVIEW ● ● ●
Think of five places you went to last week and why you went there. Work in pairs. Say why you went there, but not the name of the place: *I went there to buy some tickets.* Your partner guesses the place: *A bus station?*

Reading and Vocabulary

1 **a)** Do you know the words in **bold** in these sentences? Check new words in **V8.3** p134.

1 You shouldn't shake hands in a **doorway** in Russia.
2 In Thailand it's OK to **point** your feet **at** someone.
3 If a Japanese person gives you a **business card**, you should put it in your pocket immediately.
4 It's OK to **blow your nose** in public in Japan.
5 In China you shouldn't leave any food on your **plate**.
6 In most Asian countries you must **take off** your shoes when you enter someone's home.
7 If you **admire** something in an Arab person's home, they feel they should give it to you.

b) Work in pairs. Do you think these sentences are true or false?

2 **a)** Read the article and check your answers to **1b**).

b) Read the article again. Choose the four things that you think are the most surprising. Then compare ideas in groups.

Help with Vocabulary   Verb patterns

3 **a)** Look at the four <u>underlined</u> verbs in the article. Which verb forms come after these verbs?

b) Find these verbs in the article and <u>underline</u> the verb form that follows them. Then write the verbs in the table.

| would like | can | must | like | need | try | start |
| finish | forget | might | will | prefer | decide | |

+ infinitive	+ infinitive with *to*	+ verb+*ing*
should(n't)	*plan*	*enjoy*

c) Do you know any other verbs you can put in the table?

d) Check in **V8.4** p134.

Culture shock!

If you <u>plan</u> to go abroad this year, travel writer **Neil Palmer** would like to give you some advice on things you <u>should</u> and <u>shouldn't</u> do around the world.

■ ■ ■ Body language

Travellers <u>enjoy</u> meeting new people, but sometimes you can be rude without saying anything. In Russia, for example, you shouldn't shake hands in a doorway, and in Thailand you must never touch people's heads or point your feet at anyone. When the Japanese meet new people they like giving business cards – but you need to read the card carefully, not just put it in your pocket. And never blow your nose in public in Japan – people think that's disgusting.

■ ■ ■ Eating out

In restaurants in China you should always try to leave some food on your plate, but it's OK to start smoking before other people finish eating, which is very rude in England. If you're in India, don't forget to eat with your right hand – the left hand is 'dirty'. Also don't leave empty bottles on the dinner table in Russia – that's bad luck.

a) Fill in the gaps with the correct form of the verbs in brackets.

1 What do you enjoy _____ (do) in your free time?
2 Are you planning _____ (do) anything next weekend?
3 When did you start _____ (come) to this school?
4 Have you ever tried _____ (learn) another language?
5 Do you prefer _____ (study) in the morning or the evening?
6 Do you think you'll _____ (study) English next year?
7 What do you need _____ (do) when you get home?
8 Where would you like _____ (go) for your next holiday?

b) Work in pairs. Take turns to ask and answer the questions. Continue the conversation if possible.

Listening

 a) Work in groups. Discuss these questions.

1 What was the last present you gave? Who did you give it to? Why?
2 What was the last present you received? Who was it from?

b) Check these words with your teacher or in a dictionary.

refuse	accept	greedy	knives	a set of glasses
death	a funeral	an odd/even number		

 R8.6 Listen to a radio interview with the travel writer, Neil Palmer. Put the topics he talks about in order.

- things you shouldn't give to people
- accepting and refusing presents
- giving flowers
- opening presents

In the home

If you're travelling in Asia, someone might invite you to visit them at home. If so, don't forget to take off your shoes. And if you visit an Arab family's home, remember that it's polite to drink three cups of coffee. Also try not to admire anything valuable because your Arab host will feel he should give it to you as a present.

With so much to think about, it's not surprising many people prefer going on holiday in their own countries – or you might decide to stay at home!

 Listen again. Choose the correct words/phrases in these sentences.

1 In China you *should/shouldn't* accept a present immediately.
2 You should give presents in China with *one hand/both hands*.
3 In Thailand you *should/shouldn't* open a present when you get it.
4 Knives are a *good/bad* present to give in Japan.
5 You should give Japanese people an *odd/even* number of glasses.
6 You shouldn't give your Turkish host *white/red* flowers.

Help with Listening Understanding fast speech

 a) R8.7 Listen to these sentences. Notice the different types of linking and the way we say *t* at the end of words.

But it isn't as easy_/j/_as that,_is it?

If you_/w/_accept it immediately, people migh[t] think you're greedy.

And is there_/r/_anything you shouldn'[t] give as a present?

b) R8.8 Listen and write four sentences from the interview. You will hear each sentence twice.

c) R8.6 Look at R8.6, p153. Listen to the interview again. Notice the linking and the way we say /t/ at the end of words.

 a) Work in groups, if possible with people from the same country. Write your top ten tips about how to behave in your country. Use these ideas.

- giving and receiving presents
- behaviour in the street/in restaurants
- meeting and greeting people
- what (not) to wear in different situations
- going to a wedding
- other dos and don'ts

You must refuse a present three times before you accept it.
When you meet a friend you should kiss them on both cheeks.

b) Compare your tips with a student from a different group. Are any of your tips the same?

Real World asking about places: *What … like?*
Vocabulary adjectives to describe places
Review *should/shouldn't*

QUICK REVIEW ● ● ●
Work in pairs. What should/shouldn't you do when you are in these countries: Russia, Thailand, Japan, China, India, Saudi Arabia, Turkey?

1 Write these words in the table. Some words can go in more than one group. Check in V8.5 p135.

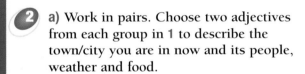

industrial   welcoming   wet   delicious
polluted   spicy   crowded   helpful
touristy   bland   cosmopolitan   freezing
relaxed   changeable   healthy   dangerous
reserved   windy

towns/cities	people	weather	food
industrial			

2 **a)** Work in pairs. Choose two adjectives from each group in **1** to describe the town/city you are in now and its people, weather and food.

b) Compare adjectives with other students. Do you agree?

3 **a)** Work in groups. What do you know about Scotland? Answer the questions.

1 What's the capital city?
2 What's the currency?
3 What languages do they speak?
4 What's a kilt?
5 What are bagpipes?
6 What Scottish drink is famous?
7 What's haggis?
8 When is the Edinburgh Festival?

b) R8.9 Bruce McMullen is in Sweden on business. He is talking to a Swedish colleague, Marlen. Listen and check your answers to **3a)**. Which group had the most correct answers?

c) Listen again. Tick the adjectives in **1** Bruce uses to describe: Edinburgh, the food, the people, the weather.

Real World **Asking about places:** *What … like?*

4 **a)** Match questions 1 and 2 with answers a) and b). Which question means: *Tell me what you know about Edinburgh?*

1 What's Edinburgh like?   a) Yes, I love it.
2 Do you like Edinburgh?   b) It's very cosmopolitan.

b) Fill in the gaps in these questions with *'s* or *are*.

1 What .... the city like?
2 What .... the people like?
3 What .... the weather like?
4 What .... the food like?

c) Do we use *like* in the answers to the questions in **4b)**?

d) Check in RW8.1 p136.

8 Review

Language Summary 8, p134

1 **a)** Match these words to the words in **bold** in 1–6. **V8.1**

~~quiet~~	garden	ground floor
central heating	small	unusual

1 It's on a **noisy** road. *quiet*
2 It's on the **top floor**.
3 It's a **typical** London house.
4 It's quite **spacious**.
5 It's got **air conditioning**.
6 It's got a lovely sunny **balcony**.

b) Take turns to describe a house that you like, but not your own. Use words from **1a)**.

2 **a)** Fill in the gaps with *for* or *since*. **G8.1**

1 _____ six months
2 _____ five years
3 _____ last summer
4 _____ a few days
5 _____ I was a child
6 _____ Friday
7 _____ a long time
8 _____ 2002

b) Write three true and three false sentences. Use the Present Perfect and phrases in **2a)**.

I've studied here for six months.

c) Work in pairs and swap papers. Guess which sentences are false.

3 **a)** Write the name of five things you really like. Use these ideas or your own.

- a book ● a film ● a restaurant
- a city ● a shop ● a nightclub
- a band ● a bar ● a café

b) Work in pairs. Take turns to give advice about the things on your list. Say why you liked them. **G8.3**

*You must/should read 'True Lives'.
Why's that?
It's really funny.*

4 **a)** Think of six places or shops in a town/city.

b) Work in pairs. Say why people go to these places. Your partner guesses the place. **G8.4**

*You go there to buy bread.
A baker's.*

5 Correct the <u>underlined</u> verb patterns. **V8.4**

I ¹<u>need losing</u> some weight – I'²<u>d like be</u> 70 kilos. So last month I ³<u>started eat</u> healthy food. Normally I ⁴<u>prefer eat</u> burgers and chips, but I've really ⁵<u>tried have</u> things like fruit instead. I also ⁶<u>enjoy to do</u> exercise, so I've ⁷<u>decided going</u> to the gym.

6 **a)** Fill in the missing letters in these adjectives. **V8.5**

1 d _ n _ _ r o _ s
2 d e l _ _ i _ _ s
3 f r _ _ z i _ _
4 p o _ _ u t _ _
5 r _ _ a x _ _
6 w _ l c _ m _ n g

b) Work in pairs. Which of these adjectives usually have:
a) a positive meaning?
b) a negative meaning?

Progress Portfolio

a) Tick the things you can do in English.

☐ I can describe my home and where I live.

☐ I can say how long something has happened.

☐ I can give and ask for advice.

☐ I can give reasons why I do things.

☐ I can talk about how people behave in my country.

☐ I can ask and answer questions about places, food, weather and people.

b) What do you need to study again? **● 8A–D**

---

5 **R8.10** **P** Listen and practise the questions in **4b)**.
What's the city like?

6 Choose a town/city you know well, but not the one you are in now. Write adjectives from **1** and other adjectives you know to describe:

- the town/city
- the people
- the weather
- the food
- the public transport
- the shops

7 **a)** Work in groups of four. Take turns to ask and answer questions with *What's/What are … like?* about the places you chose in **6**.

> What's Stockholm like?
>> It's a beautiful city, but it's freezing in winter.

b) Work on your own. Put the places you talked about in order from 1 to 4 (1 = the best place).

c) Work in the same groups of four. Compare lists and give reasons for your order.

d) Tell the class which place is the most popular and why.

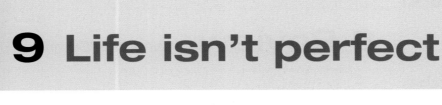

9 Life isn't perfect

9A Problems, problems

Vocabulary everyday problems
Grammar first conditional; future time clauses with *when, as soon as, before, after, until*
Review *What ... like?* questions

QUICK REVIEW ●●●
Work in pairs. Find one place you've been to that your partner hasn't. Then take turns to ask about: the place, the food, the people, the weather. *What's New York like? It's very cosmopolitan.*

Vocabulary Everyday problems

 a) Complete the phrases with the verbs in the boxes. Check new words/phrases in V9.1 p137.

oversleep	leave	get

1 *oversleep* on Monday mornings
2 .... lost
3 .... your wallet at home

run	lose	miss

4 .... a plane/a train
5 .... your keys
6 .... out of money/time

have	get	forget

7 .... someone's birthday
8 .... an accident
9 .... stuck in traffic

b) Work in pairs. Test your partner.

(a plane)
(miss a plane)

2 **a)** Tick the phrases in **1a)** that you often do or have done in the past.

b) Work in groups. Compare answers. Which phrases did everyone tick?

(I often lose my keys.)
(Yes, so do I.)

Brian and Eleanor

Ⓐ

Listening and Grammar

3 **a)** Look at the pictures. What problems do these people have?

b) R9.1 Listen and match the conversations to the pictures.

c) Work in pairs. Who said these sentences?

1 If I'm late again, I'll lose my job.
2 We'll miss the film if we don't find them soon.
3 If we don't get there by five, we'll miss the plane.
4 What will we do if we're too late?
5 You'll be OK if you get a taxi.

d) Listen again and check.

Help with Grammar First conditional

4 **a)** Look at this sentence. Notice the two different clauses.

if clause   main clause
If I'm late again, I'll lose my job.

b) Look at the sentences in **3c)** and answer these questions.

1 Do these sentences talk about the present or the future?
2 Does the *if* clause talk about things that are possible or certain?
3 Which verb form is in the *if* clause?
4 Which verb form is in the main clause?
5 Is the *if* clause always first in the sentence?

c) Check in G9.1 p138.

Rebecca and Natalie

Alan and Kathryn

5 R9.2 P Listen and practise. Copy the stress.

I'll lŏse my jŏb → *If I'm lăte agăin, I'll lŏse my jŏb.*

6 Fill in the gaps with the correct form of the verbs in brackets.

1 A If you _don't hurry_ (not hurry), you _'ll be_ (be) late.
   B OK, I'm going. I _____ (ring) you if there _____ (be) a problem.

2 A Don't worry. If she _____ (miss) the last bus, she _____ (get) a taxi.
   B But look at the time. If she _____ (not be) home soon, I _____ (start) worrying.

3 A If he _____ (not get) here in the next ten minutes, I _____ (go) without him.
   B If I _____ (see) him, I _____ (tell) him you're waiting.

7 a) Alan is going on a business trip. Read sentences a)–e). Then put the things on the list in the order he is going to do them.

   a) I'll pack **before** I go to bed.
   b) I won't leave the office **until** I finish this report.
   c) I'll phone the hotel **after** I talk to him.
   d) **As soon as** I finish the report, I'll go to the bank.
   e) I'll call Frank **when** I get home.

   b) R9.3 Listen and check.

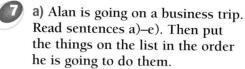

To do

- phone hotel – check reservations
- call Frank about plane tickets
- pack for trip
- finish report 1
- go to bank

Help with Grammar Future time clauses with *when, as soon as, before, after, until*

8 a) Look at the sentences in 7a) and answer these questions.

1 Do these sentences talk about the present or the future?
2 Which verb form comes after *when, as soon as, before, after* and *until*?
3 Which verb form is in the main clause?

b) Choose the correct words/phrases in the rules.

- We use *if/when* to say we are certain something will happen.
- We use *if/when* to say something is possible, but it isn't certain.
- We use *as soon as /until* to say something will happen immediately after something else.
- We use *until/after* to say something stops happening at this time.

c) Check in G9.2 p138.

9 a) Choose the correct words/phrases. Then fill in the gaps with the correct form of the verbs in brackets.

1 I'll probably work *as soon as/until* I _____ (be) sixty-five.
2 I _____ (do) my homework *before/as soon as* the class finishes.
3 *When/If* I _____ (get) home today, I'll probably watch TV.
4 Maybe I _____ (phone) some friends *if/after* I have dinner.
5 I'll probably read a book *before/after* I _____ (go) to sleep.
6 I _____ (study) English next year *if/until* I have time.

b) Tick the sentences that are true for you. Compare sentences with another student.

Get ready ... Get it right!

10 Work in pairs. Student A → p105. Student B → p113. Follow the instructions.

9B Sleepless nights

Vocabulary adjectives to describe feelings
Grammar too, too much, too many, (not) enough
Review should/shouldn't

QUICK REVIEW ●●●
Work in pairs. Write all the phrases for everyday problems you can remember. Which of these problems have you had in the last three months?

Vocabulary
Adjectives to describe feelings

1 **a)** Tick the words you know. Check new words in **V9.2** p137.

> bored   worried   stressed
> excited   depressed   angry
> pleased   embarrassed   tired
> satisfied   guilty   upset   lonely
> nervous   confident   fed up
> sad   calm   annoyed

b) Work in pairs. Which words describe positive feelings? Which describe negative feelings?

2 **a)** Choose six adjectives from **1a)**. Write when you feel like this on a piece of paper. Do not write the adjectives.

before an exam

b) Work in pairs. Swap papers. Take turns to guess the adjectives.

> Do you feel confident before an exam?

> No, not usually.

> Do you feel nervous?

> Yes, I do!

Listening and Grammar

3 Work in groups. Discuss these questions.

1 What's the best age to have children? Why?
2 How does your life change when you have your first baby, do you think?
3 Do you know people with babies or young children? Tell the other students about them.
4 Do you ever look after children for friends or someone in your family? If yes, do you like doing it?

Martin

Meg

Vicky

4 **a)** Look at the photo. How do the parents feel, do you think?

b) **R9.4** Listen and tick the things Vicky and Martin talk about.

	Vicky	Martin
1 feeling depressed	✓	
2 sleep problems		
3 feeling lonely		
4 social life		
5 money		
6 moving house		
7 good things about being a parent		
8 having more children		

5 **a)** Work in pairs. Who said these things, Vicky or Martin?

1 I feel a bit guilty, so I try not to get home **too late**.
2 I get upset when he says he's got **too much work** to do.
3 I've always got **too many things** to do.
4 She's **not old enough** to talk.
5 I do**n't** have **enough energy** to do anything in the day.
6 I earn **enough money** for the whole family.
7 I think this place is **big enough** for us.

b) R9.4 Listen again and check.

Help with Grammar *too, too much, too many, (not) enough*

6 **a)** We use *too, too much* and *too many* to say something is <u>more</u> than we want. Look at sentences 1–3 in **5a**). Then fill in the gaps with *countable noun, uncountable noun* or *adjective*.

- *too* + ...
- *too much* + ...
- *too many* + ...

b) We use *not enough* to say something is <u>less</u> than we want. Look at sentences 4 and 5 in **5a**). Then fill in the gaps with *noun* or *adjective*.

- *not* + ... + *enough*
- *not* + *verb* + *enough* + ...

c) We use *enough* to say something is the <u>correct</u> number or amount. Look at sentences 6 and 7 in **5a**). Then fill in the gaps with *noun* or *adjective*.

- *enough* + ...
- .... + *enough*

d) Do we use the infinitive with *to* or *verb+ing* after the phrases in sentences 1–5 in **5a**)?

e) Check in G9.3 p138.

7 R9.5 P Listen and practise.

gẻt hỏme tỏỏ lảte → I trỷ nỏt to gẻt hỏme tỏỏ lảte.

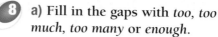

8 **a)** Fill in the gaps with *too, too much, too many* or *enough*.

1 Two children are <u>enough</u>. More than two is ....
2 Fathers don't spend .... time with their children.
3 Children watch .... TV. They should play outside more.
4 Eighteen-year-olds aren't mature .... to have children.

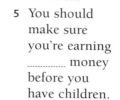

5 You should make sure you're earning .... money before you have children.

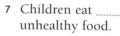

6 Forty isn't .... old to have a child.
7 Children eat .... unhealthy food.

b) Tick the sentences you agree with.

c) Work in groups. Compare your answers and give reasons. Which sentences do you all agree or disagree with?

Get ready … Get it right!

9 Write six sentences about problems in your life. Use these ideas or your own, adjectives from **1a**) and *too, too much, too many, (not) enough*.

| money | work | house/flat | family | the weather |
| relationships | clothes | friends | free time | learning English |

I haven't got enough money to go on holiday.
I'm very stressed because I've got too much work to do.

10 **a)** Work in groups. Tell the other students about your problems. Give advice with *You should/shouldn't …* and *Why don't you … ?*.

> I've got too much work to do.

> You should talk to your boss.

> Why don't you ask someone to help you?

b) What was the best piece of advice other students gave you? Tell the class.

9C In the neighbourhood

Vocabulary phrasal verbs
Skills Reading: a letter
to a newspaper; Listening:
a news report
Help with Listening fillers
Review *too, too much, too
many, (not) enough*; adjectives
to describe feelings

QUICK REVIEW ● ● ●
Work in pairs. Make a list of adjectives to describe feelings: *excited*, *stressed*, etc.
Choose four of your adjectives. Take turns to tell your partner about the last
time you felt like this.

Vocabulary Phrasal verbs

1 Work in groups. Tell the other students about your neighbours. Who are they? What are they like? Do you have any problems with them?

2 **a)** Read this letter and answer these questions.

1 What problem does Yvonne have?
2 How has she tried to solve the problem?
3 How has this problem changed her day-to-day life?
4 How does she feel now?

b) Work in pairs. What advice can you give Yvonne?

NIGHTMARE NEIGHBOURS

I've lived in a rented flat for the last six months and until recently life has been very quiet and peaceful. But now a new couple have **moved in** next door and they are making my life impossible. The main problem is that they have parties during the week that **go on** all night. Sometimes their friends **turn up** at their flat at two or three in the morning and when I complain they just tell me to **go away**. My two children can't sleep because of the noise, so I don't get enough sleep either. I was doing evening classes twice a week, but I've had to **give them up** because I'm too tired to go. Now when I get home I just **take off** my coat, **sit down** in front of the TV and fall asleep – until the party starts next door, of course.

All this is making me very depressed and fed up and I just can't **put up with** the noise any longer. I like living here and I **get on** well **with** all my other neighbours, but these people are a nightmare. I don't want to **go back** to my parents' house where we were living before, but I don't know what else to do. Do your readers have any advice for me?

Mrs Yvonne Chapman,
Catford

3 Read the letter again. Match the phrasal verbs in **bold** to their meanings a)–j).

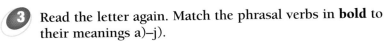

a) start living in a new home *move in*
b) like someone and be friendly to him/her *get on with*
c) be standing and then sit in a chair
d) tolerate
e) stop doing
f) leave a place
g) continue
h) arrive at a place
i) return
j) remove

Help with Vocabulary Phrasal verbs

4 **a)** Phrasal verbs have two or three parts: a verb and one or two particles. Look at the table. Then write phrasal verbs c) and d) in **3** in the table.

verb	particle(s)
move	in
get	on with

b) Read about phrasal verbs.

● Some phrasal verbs are **literal**. We can understand the meaning from the verb and the particle(s):

*A new couple have **moved in** next door.*

● Some phrasal verbs are **non-literal**. We can't always understand the meaning from the verb and the particle(s):

*I **get on** well **with** all my other neighbours.* (= like and be friendly)

c) Look at phrasal verbs c)–j) in **3**. Which are: literal (L)? non-literal (NL)?

d) Check in V9.3 p137.

5 R9.6 P Listen and practise. Copy the linking.

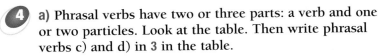

A new couple have moved in next door.

6 Work in groups. Group A → p109. Group B → p117. Follow the instructions.

9 **a)** Think about the problems in your neighbourhood. Make eight sentences with *too much, too many, (not) enough*. Use the words/phrases in the box or your own ideas.

> traffic   cinemas
> places for children to play
> places to park   noise at night
> trains   buses   pollution
> rubbish   dogs   late-night bars
> good schools   parks
> sports centres   police

There's too much traffic.
There aren't enough cinemas.

b) Work in groups. Compare your ideas. How many are the same? What are the three biggest problems?

Listening

 a) [R9.7] Listen to five people talking about their neighbours. Put pictures A–E in order.

b) Listen again. Answer these questions.

1 What do the first person's neighbours do when she goes away?
2 What is the second person thinking of doing?
3 How far away is the third person's nearest neighbour?
4 Why does the fourth person think the children get into trouble?
5 Why is it important for the fifth person to park near her house?

c) Work in pairs. Who do you think has the biggest problem with their neighbours?

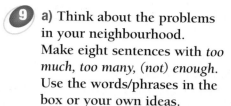

10 **a)** Make a list of five things you would like to do to improve your town/city (or the town/city you're studying in).

improve public transport
build a new cinema

b) Work in pairs. Explain why you have chosen the things on your list. Then choose the five best things from both lists.

> I'd like to improve public transport because there are too many cars.

> Yes, that's a good idea. I've got that on my list too.

c) Work in large groups or with the whole class. Agree on a final list of five things. Which is the most important, do you think?

Help with Listening Fillers

• In spoken English we often use words/phrases to give us time to think (*well*, etc.). These fillers don't have any meaning.

8 **a)** <u>Underline</u> the fillers in these sentences.

1 <u>Well</u>, I kind of get on well with all my neighbours er except one.
2 They've er got a teenage son, you see, and he's, like, learning to play the drums.
3 And, you know, that's um just the way I want it.

b) [R9.7] Look at R9.7, p154. Listen again and <u>underline</u> all the fillers.

9D Invitations

Real World invitations and making arrangements
Help with Listening intonation (2)
Review Present Continuous for future arrangements

QUICK REVIEW ●●●
Work in pairs. Write all the phrasal verbs you know. Compare answers with another pair. Who has got the most? Do you know the meaning of all the phrasal verbs?

1 a) Write the names of two friends from different times in your life. When did you last see them? What did you do together?

b) Work in groups. Tell the other students about your friends and the last time you saw them.

2 R9.8 Listen to Martin's phone conversations with Lucy and Dave. Answer the questions.

1 Why is Martin phoning Lucy and Dave?
2 Are Lucy and Dave free that evening?
3 What arrangement do Martin and Dave make?

3 a) Work in pairs. Find five mistakes in this paragraph.

Martin and Vicky are having a dinner party on Saturday. It starts at 7.30. Lucy is coming to the party. Dave can't come because he's working at the weekend. Martin and Dave are meeting after work on Wednesday. They're meeting in a restaurant on Market Street at 6.30.

b) R9.8 Listen again and check your answers to 3a).

Real World Invitations and making arrangements

4 a) Match headings a)–d) to sentences 1–10.

a) asking about people's arrangements
b) inviting someone to do something
c) saying yes or no
d) arranging a time and place

1 Are you doing anything next Friday? *a)*
2 Would you like to come?
3 Yes, I'd love to.
4 I'd love to, but I can't.
5 Why don't we meet for a drink?
6 Yes, that'd be great.
7 Are you free on Wednesday?
8 What are you doing on Tuesday?
9 Where/What time shall we meet?
10 How about 6.30?

b) Answer these questions.

1 Look at sentences 1 and 8. Which verb form do we use to ask about people's arrangements?
2 Look at sentence 2. Which verb form comes after *Would you like ... ?*
3 Look at sentence 5. Which verb form comes after *Why don't we ... ?*

c) Check in RW9.1 p138.

Help with Listening Intonation (2)

● Remember: we know if people are interested by how much their voices move up and down.

5 R9.9 Listen to the same sentences said twice. Which voice sounds interested, a) or b)?

1 a) b)   4 a) b)
2 a) b)   5 a) b)
3 a) b)   6 a) b)

6 R9.10 P Listen and practise the sentences in 4a). Copy the polite intonation.

Are you doing anything next Friday?

7 **a)** Martin phones another friend, Ian, to invite him to the dinner party. Work in pairs and write their conversation. Use sentences from **4a)** and your own ideas.

b) Practise the conversation in pairs until you remember it.

c) Role-play the conversation for other students.

8 **a)** Draw a diary page for next week. Write four arrangements. If you don't have any, invent them!

Mon	cinema – Eva
Tues	meet Jan 1p.m.
Wed	
Thurs	tennis Magda 6.30
Fri	
Sat	party – Tomek's house
Sun	

b) Think of three more things you would like to do next week. <u>Don't</u> write them in your diary.

c) Work in groups or with the whole class. Invite other students to do the things from **8b)**. If they say yes, arrange a day/time/place to meet. Write the new arrangements in your diary.

d) Work in pairs. Take turns to tell your partner what you are doing next week. Who is the busiest?

♪ **R9.11** Look at the song *What the World Needs Now* on p101. Follow the instructions.

9 Review   Language Summary 9, p137

1 **a)** Cross out the incorrect word/phrase. **V9.1**

1 oversleep *on Friday/this morning/in traffic*
2 get *an accident/stuck in traffic/lost*
3 lose *your keys/a bus/your wallet*
4 run out of *your wallet/coffee/money*
5 miss *a bus/your keys/a train*

b) Work in pairs. Take turns to ask and answer questions with the phrases in **1a)**.
When was the last time you overslept?

2 **a)** Fill in the gaps with the correct form of the verbs in brackets. **G9.1**

1 If I *don't leave* now, I .... late. (not leave, be)
2 If I .... late, my girlfriend .... for me. (be, not wait)
3 If she .... for me, I .... annoyed. (not wait, get)
4 If she .... I'm annoyed, she .... angry. (know, get)
5 If she .... angry, I .... apologise! (get, have to)

b) Work in pairs. Make a story like the one in **2a)**. Begin with:
If James works harder, he'll ...

c) Work with another pair. Take turns to tell your stories.

3 **a)** Cross out the incorrect words/phrases. Sometimes both are possible. **G9.2**

1 I'll do the washing up *before/as soon as* I go to bed.
2 I won't leave *before/until* you get here.
3 I'll stay *until/before* you arrive.
4 I'll tell him *when/until* she comes.
5 *As soon as/When* you get home, will you phone me?

b) Work in pairs. Compare answers.

4 **a)** Complete these sentences about today's world. **G9.3**

1 There are too many …
2 People are too …
3 There's too much …
4 There isn't enough …
5 There aren't enough …

b) Work in pairs. Discuss your ideas. Do you agree?

5 **a)** Complete the phrasal verbs with these particles. **V9.3**

up (x 2)   away
with   on

1 I haven't been .... for the weekend for ages.
2 I'm going to give .... English next year.
3 My friends never turn .... on time. They're always late.
4 I'm planning to go .... learning English until I'm fluent.
5 I get on .... all my relatives.

b) Make the sentences true for you. Then compare with a partner.

Progress Portfolio

a) Tick the things you can do in English.

☐ I can talk about everyday problems.
☐ I can talk about possible future events.
☐ I can say how I feel about things.
☐ I can invite people to dinner, a party, etc.
☐ I can accept and refuse an invitation politely.
☐ I can arrange where and when to meet people.

b) What do you need to study again? ● **9A–D**

10A Going, going, gone!

QUICK REVIEW ●●●
Imagine you are having a party sometime next week. Decide on the day and time. Invite other students to your party. How many people can come?

Reading and Grammar

 1 Work in groups. Discuss these questions.

1 What were the last three things you bought (not food or drink)? Where did you buy them?

2 Have you ever been to an auction? If yes, did you buy anything?

 2 a) Read the article and answer these questions.

1 Do Christie's and Sotheby's only sell art?
2 Which two items did Sotheby's sell in May 2004?
3 What is 'memorabilia'?
4 Where can you buy memorabilia?

b) Read the article again. Then fill in gaps 1–7 with these prices.

£56,000	£73,000	£157,000	£58,000,000
£700,000	£1,770,000	£117,000	

c) **R10.1** Listen and check.

THE MEMORABILIA BUSINESS

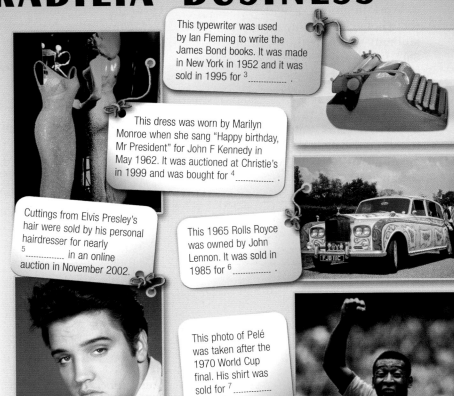

Christie's and Sotheby's are known all over the world for their sales of fine art. In May 2004, for example, a painting by Picasso called *Boy with a Pipe* was sold by Sotheby's for a record-breaking [1] _____ . But these two famous auction houses also make a lot of money selling memorabilia from the world of music, sport and cinema. Beatles memorabilia is very valuable and is collected by fans all over the world — one of George Harrison's guitars was sold at Sotheby's for [2] _____ in the same week as the Picasso painting. But you don't have to go to an auction house to buy something that was owned by your favourite star — thousands of items of memorabilia are bought and sold every day on Internet sites like eBay. Take a look at some of the things that people have bought over the years.

This typewriter was used by Ian Fleming to write the James Bond books. It was made in New York in 1952 and it was sold in 1995 for [3] _____ .

This dress was worn by Marilyn Monroe when she sang "Happy birthday, Mr President" for John F Kennedy in May 1962. It was auctioned at Christie's in 1999 and was bought for [4] _____ .

Cuttings from Elvis Presley's hair were sold by his personal hairdresser for nearly [5] _____ in an online auction in November 2002.

This 1965 Rolls Royce was owned by John Lennon. It was sold in 1985 for [6] _____ .

This photo of Pelé was taken after the 1970 World Cup final. His shirt was sold for [7] _____ in 2002.

3 **a) Work in pairs. Don't look at the article. How much can you remember?**

1 Where was Ian Fleming's typewriter made?
2 When was the photo of Pelé taken?
3 Who were Elvis's hair cuttings sold by?
4 When was Marilyn Monroe's dress sold?
5 How much was the Picasso painting sold for?

b) Read the article again and check.

Help with Grammar Present Simple passive; Past Simple passive

4 **a) Look at these sentences. Then answer the questions.**

active	Ian Fleming used this typewriter.
passive	This typewriter was used by Ian Fleming.

1 In which sentence are we more interested in: a) Ian Fleming? b) the typewriter?
2 What is the subject in each sentence?

b) Choose the correct words in these rules.

- The person doing the action is the subject in *active/passive* sentences.
- We often use the *active/passive* when we are more interested in what happened to someone or something than in who did the action.
- In *active/passive* sentences we can use *by* to say who or what did the action (the agent).

c) Fill in the gaps with *past participle*, *are*, and *were*.

- To make the Present Simple passive we use: subject + *am*, *is* or _____ + _____ .
- To make the Past Simple passive we use: subject + *was* or _____ + _____ .

d) Look at 3a). How do we make questions in the passive?

e) Check in G10.1 **p140.**

5 R10.2 P **Listen and practise.**
Christie's and Sotheby's are known all over the world.

6 **a) Read the article again and underline all the passive sentences. Which are: in the Present Simple? in the Past Simple?**

b) Work in pairs. Check your answers.

---

 7 **Read about eBay. Put the verbs in brackets in the correct active or passive form.**

Pierre Omidyar ¹*started* (start) eBay in his apartment in 1995. At that time his website ² _____ (call) AuctionWeb, but he ³ _____ (change) the name to eBay in 1997. On its first day AuctionWeb ⁴ _____ (not visit) by a single person, but eBay has become one of the most successful Internet businesses in the world. It now ⁵ _____ (have) over 27,000 categories and it ⁶ _____ (use) by over 114 million people. About 100,000 people ⁷ _____ (make) their living by selling things on eBay. Many people ⁸ _____ (go) to eBay to buy and sell unusual things. One person ⁹ _____ (buy) a piece of French toast, half-eaten by singer Justin Timberlake, for $1,025, and a game of golf with Tiger Woods ¹⁰ _____ (buy) by a fan for $425,000. One person even ¹¹ _____ (try) to sell 'absolutely nothing' – he got $1.03!

b) Work in pairs. Which information about eBay do you think is the most suprising?

Vocabulary Verbs often used in the passive

8 **a) Work in pairs. Which nouns can you use with these verbs?**

manufacture	paint	direct	publish
write	build	invent	grow	make

You can write a book.

b) Do the exercise in V10.1 **p139.**

9 **a) What are the past participles of the verbs in 8a)?**

b) Fill in the gaps with the correct form of the verbs in 8a). Then complete the sentences to make them true for you.

1 My favourite book _____ by _____ .
2 My mobile phone _____ in _____ .
3 My favourite film _____ by _____ .
4 My house/flat _____ about _____ ago.
5 My favourite shoes _____ in _____ .

c) Compare sentences with a partner. How many are the same?

Get ready … Get it right!

10 Work in two groups. Group A → p103. Group B → p111. Follow the instructions.

10B Changing trends

Vocabulary *anything, someone, no one, everywhere,* etc.
Grammar *used to*
Help with Listening *used to*
Review Past Simple

QUICK REVIEW ● ● ●
Think of five famous buildings, paintings or books from your country. Work in pairs. Tell your partner when these things were built/painted/written and who by.

Listening and Grammar

1 **Work in pairs. Discuss these questions.**

1 What type of things do you like (and hate) shopping for?
2 Who goes shopping more often in your country, men or women? What do they buy?
3 Is it a good idea for men and women to go shopping together? Why?/Why not?
4 What was the last thing you bought (not food or drink)?

2 **a)** R10.3 **Listen to an interview with Sam Bennett about his radio programme, *Real Men Shop!*. Put the things he talks about in order.**

a) skincare products for men
b) a department store
c) a men's clothes shop
d) food shopping in the 1970s

b) Listen again. Fill in the gaps in these sentences.

1 Selfridges opened in ....
2 Selfridges used to have a special room only for ....
3 In the 1970s most married men never used to do the .... shopping.
4 'Shopping girlfriends' used to help men choose ....
5 .... years ago you didn't use to see skincare products for men.

c) How have shopping trends changed in your country?

Help with Grammar *used to*

3 **a) Look at sentences 2–4 in 2b). Then choose the correct words in the rules.**

● We use *used to* to talk about *present/past* habits and repeated actions.
● We *can/can't* use *used to* with state verbs (*be, like, have, want,* etc.).
● After *used to* we use *the infinitive/verb+ing*.

b) Look at sentence 1 in 2b). Why can't you use *used to* in this sentence, do you think?

c) Look at sentence 5 in 2b). How do we make the negative of *used to*?

d) Make questions with these words. What are the positive and negative short answers for question 2?

1 single men / do / did / What / use to ?
2 men / buy / use to / skincare products / Did ?

e) Check in G10.2 **p140.**

Help with Listening *used to*

 a) R10.4 Listen to these sentences. Notice how we say the different forms of *used to*.

They used to /juːstə/ have a special room.
Men didn't use to /juːstə/ do anything like that.
What did single men use to /juːstə/ do?

b) R10.3 Look at R10.3, p155. Listen to the interview again and notice how we say the different forms of *used to*.

 a) Read sentences 1–8 about shopping in the UK in the 1930s. Fill in the gaps with the correct form of *used to* and these verbs.

| ~~drink~~ | eat | open | not sell |

1 Most people *used to drink* tea not coffee.
2 Shops never .... on Sundays.
3 People .... less sugar.
4 Shops .... frozen food.

| buy | not be | take | not have |

5 There .... any supermarkets.
6 People .... food every day.
7 People .... credit cards.
8 People always .... their own shopping bags.

b) R10.5 P Listen and check. Then listen again and practise.

Most people used to /juːstə/ drink tea not coffee.

 a) Write four sentences with *used to/ didn't use to* about your (or your family's) shopping habits ten years ago.

I used to go shopping at lunchtime.

b) Work in groups. Compare sentences. Are any the same?

Help with Vocabulary *anything, someone, no one, everywhere, etc.*

 a) Look at these sentences from the interview. Which words in **bold** talk about: a) people? b) places? c) things?

*Men didn't use to do **anything** like that.*
***Someone** bought their clothes for them.*
***No one**'s surprised anymore.*
*Now you can buy them **everywhere**.*

b) Fill in the gaps in the table.

	1	2	3	4
people	someone		no one	
places				everywhere
things		anything		

c) Look at columns 1 and 2. Which do we usually use in: a) positive sentences? b) negative sentences and questions?

d) Check in V10.2 p139.

 a) Choose the correct words in these sentences.

1 *Everything/No one* used to buy food in supermarkets.
2 You could buy fresh fruit *everywhere/something*.
3 *Everything/Someone* used to cost less than it does now.
4 There didn't use to be *nothing/anything* to do at the weekends.
5 You couldn't travel *anywhere/somewhere* by plane.
6 *Anyone/Everyone* used to use the same currency as they do now.

b) Tick the sentences that you think are true about your country in the 1930s. Compare answers with a partner.

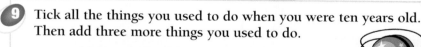
Get ready ... Get it right!

9 Tick all the things you used to do when you were ten years old. Then add three more things you used to do.

- spend hours reading/playing computer games
- have a favourite toy/TV programme
- put posters of pop stars/footballers on my bedroom wall
- be very shy/moody
- get into trouble with my parents/the teachers
- be good or bad at maths/languages
- play on my own/with my friends a lot
- study very hard/do sports at school

10 Work in groups. Talk about things you used to do when you were ten. Ask follow-up questions if possible.

I used to spend hours playing computer games.

So did I. Which games did you use to play?

Vocabulary use of articles: *a*, *an*, *the*, no article
Skills Reading: a magazine article; Reading and Listening: a profile
Review Past Simple passive; *have to*

VOCABULARY AND SKILLS

QUICK REVIEW ●●●
Work in pairs. Find six things that you both used to do five years ago that you don't do now.

Reading and Vocabulary

1 Work in groups. Discuss these questions.

1 How important are clothes to people in your country, do you think?
2 Do you think people spend too much money on clothes?
3 How many 'designer labels' can you name? What do these companies sell?

2 Read the magazine article about the Gucci family. Fill in gaps a)–f) in the family tree.

3 Read the magazine article again and tick the correct sentences. Change the incorrect sentences.

1 Guccio Gucci designed clothes.
2 Rodolfo was good friends with Paolo.
3 Paolo wanted to start his own business.
4 Paolo gave information about his father to the police.
5 Maurizio was a successful businessman.
6 Patrizia shot Maurizio.

THE GUCCI STORY

Guccio Gucci 1881–a)_____   Aida Gucci

Aldo Gucci 1904 –b)_____   Ugo Gucci   c)_____ Gucci   Rodolfo Gucci

Roberto Gucci   d)_____ Gucci   Patrizia e)_____   Maurizio Gucci 1954 –f)_____

Lots of people love buying ¹**clothes** and Gucci is one of ²**the most famous** fashion houses in ³**the world**. It was started in ⁴**Italy** in 1921 by a man named Guccio Gucci. He was ⁵**a designer** who made leather bags and suitcases and he had ⁶**a small shop** in Florence. ⁷**The shop** was the beginning of the family business and by 1953 Guccio's four sons, Aldo, Ugo, Vasco and Rodolfo, were all working for the company.

When Guccio died in 1953, his eldest son Aldo became ⁸**the head** of Gucci and took the Gucci label to ⁹**America**, while Rodolfo managed the Italian side of the business. Aldo's son, Paolo, didn't get on with his father or his uncle, Rodolfo, so he made plans to start his own company called Paolo Gucci. When Aldo discovered this, he sacked Paolo and made it impossible for his son to start his own fashion business. Paolo was so angry that he told the Italian police his father wasn't paying enough tax. Aldo was sent to prison for a year and a day.

After Aldo died in 1990, his nephew, Maurizio, became the head of Gucci. Unfortunately Maurizio wasn't ¹⁰**a very good businessman** and in 1991 the company lost $60 million.

This was ¹¹**the worst** year in Gucci's history. Maurizio was also having problems with his marriage. One day he went on a business trip and decided not to go back to his wife, Patrizia Reggiani. They finally got divorced in 1994 and a year later Patrizia hired ¹²**a gunman** to murder her ex-husband. On 27ᵗʰ March 1995, ¹³**the gunman** shot and killed Maurizio while he was walking to work. Patrizia was sent to prison for 26 years.

Gucci ¹⁴**products** are still sold all over the world, but there are no members of the Gucci family in the successful company we know today.

Help with Vocabulary Use of articles: *a, an, the*, no article

4 **a)** Look at the words/phrases 1–7 in the first paragraph of the article. Match one word/phrase to each of these rules.

- We use *a* or *an*:
  a) with jobs. *a designer*
  b) to talk about a person or a thing for the first time.
- We use *the*:
  c) to talk about a person or a thing for the second/third/fourth, etc. time.
  d) when there is only one (or one in a particular place).
  e) with superlatives.
- We don't use an article:
  f) to talk about people or things in general.
  g) for most cities and countries.

b) Check in V10.3 p139.

5 Look at the rest of the article. Match one of the words/phrases 8–14 with each rule a)–g) in **4a)**. There is one word/phrase for each rule.

Reading and Listening

6 **a)** Read about another Italian fashion designer, Gianni Versace. Fill in the gaps with *a, an, the* or – .

GIANNI VERSACE – fashion designer

Gianni Versace was born in 1946 in a town called ¹_____ – Reggio Calabria. Even when he was ²_____ child he loved ³_____ clothes. When he was 25 he decided to go to ⁴_____ Milan and become ⁵_____ fashion designer, and in 1982 he won his first award for being ⁶_____ best designer of ⁷_____ women's clothes. He created ⁸_____ new perfume for men called 'Versace l'Homme' in 1984.

In 1995 he organised ⁹_____ party with Elton John to raise money for ¹⁰_____ AIDS patients. At ¹¹_____ party he signed copies of his new book, *Men without Ties*, and gave all ¹²_____ money from ¹³_____ book to charity.

On July 15ᵗʰ 1997 Versace was murdered in ¹⁴_____ Miami. No one really knows ¹⁵_____ reason why he was killed.

b) R10.6 Read and listen to the information about Versace. What extra information is in the recording?

7 **a)** Do the questionnaire.

Are you a fashion victim?

1 How important is it for you to wear clothes that are in fashion?
a) Very important.
b) Quite important.
c) Not at all important.

2 How many designer clothes have you got?
a) One or two things for special occasions.
b) None – they're too expensive.
c) Quite a lot – I love designer clothes.

3 How often do you go shopping for clothes?
a) Two or three times a year.
b) Once or twice a month.
c) Every week, if possible.

4 What kind of clothes do you look for when you go shopping?
a) Things I've seen in fashion magazines.
b) Things that I think will look good on me.
c) Things that are cheap or in a sale.

5 There's a party at the weekend. Do you buy some new clothes?
a) Maybe, if I haven't got anything nice to wear.
b) No, of course not.
c) Yes, I always buy something new for a party.

6 How many pairs of shoes have you got?
a) 5–15 pairs.
b) More than 15 pairs.
c) 1–5 pairs. I've only got one pair of feet!

b) Work in pairs. Take turns to ask and answer the questions. How many of your answers are the same?

c) Check your answers on p158. Are you and your partner fashion victims?

d) Work in groups. Do you agree with the description of you on p158? Why?/Why not?

10D Can I help you?

Real World in a shop
Vocabulary shopping
Help with Listening what shop assistants say
Review clothes; articles

QUICK REVIEW ●●●

Work in pairs. Make a list of all the clothes vocabulary you can remember. Compare lists with another pair. Who has the most words? Which students in the class are wearing the things on your list?

1 a) Look at the picture. How many things do you know in English?

b) Work in pairs. Compare answers. Do you have the same things?

c) Tick the words/phrases you know. Then do the exercise in V10.4 p139.

size	extra large	large	medium
small	a fitting room		try on
it doesn't fit	sign here		a receipt
cash	here's your change		

Help with Listening
What shop assistants say

 2 a) R10.7 Listen to two conversations in a shop. Put the sentences in the order you hear them.

1
a) Here's your change and your receipt.
b) I'll have a look ... yes, here's a medium.
c) The fitting room's over there.
d) Can I help you?
e) Does it fit?
f) What size is that one?

2
a) How would you like to pay?
b) What size do you want?
c) Check the amount and sign here, please.
d) Here you are. That's £19.75 altogether.
e) Who's next, please?

b) Work in pairs. Compare answers.

 3 R10.7 Listen again. Choose the correct answers.

1 The first customer wants a *bigger/smaller* size.
2 She *tries/doesn't try* it on.
3 The T-shirt costs *£5/£15*.
4 The second customer buys a *map/postcard* and *batteries/a camera*.
5 He pays *cash/by credit card*.

Real World In a shop

4 a) Fill in the gaps with these words.

sell	size	looking	take	Excuse	try	Could

1 I'm just _____ , thanks.
2 _____ me.
3 Have you got this T-shirt in a smaller _____ ?
4 Can I _____ it on, please?
5 OK, I'll _____ it.
6 _____ I have this map, please?
7 Do you _____ batteries?

b) Check in RW10.1 p140.

 5 R10.8 P Listen and practise the sentences in 4a). Copy the polite intonation.

I'm just looking, thanks.

1 **a)** Fill in the gaps with the correct active or passive form of the verbs in brackets. Then choose the correct answer. G10.1

1 Pablo Picasso/Henri Matisse __painted__ (paint) Guernica.
2 Rolex watches _____ (make) in *Japan/Switzerland*.
3 Marie Curie _____ (discover) *penicillin/radium*.
4 Porsche cars _____ (manufacture) in *Germany/ Sweden*.
5 The 2002 World Cup _____ (win) by *Brazil/ Germany*.
6 Frankenstein _____ (write) by *Bram Stoker/Mary Shelley*.

b) Work in pairs. Compare answers. Then check on p158.

2 In which sentences can you use *used to*? Change the verbs in **bold** if possible. G10.2

1 I **went** shopping every weekend. ✓
   I used to go shopping every weekend.
2 But in May I **lost** my job. ✗
3 After that I **didn't go** shopping very often.
4 I **got** quite depressed.
5 I **didn't have** very much money.
6 Then one day I **found** the perfect job.
7 I **became** a buyer for a big department store.

3 **a)** Write six sentences with *used to/didn't use to* to describe how life has changed in your country/city/town over the years. G10.2

There didn't use to be as many cafés as there are now.

b) Work in pairs. Discuss the changes. Are any the same?

4 **a)** Choose the correct word. V10.2

1 I haven't got *anything/nothing* to do when I get home.
2 I know *someone/anyone* who works at home.
3 I'm not going *anything/ anywhere* this weekend.
4 I take my mobile phone *everywhere/somewhere*.
5 *Anyone/No one* in my family is over 70 years old.

b) Make the sentences true for you.

c) Work in pairs. Compare sentences. Are any the same?

5 **a)** Fill in the gaps with *a, the* or –. V10.3

I had [1] _a_ car accident last year. [2] _____ accident happened at [3] _____ night when [4] _____ weather was really bad and I had to buy [5] _____ new car. I got it from [6] _____ friend who's [7] _____ car salesman in [8] _____ London. I used to buy [9] _____ expensive cars, but this time I got [10] _____ cheapest car there was!

b) Work in pairs. Compare and say why you chose your answers.

I put 'the' because it's the second time the person talks about it.

6 **a)** Work in pairs. Use the prompts to write a conversation in the shop. Remember to use *please* and *thank you*.

SHOP ASSISTANT	Can / help you?
CUSTOMER	/ this shirt in blue?
SHOP ASSISTANT	/ have / look. Yes, here / blue one.
CUSTOMER	/ try / on?
SHOP ASSISTANT	Sure. / fitting room / over there.
SHOP ASSISTANT	/ fit?
CUSTOMER	Yes, / take it.
SHOP ASSISTANT	/ £... / please. How / like / pay?
CUSTOMER	/ credit card.
SHOP ASSISTANT	Check / amount / sign here. Here / receipt.

b) Practise the conversation until you remember it.

c) Work with another pair. Take turns to role-play your conversation.

7 Work in pairs. Student A → p107. Student B → p115. Follow the instructions.

Progress Portfolio

a) Tick the things you can do in English.

☐ I can talk about where things were made, grown, etc.

☐ I can talk about how things are different now compared to the past.

☐ I can talk about my childhood.

☐ I can understand a simple profile of someone's life.

☐ I can have a simple conversation in a shop.

b) What do you need to study again? ● 10A–D

11 Gossip and news

Guess what?

Vocabulary verb-noun collocations (3)
Grammar Present Perfect for giving news with *just*, *yet* and *already*
Help with Listening /t/ at the end of words (2)
Review *will*

QUICK REVIEW ●●●
Work in pairs. Take turns to role-play a conversation between a shop assistant and a customer in a clothes shop. Try to continue each conversation for two minutes.

Vocabulary
Verb-noun collocations (3)

1 **a) Cross out the incorrect words/phrases. Check in V11.1 p141.**

1 get *sacked/an accident/ promoted/lost*
2 have *an accident/an operation/ 18 years old/a problem*
3 lose or find *an exam/a job/ a wallet/your keys*
4 pass or fail *a driving test/ a job/an exam/a course*

b) Use the verbs and words/ phrases in 1a) to make four sentences about yourself.

c) Work in pairs. Listen to your partner's sentences. Ask follow-up questions.

> I got promoted last year.

> Really? What's your new job?

Reading and Grammar

2 **Read Sharon's messages A–D. Answer the questions.**

1 Why is Tim in hospital?
2 What has Ted done that Jill hasn't?
3 What does Robin Hall want?
4 Who got sacked?
5 Which people are happy and which people aren't?

(A) Dear Sharon,
I tried to ring you but you were in a meeting. I've just heard that Tim's in hospital. **He's had a car accident.** He's already had an operation and he's doing well, but I don't know all the details yet. I'll phone you when I have some more news.
Love,
Deborah

(B) 10 a.m.
Robin Hall's just phoned. He hasn't received the money for the work he did for you last month. Have you sent him the cheque yet?

(C) Pippa's just lost her job! Give her a call.

(D) Hi Sharon!
We're having a great time here. It's a really beautiful island and the weather's wonderful. Ted's already done three dives and says it's amazing. I haven't done any yet, but I'm going to do my first one tomorrow. See you soon.
Love Jill and Ted

Help with Grammar Present Perfect for giving news with *just*, *yet* and *already*

3 **a)** Look at the sentences in **bold** in Sharon's messages. Which verbs are in the Present Perfect? Which verb is in the Past Simple?

b) Choose the correct verb forms in the rules.

- We use the *Present Perfect/Past Simple* for giving news about things that happened in the past, but are connected to now. We don't say the exact time they happened.
- We use the *Present Perfect/Past Simple* when we say the exact time something happened.

c) Look at the email (A) again. Find *just*, *yet* and *already*. Then fill in the gaps in the rules with these words.

- We use .... to say something hasn't happened, but we think it will happen in the future.
- We use .... to say something happened a short time ago but we don't know exactly when.
- We use .... to say something happened some time in the past (perhaps sooner than we expected).

d) Find *just*, *yet* and *already* in messages B–D. Then answer the questions.

1 Which of these words do we usually use in: positive sentences? negative sentences? questions?
2 Which words usually go: a) between the auxiliary and the past participle? b) at the end of the sentence or clause?

e) Check in G11.1 p142.

4 R11.1 P Listen and practise.

I've just heard that Tim's in hospital.
He's already had an operation.
I don't know all the details yet.

5 **a)** Put the words in brackets in the correct places in the sentences.

1 I've sent him a cheque. (just)
2 We've been here a week. (already)
3 I haven't been to visit him. (yet)
4 Ted's gone for another dive. (just)
5 Have you called her? (yet)
6 I've talked to his parents. (already)

b) Work in pairs. Match the sentences in 5a) with Sharon's messages A–D.

6 **a)** R11.2 Listen to Sharon talking to Pippa. Has Pippa got any good news?

b) Listen again and tick the things Pippa's already done.

To do
- clear desk
- check bank account
- tell Andrew the news
- phone Ed Burrows
- look for holiday on the Net
- book holiday

c) Work in pairs. Compare answers. What hasn't Pippa done yet?

Help with Listening /t/ at the end of words (2)

- Remember: in spoken English sometimes you don't hear /t/ at the end of a word when the next word starts with a consonant sound.

7 **a)** R11.3 Listen to these sentences. In which sentences do you hear the *t* in **bold**?

1 I've jus**t** got your message.
2 And wha**t** abou**t** Andrew?
3 He isn'**t** back from Germany until Friday.
4 I've jus**t** opened an email from Ed Burrows.

b) R11.2 Look at R11.2, p155. Listen to Sharon and Pippa's conversation again. Notice when we don't say /t/ at the end of words.

8 **a)** Make sentences with these words. Use the Present Perfect.

1 I / lunch / have / just
I've just had lunch.
2 yet / I / a holiday / not book / this year
3 already / this year / I / on holiday / go
4 what to do / yet / I / not decide / next weekend
5 a new job / just / I / find
6 look at / already / I / for this lesson / the CD-ROM

b) Tick the sentences that are true for you. Compare answers with a partner.

Get ready ... Get it right!

9 Work in pairs. Student A → p102. Student B → p110. Follow the instructions.

11B Murder mystery

Vocabulary crime
Grammar relative clauses with *who*, *which*, *that* and *where*
Review Present Perfect; Past Simple passive

QUICK REVIEW ●●●
Think of four pieces of news about you and people you know. Work in groups. Tell the other students your news: *My sister's just taken some exams.* Ask questions about your partners' news: *Has she got the results yet?*

Vocabulary Crime

1 Work in groups. Discuss these questions.

1 Do you like watching TV crime dramas or programmes about real-life crime? If yes, which ones?

2 Do you ever read crime novels? If yes, which authors and books are your favourites?

2 Tick the words you know. Then do the exercise in V11.2 p141.

rob	steal	burgle	murder
break into	shoot	bullets	
arrest	a victim	a suspect	

3 Fill in the gaps in the table with these words. Check in V11.3 p141.

steal	murderer	burgle	robbery
thief	robber	murder	burglary

verb	criminal	crime
rob		
steal		theft
	burglar	
murder		

4 Choose the correct words in these sentences.

1 Three men *robbed/stole* a bank in London last night and *robbed/stole* over £500,000. This was the third bank *robbery/burglary* in the city this month.

2 Last night my car was *burgled/broken into* and my CD player was *robbed/stolen*.

3 A man was *stolen/murdered* yesterday in Los Angeles. The police have *arrested/robbed* two *suspects/victims* in connection with the *murder/murderer*.

4 My brother's flat was *stolen/burgled* last week and his TV was *stolen/burgled*.

Listening and Grammar

5 a) R11.4 There has been a murder in Yately, a village in England. Listen to the conversation and match the people to their descriptions.

Mary — the murder victim
Alice — the new person in the village
Barry Clark — Ellen and Jack's son
Ellen — the owner of the flower shop
Jack Miller — Jack's wife
Adam — Jack's business partner

b) Work in pairs. Who are the people in pictures A–C?

6 Listen again and answer these questions.

1 When did the murder happen?
2 Where was the body found?
3 When did the Garden Centre open?
4 How was the victim killed?
5 What were Jack and Barry arguing about yesterday?
6 Who wanted to get divorced?
7 Why was Adam sent to prison?
8 When did he come out of prison?

Help with Grammar Relative clauses with *who, which, that* and *where*

7 **a)** Look at these sentences. The <u>underlined</u> clauses are called relative clauses. They tell you which person, thing or place we are talking about.

*That's the place **where** <u>they found the body</u>.*
*He's the man **who/that** <u>was murdered</u>.*
*Her marriage is the only thing **which/that** <u>makes her happy</u>.*

b) Complete the rule with the words in **bold**.

- To introduce relative clauses we use:
  a) .... or .... for people.
  b) .... or .... for things.
  c) .... for places.

c) Check in G11.2 p142.

8 Complete these sentences with *who, which, that* or *where*. Sometimes more than one answer is possible.

1 Jack Miller is the man ...*who*... was murdered.
2 The big house at the end of the village is .... the Miller family lives.
3 Alice is the woman .... owns the flower shop.
4 The only person .... has been in prison is Adam.
5 The police never found the money .... Adam stole.
6 Mary thought Yately was a sleepy village .... nothing ever happened.

9 **a)** Work in groups. Make a list of suspects. Who murdered Jack Miller, do you think? Why?

b) Compare answers with the whole class.

Get ready ... Get it right!

10 Work in two groups. Group A → p108. Group B → p116. Follow the instructions.

11 **a)** Work in pairs with a student from the other group. Take turns to point to the things in the picture and tell your partner what you know about them. Use relative clauses.

> This is the person who ...

> This is the gun that ...

> That's the place where ...

b) Who do you think murdered Jack Miller now? How and why did the murderer do it, do you think?

12 **a)** R11.5 Listen to a news report about the murder trial. Who is the murderer?

b) Look at R11.5, p156. Read and listen to the news report again. How did the murder happen? Why did the murderer kill Jack Miller?

Vocabulary guessing meaning from context
Skills Listening: the news; Reading: a newspaper article
Help with Listening sentence stress (2)
Review Present Perfect; Past Simple

VOCABULARY AND SKILLS

QUICK REVIEW ●●●
Write five definitions of people, things or places using relative clauses. Work in pairs. Take turns to say your definitions: *It's a place where you do exercise.* Your partner guesses the answer: *Is it a gym?*

(A) **Murder Mystery of Dolphin Lover**

(B) **Workmen steal Van Gogh**

(C) **Police and Protesters Clash at World Trade Conference**

(D) **TEA CAN STOP CANCER**

Listening

1 a) Read newspaper headlines A–D. Check new words with your teacher or in a dictionary. Which is the most interesting story, do you think?

b) R11.6 Listen to the news. Put the headlines in order.

2 a) Match two pieces of information to each of the headlines A–D.

1 they tried to stop cars arriving
2 swim-with-dolphin centres
3 they have to test all new products
4 two men dressed as gas inspectors
5 over $20 million
6 found dead in her car
7 over 40 arrests
8 an American cream

b) Work in pairs. How is the information in **2a)** connected to the headlines?

c) R11.6 Listen again and check.

Help with Listening
Sentence stress (2)

● You can often understand the general idea of a story by listening to the stressed words.

3 a) R11.6 Look at R11.6, p156. Listen again and follow the stressed words in the first three stories.

b) Look at the fourth story on p156. Decide which words are stressed.

c) Listen again and check.

Reading and Vocabulary

4 a) Match these words to the pictures.

a kangaroo   a storm   an unconscious person   a fence

b) Work in pairs. Don't read the article yet. What do you think happens in the story? Put the pictures in order.

c) Read the article and check.

5 Read the article again. Tick the true sentences. Correct the false ones.

1 Lulu found Mr Richards first.
2 Lulu went to find Mr Richards's daughter.
3 Lulu has lived on the farm for ten years.
4 Lulu's mother also lives on the farm.
5 Dr Wirth wants Lulu to get a medal.

Help with Vocabulary Guessing meaning from context

- Sometimes you can guess the meaning of a word by:
  a) knowing what type of word it is (noun, verb, adjective, etc.).
  b) understanding the general meaning of the story and the rest of the sentence.

6 a) Look at the words in **bold** in the article. Are they nouns, verbs or adjectives?

b) Choose the correct meanings a) or b). What information in the article helped you decide?

		a)	b)
1	severe	a) very bad	b) not very bad
2	damage	a) when things are broken	b) when things are very old
3	branch	a) a young bird	b) the 'arms' of a tree
4	barked	a) looked like a dog	b) made a noise like a dog
5	weird	a) unusual	b) normal
6	blind	a) you can't see	b) you can't hear

c) Check in V11.4 p141.

7 a) Look at R11.6, p156. Find these words.

demonstrators	prevent	
injured	cruel	residents
apartment block	leak	worth

b) Work in pairs. Are these words nouns, verbs or adjectives? Try to guess the meanings.

c) Work with another pair. Compare ideas. Check your answers with your teacher or in a dictionary.

8 a) Work in groups. Make a list of the stories you can remember from this week's news. What can you remember about each story?

b) Work in pairs with a student from another group. Take turns to tell your partner about your stories. Which do you think is the most interesting?

Kangaroo rescues farmer

A kangaroo named Lulu was called a hero today after she helped to save farmer Len Richards's life.

Mr Richards, 52, was checking the fences around his farm near Melbourne after **severe** storms. While he was walking around looking at the **damage**, a large **branch** from a nearby tree fell on his head.

"Lulu stood next to Dad's unconscious body and **barked** like a dog to get help," said the farmer's daughter, 17-year-old Celeste Richards. "She made this **weird** noise for about 15 minutes, so we went outside to see what the problem was," she added. "She was trying to get our attention. When we got there we saw Lulu standing over Dad's body. Without her, my Dad might be dead."

Lulu, who is **blind** in one eye, became the Richards's family pet about ten years ago. The kangaroo's mother was killed by a car and the Richards family found the baby kangaroo in her mother's pouch. They took her home and looked after her, and the farm soon became her home. "Lulu and Dad are very close and she follows him everywhere," Celeste explained.

The Australian RSPCA* has recommended Lulu for a national bravery award. "From my point of view it's a really good story and I hope Lulu gets a medal," said Dr Hugh Wirth, the organisation's president.

*RSPCA = The Royal Society for the Prevention of Cruelty to Animals

Adapted from *The Guardian* 22/09/03

11D Did you?

Real World echo questions
Help with Listening intonation (3)
Review auxiliary verbs; crime words

QUICK REVIEW ●●●

Work in pairs. Make a list of all the crime words you know (*rob*, *thief*, etc.). Compare lists with another pair. Which words are: verbs, criminals, crimes?

 1
a) Look at the picture. Where are the people? What are they doing?

b) Complete conversations A–D with these echo questions.

Didn't you?	Are you?
Doesn't he?	Has she?

c) R11.7 Listen and check.

 2 R11.7 Listen again. Choose the correct answers.

1 The old man is going to Rome to *study/live*.
2 Max's family's owned the company for *18/80* years.
3 Angus used to *live/work* with his friend, Josh.
4 Hannah's had two *boys/girls*.

Real World Echo questions

 3
a) Choose the correct phrase in the rule.

● We use echo questions when we *are interested or surprised/ didn't hear what people said*.

b) Look again at conversations A–D. Then choose the correct words in the rules.

● We usually use the *main verb/auxiliary* in echo questions.

● We only use *names/subject pronouns* in echo questions.

● If the sentence is positive, the echo question is *positive/negative*.

● If the sentence is negative, the echo question is *positive/negative*.

c) What are the echo questions for these sentences?

1 I work for a TV company. *Do you?*
2 His mother really likes it here.
3 They went to Sydney last week.
4 He's got four sisters.
5 My car's twenty years old.

d) Check in RW11.1 p142.

Max doesn't want to sell the company.

I'm going to Rome next month.

Help with Listening Intonation (3)

● Remember: we know if people are interested or surprised by how much their voices move up and down.

4 R11.8 Listen to six conversations. Which people sound interested (I) or not interested (NI)? Notice the intonation in the echo questions.

1	Ⓘ	NI	4	I	NI
2	I	NI	5	I	NI
3	I	NI	6	I	NI

5 R11.9 P Listen and practise. Copy the intonation.
Hàs she?

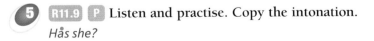

6 Which people from conversations A–D said these sentences, do you think?

1 I'm going to live with an Italian family.
2 Her brother's got twins too.
3 The company lost £6 million last year.
4 She wants to have six children.
5 I've never been to Italy before.
6 He can't borrow any more from the bank.

I didn't go to work today.

Have you heard? Hannah's had twins!

7 **a)** Write echo questions for the sentences in **6**.

b) Work in pairs. Take turns to say the sentences and echo questions.

8 R11.10 Listen to Angus talking about his friend, Josh. Respond with an echo question.

9 **a)** Write six interesting things about yourself or people you know.

b) Work in pairs. Take turns to say your sentences to your partner. Continue the conversation with an echo question and follow-up questions.

🎵 R11.11 Look at the song *You've Lost That Lovin' Feelin'* on p101. Follow the instructions.

11 Review   Language Summary 11, p141

1 **a)** Choose the correct verb. V11.1

1 *get/have* sacked
2 *lose/pass* a driving test
3 *fail/have* an accident
4 *pass/have* an operation
5 *have/get* lost
6 *get/lose* promoted

b) Work in pairs. Which things have happened to you?

2 Fill in the gaps with the correct form of the verb. Put *just*, *yet* and *already* in the correct place in the sentences. G11.1

1 Sharon *has just been* to the bank. (go, just)
2 She .... to the supermarket. (not go, yet)
3 She .... Deborah. (phone, already)
4 She .... an email to Tim. (send, just)
5 She .... a letter to Jill. (write, already)
6 .... she .... Pippa to dinner? (invite, yet)

3 **a)** Fill in the missing letters for these crimes. V11.2 V11.3

1 m _ r d _ r   3 r _ b _ e _ y
2 b u _ g _ a r _   4 t h _ f _

b) Work in pairs. Write the criminal and the verb for each crime in **3a)**.

c) Fill in the gaps with a word from **3a)** or **3b)**.

1 My house was *burgled* last week. There have already been three .... in our area this month.
2 There was a bank .... yesterday. The .... had guns.
3 A man was murdered, but they haven't caught the .... yet.
4 I was .... in the street. The thief .... my bag.

4 **a)** Fill in the gaps with *who*, *which*, *that* or *where*. G11.2

1 The place .... I usually go for a haircut.
2 The person .... lives next door to me.
3 A restaurant .... they have delicious food.
4 A present .... I got last birthday.
5 The thing .... I spend most of my money on.
6 The teacher .... helped me most at school.

b) Write the answers to 1–6 in **4a)** on a piece of paper. Don't write them in order.

c) Work in pairs. Swap papers. Guess who or what the people/ things/places are.

5 **a)** Complete the sentences for you with something surprising.

1 My best friend has got …
2 Last weekend I went to …
3 I'm never going to … again.
4 I used to …
5 I didn't use to …

b) Work in pairs. Take turns to say your sentences. Respond with an echo question and follow-up questions. RW11.1

Progress Portfolio

a) Tick the things you can do in English.

☐ I can talk about things I've done or haven't done yet.

☐ I can understand simple messages.

☐ I can talk about different crimes.

☐ I can say which person, thing or place I am talking about.

☐ I can understand the main points of simple news items.

☐ I can show I'm interested in a conversation.

b) What do you need to study again? ⊙ 11A–D

12A A year off

Vocabulary money
Grammar reported speech
Help with Listening /h/ at the beginning of words
Review present and past verb forms; *going to*; *will*; *can*

QUICK REVIEW ●●●
Imagine you are a famous person. Write four sentences about your life. Work in pairs. Take turns to say your sentences. Answer with an echo question and follow-up questions: A *I was on TV yesterday.* B *Were you? Which programme were you on?* Guess who your partner is.

Vocabulary Money

1 a) Tick the phrases in **bold** you know. Check new phrases in **V12.1** p143.

1 I **lent some money** to a friend last week.
2 I try to **save money** every month.
3 I **waste** a lot of **money on** things I don't need.
4 I've got a favourite possession that didn't **cost a lot of money**.
5 I **borrowed money from** someone last month.
6 I don't think I **earn** enough **money**.
7 I **got** some **money out of** the bank last weekend.
8 I've never **won** any **money** in my life.
9 I **spend** a lot of **money on** clothes.
10 I **lost** some **money** last week.
11 I **owe money to** someone, but I'm going to **pay** it **back**.

b) Which sentences are true for you? Compare answers in groups.

Listening and Grammar

2 a) **R12.1** Listen to Philip talking to his aunt, Maureen. What has he just done?

b) Listen again. Fill in the gaps in Philip's sentences.

1 I'm working in a ....
2 I want to .... abroad.
3 I'm going to work for a ....
4 I'll be back next ....
5 I can save .... a week.

3 a) **R12.2** That evening Maureen told her husband, Arthur, about her conversation with Philip. Listen and put her sentences 1–5 in the order she says them.

a) He said that he wanted to work abroad.
b) He told me that he was going to work for a charity.
c) He said he was working in a restaurant.
d) He told me he could save £100 a week.
e) He said that he'd be back next June.

b) Match Philip's sentences 1–5 in 2b) to Maureen's sentences a)–e) in 3a).

Help with Grammar Reported speech

 4 **a)** Look at the sentences in 2b) and 3a). Notice how the verb changes in reported speech. Then fill in the table with these verb forms.

~~Past Simple~~   would   could   Past Continuous   *was/were going to*

verb form in direct speech	verb form in reported speech
Present Simple (*want*)	*Past Simple*
Present Continuous (*am working*)	
will	
can	
am/are/is going to	

b) Look again at sentences a)–e) in 3a). Then complete the rules with *always* or *never*.

- *say* _____ has an object:
  He said (that) … not ~~He said me (that) …~~ .
- *tell* _____ has an object:
  He told me (that) … not ~~He told (that) …~~ .

c) Fill in the gaps with the correct subject pronoun (*I*, *you*, etc.) or possessive adjective (*my*, *your*, etc.).

1 "I don't see my aunt very often." → Philip said that _____ didn't see _____ aunt very often.

2 "I don't see my nephew very often." → Maureen said that _____ didn't see _____ nephew very often.

d) Check in G12.1 p144.

 5 R12.3 P Listen and practise.

he wånted to wõrk abroåd → *He saìd that /ðət/ he wånted to wõrk abroåd.*

6 **a)** R12.4 Listen to the rest of Maureen and Arthur's conversation. Answer these questions.

1 How much is the flight?
2 How much does Philip earn a week?
3 What did Maureen do this afternoon?
4 What does Arthur think of what she's done?

b) What did Maureen say to Arthur? Write the sentences in reported speech. Use the verbs in brackets.

1 PHILIP   The flight is about £700. (say)
   He said (that) the flight was about £700.

2 PHILIP   I don't earn very much. (tell)

3 MAUREEN It's going to take you ages to save enough money. (say)

4 PHILIP   I'm working seven days a week. (say)

5 MAUREEN We'll pay for your ticket. (tell)

6 PHILIP   I can pay you back next year. (say)

c) Listen again and check.

Help with Listening
/h/ at the beginning of words

- In spoken English sometimes you don't hear /h/ at the beginning of words.

7 **a)** R12.5 Listen to these sentences. Circle each *h* in **bold** you hear.

1 Anyway, **h**e said that the flight was about seven **h**undred pounds.
2 And **h**e told me that **h**e didn't earn very much.
3 And then **h**e said that **h**e was working seven days a week.
4 Yes, **h**e was very **h**appy, I can tell you.

b) Choose the correct words in these rules.

- We usually hear /h/ after a *vowel/consonant* sound.
- We don't usually hear /h/ after a *vowel/consonant* sound.

c) R12.4 Look at R12.4, p157. Listen to Maureen and Arthur's conversation again. Notice when they don't say /h/ at the beginning of words.

Get ready … Get it right!

8 Write 6–8 sentences about your life. Use these phrases or your own ideas.

- I … every day/week/weekend.
- I can/can't … quite/very well.
- At the moment I'm ……ing …
- Next weekend I'm going to …
- I (don't) like …
- When I'm old I think I'll …

9 **a)** Work in pairs. Tell your partner your sentences. Remember your partner's sentences. You can write <u>one</u> word only to help you remember each sentence.

b) Work with a new partner. Take turns to tell him/her your first partner's sentences. Use reported speech.

c) Tell the class two things you found out about the other students.

12B Taking chances

Vocabulary unusual activities
Grammar second conditional
Review reported speech

QUICK REVIEW ● ● ●
Think of six things other students have told you about themselves on this course (or your family/friends have told you recently). Work in pairs. Swap information using reported speech: *Yoko told me she wanted to learn Italian.*

Vocabulary Unusual activities

1 Work in groups. Answer these questions.

1 When was the last time you did something exciting or unusual?
2 What was it? Did you enjoy it?
3 Would you like to do it again? Why?/Why not?

2 **a)** Match these words/phrases to the pictures. Check new words in V12.2 p143.

> insects   hypnotise someone
> a reality TV programme   gloves
> a tarantula   a parachute jump
> a karaoke machine   dye your hair

b) Work in pairs. Compare answers.

Reading and Grammar

3 **a)** Look at the cards from the game *Risk-taker!*. Choose the correct answers for you.

b) Choose a partner, but don't talk to him/her yet. Guess which answers he/she chose.

c) Check your guesses with your partner. How many were correct?

(In question 1 I think you chose b).)

(No, I chose a)!)

d) Look at p158. Are you and your partner risk-takers?

RISK-TAKER!

1 If I won a parachute jump in a competition,
  a) I wouldn't do it.
  b) I'd do it.
  c) I'd do it if a friend jumped with me.

2 If someone asked me to hold a tarantula,
  a) I'd do it.
  b) I'd do it but I'd wear gloves.
  c) I'd leave the room as soon as I could.

3 If someone asked me to be on a reality TV programme,
  a) I'd definitely say no.
  b) I'd say yes immediately.
  c) I'd say maybe and think about it.

4 If someone offered me $100 to dye my hair pink,
  a) I'd do it.
  b) I wouldn't do it.
  c) I'd do it, but only for $1,000!

5 If I was in a foreign country and was given insects to eat,
  a) I'd eat them.
  b) I'd eat them if there was nothing else.
  c) I wouldn't eat them.

Help with Grammar Second conditional

4 **a)** Look at the sentences on the cards. These are called second conditionals. Choose the correct words/phrases in the rules.

- We use the second conditional to talk about *real/imaginary* situations.
- The second conditional talks about *the past/the present or the future.*

b) Look at this sentence. Then fill in the gaps in the rule with *infinitive* or *Past Simple*.

If I won a parachute jump, I'd do it.

- We make second conditionals with: *If* + subject + ... (...), subject + *'d (would)/ wouldn't* + ... (...).

c) Fill in the gaps in these questions with *if*, *do* or *would*.

1 .... someone asked you to hold a tarantula, ... you .... it?
2 What .... you .... you won a parachute jump?

d) Check in **G12.2** p144.

5 **R12.6** **P** Listen and practise.

I'd dǒ it → If I wǒn a pǎrachute jǔmp, I'd dǒ it.

6 If I went to a party and there was a karaoke machine,
a) I'd only sing if all my friends did.
b) I'd definitely sing.
c) I'd go home immediately!

7 If someone offered to hypnotise me,
a) I'd say yes immediately.
b) I'd ask my friend to try it first.
c) I'd definitely say no.

6 Make five sentences with the phrases from A, B and C.

 A
1 If I didn't have to get up early,
2 If my parents lived nearer,
3 If she worked a bit harder,
4 If my father was here,
5 If he didn't work so hard,

 B
I'd see them more often,
I'd go out tonight,
he wouldn't be so tired,
he'd know what to do,
she wouldn't do so badly at school,

C
but he really needs the money.
but he's on holiday in South America.
but she spends all her time watching TV.
but I start work at 7.30 tomorrow.
but they live 300 kilometres away.

7 **a)** Fill in the gaps with the correct form of the verbs in brackets. Then complete the sentence for you.

1 If I *could* (can) live anywhere in the world, *I'd live* (live) in ...
2 If I .... (have) more free time, I .... (like) to ...
3 If I .... (can) have any job in the world, I .... (be) a/an ...
4 If I .... (not be) in this English class now, I .... (be) ...
5 If I .... (have) more money, I .... (buy) ...
6 If I .... (can) change one thing in my life, I .... (change) ...

b) Work in pairs and compare sentences.

If I could live anywhere in the world, I'd live in the Caribbean.

Yes, me too.

Oh, I wouldn't. I'd live in the USA.

Get ready ... Get it right!

8 Work in pairs. Student A → p104. Student B → p112. Follow the instructions.

Vocabulary connecting words (2): *first, next, then*, etc.
Skills Listening: a radio interview; Reading: a magazine article
Help with Listening linking: review (2)
Review *used to*; past verb forms

QUICK REVIEW ● ● ●

What would you be if you were: a colour, a day of the week, a season, a place, an item of clothing, a drink, an animal? Work in pairs. Compare answers. Are any the same?

Vocabulary and Listening

1 a) Look at the photo. Who is he? Why was he famous?

b) Check these words/phrases with your teacher or in a dictionary. Which words can you see in the picture?

> a magician   a magic trick   hide
> a pair of handcuffs   a tank of water
> escape from something   a curtain
> a piece of wire   onstage   chains

2 a) Work in pairs. Are these sentences true or false, do you think?

1 Houdini was his real name.
2 He was born in the USA.
3 He became famous very quickly.
4 He used to do underwater escapes.
5 He died onstage.

b) **R12.7** Listen to a radio interview and check your answers.

3 Listen again. Choose the correct answers.

1 He started working as a magician when he was *17/27*.
2 He used to do *12/20* shows a day.
3 He tried to sell his magic secrets for *$20/$2,000*.
4 He practised opening handcuffs for *two/ten* hours a day.
5 He used to hide pieces of wire *in the water tank/on his body*.
6 He died because of *stomach problems/an accident*.

Help with Listening **Linking: review (2)**

4 a) Look at this sentence. Notice the different types of linking.

Well, the₋/j/₋*underwater*₋/r/₋*escape, I suppose. He was put into*₋/w/₋*a tank of water*₋/r/₋*in handcuffs and chains, then Bess pulled a curtain around it.*

b) **R12.7** Look at R12.7, on p157. Listen again and notice the linking.

Reading and Vocabulary

5 a) Work in groups. Discuss these questions.

1 Have you ever seen a magician onstage or on TV? If yes, what did he/she do?
2 Have you heard of David Blaine? If yes, what do you know about him?

b) Check these words/phrases with your teacher or in a dictionary. Which words can you find in photos A–C on p97?

> a stunt   a glass box   a pillar   frozen
> jump off   survive   a block of ice

6 a) Read about David Blaine. Put photos A–C in the order he did them.

b) Read the article again and answer these questions.

1 When did David Blaine start doing magic?
2 Which famous people is he friends with?
3 When did he become famous?
4 Why did he have to spend two weeks in hospital?
5 How did he get off the pillar?
6 What did he eat when he was in the glass box?
7 What connection does he have with Houdini?

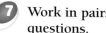

DAVID BLAINE
The New Houdini?

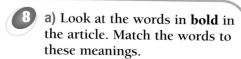

7 Work in pairs. Discuss these questions.

1 Which of David Blaine's stunts do you think was the best or the most dangerous? Why?
2 Would you like to go and watch one of his stunts? Why?/Why not?

Help with Vocabulary
Connecting words (2)

8 a) Look at the words in **bold** in the article. Match the words to these meanings.

1 words that connect things that happen at the same time
2 words that show the order of events

b) Check in V12.3 p143.

9 a) Answer these questions.

1 What are the verbs for these symbols: $+ - \times \div$?
2 How many digits are in this number: 1,750?

b) Read the number trick. Choose the correct words.

¹*First/Next* choose a number from 1 to 9 and write it down. ²*Then/When* multiply it by 2 and add 5. ³*Next/After* multiply this number by 50. ⁴*Finally/After that* add the number of years there have been in this century so far. ⁵*While/Then* add 1,750. ⁶*First/Finally*, subtract the year you were born. The final answer has three digits. The first digit is the number you first thought of, and the second two digits are your age on your birthday this year!

c) Work in pairs. Do the number trick with your partner.

10 Work in new pairs. Student A → p109. Student B → p117. Follow the instructions.

With his own type of street magic and amazing live TV shows, David Blaine has become one of the most famous magicians in the world. It's not surprising that people call him 'the new Houdini'.

Blaine was born in Brooklyn, New York, and started doing magic when he was four. **While** he was studying to be an actor, he used to do magic tricks for customers in Manhattan's expensive restaurants. **Then** he started working at parties for rich people, and became friends with actors like Robert de Niro and Leonardo di Caprio. He also went out with Madonna for a short time. He became famous **after** he made a TV show called *David Blaine: Street Magic*, where he did magic tricks in the street in front of ordinary people.

Since then he has done a number of spectacular stunts that were shown live on TV. **First** he was frozen inside a six-ton block of ice in New York's Times Square. He stayed there for over 61 hours. **When** he was released from the ice he couldn't walk and he had to spend two weeks in hospital. **Next** he stood on a 25-metre pillar for 35 hours – again without food or water. The pillar was only 56 cm wide and he couldn't eat, sleep or sit down. **Finally**, he jumped off the pillar – onto a pile of boxes. **After that** he lived without food for 44 days in a glass box by the River Thames in London. He survived only on water from a tube and lost 24 kilos.

David is now a millionaire and lives in Hollywood. Who used to live in his house, do you think? Yes, you've guessed it – Harry Houdini!

a) Fill in the puzzle with 'money' verbs. What is the hidden phrase? V12.1

	¹B		R			W
	²W			S	T	
	³		A	R		
	M	O	N	E	Y	
	⁴L		S			
⁵L		D				
⁶S		V				
⁷P			B		C	

b) Choose the correct verb.

1 I don't *lend/spend* much on clothes.
2 Can you *borrow/lend* me £10?
3 I'll *pay/waste* you back soon.
4 I already *save/owe* Joe a lot.
5 How much do you *earn/win* as a doctor?
6 We need to *save/get* some money out of the bank.
7 I *borrowed/lent* £50 from Jeff last week.

 a) Make these sentences true for you.

1 I'm going to look at the CD-ROM tonight.
2 I'll need English for my work/studies in the future.
3 I want to study English again next year.
4 I've got a good English dictionary.
5 I can understand a lot of English songs.
6 I read something in English every day.

b) Work in pairs. Take turns to say your sentences. Remember what your partner says.

c) Work with a different student. Tell him/her what your first partner said. Use *say* and *tell*. G12.1

Nadine said she was going to look at the CD-ROM tonight.

 a) Fill in the gaps with the correct form of the verbs in brackets. G12.2

Life would be better if ...
1 ... there *weren't* (not be) any cars.
2 ... everyone .... (retire) at fifty.
3 ... the weekend .... (be) three days long.
4 ... everyone .... (speak) the same language.
5 ... we .... (have) more women politicians.

b) Work in groups. Choose the three best ideas.

 a) Replace the * in the story with these connecting words. V12.3

then	first	after that
finally	next	while

* the magician put a woman in a box. * he locked it. * the magician asked a man to hold the woman's hand, * the man was holding her hand the magician cut the box in half with a saw. * the man walked round the two halves of the box. * the magician put the box back together and the woman got out.

b) Work in pairs. Compare answers.

Progress Portfolio

a) Tick the things you can do in English.

☐ I can talk about money.
☐ I can report what other people have said.
☐ I can talk about imaginary situations in the present or future.
☐ I can understand a simple magazine article.
☐ I can use connecting words (*next,* etc.).

b) What do you need to study again? ⊙ 12A–C

Work in groups of four. Read the rules. Then play the game!

Rules

You need: One counter for each student; one dice for each group.

How to play: Put your counters on *START HERE*. Take turns to throw the dice, move your counter and follow the instructions on the square. The first student to get to *FINISH* is the winner.

Grammar and Vocabulary squares: The first student to land on a Grammar or Vocabulary square answers question 1. The second student to land on the same square answers question 2. If the other students think your answer is correct, you can stay on the square. If the answer is wrong, move back to the last square you were on. You can check your answers with your teacher. If a third or fourth student lands on the same square, he/she can stay on the square without answering a question.

Keep Talking squares: If you land on a Keep Talking square, talk about the topic for 30 seconds. Another student can check the time. If you can't talk for 30 seconds, move back to the last square you were on. If a second or third student lands on the same square, he/she also talks about the same topic for 30 seconds.

End of Course Review

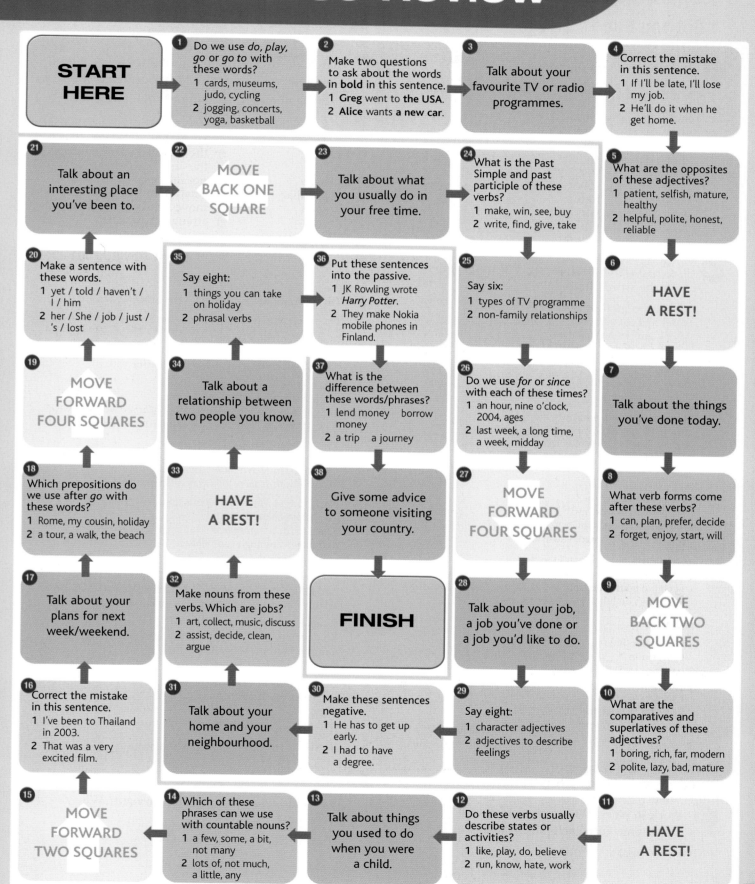

START HERE

1 Do we use *do, play, go* or *go to* with these words?
1 cards, museums, judo, cycling
2 jogging, concerts, yoga, basketball

2 Make two questions to ask about the words in **bold** in this sentence.
1 **Greg** went to **the USA**.
2 **Alice** wants **a new car**.

3 Talk about your favourite TV or radio programmes.

4 Correct the mistake in this sentence.
1 If I'll be late, I'll lose my job.
2 He'll do it when he get home.

21 Talk about an interesting place you've been to.

22 MOVE BACK ONE SQUARE

23 Talk about what you usually do in your free time.

24 What is the Past Simple and past participle of these verbs?
1 make, win, see, buy
2 write, find, give, take

5 What are the opposites of these adjectives?
1 patient, selfish, mature, healthy
2 helpful, polite, honest, reliable

20 Make a sentence with these words.
1 yet / told / haven't / I / him
2 her / She / job / just / 's / lost

35 Say eight:
1 things you can take on holiday
2 phrasal verbs

36 Put these sentences into the passive.
1 JK Rowling wrote *Harry Potter*.
2 They make Nokia mobile phones in Finland.

25 Say six:
1 types of TV programme
2 non-family relationships

6 HAVE A REST!

19 MOVE FORWARD FOUR SQUARES

34 Talk about a relationship between two people you know.

37 What is the difference between these words/phrases?
1 lend money   borrow money
2 a trip   a journey

26 Do we use *for* or *since* with each of these times?
1 an hour, nine o'clock, 2004, ages
2 last week, a long time, a week, midday

7 Talk about the things you've done today.

18 Which prepositions do we use after *go* with these words?
1 Rome, my cousin, holiday
2 a tour, a walk, the beach

33 HAVE A REST!

38 Give some advice to someone visiting your country.

27 MOVE FORWARD FOUR SQUARES

8 What verb forms come after these verbs?
1 can, plan, prefer, decide
2 forget, enjoy, start, will

17 Talk about your plans for next week/weekend.

32 Make nouns from these verbs. Which are jobs?
1 art, collect, music, discuss
2 assist, decide, clean, argue

FINISH

28 Talk about your job, a job you've done or a job you'd like to do.

9 MOVE BACK TWO SQUARES

16 Correct the mistake in this sentence.
1 I've been to Thailand in 2003.
2 That was a very excited film.

31 Talk about your home and your neighbourhood.

30 Make these sentences negative.
1 He has to get up early.
2 I had to have a degree.

29 Say eight:
1 character adjectives
2 adjectives to describe feelings

10 What are the comparatives and superlatives of these adjectives?
1 boring, rich, far, modern
2 polite, lazy, bad, mature

15 MOVE FORWARD TWO SQUARES

14 Which of these phrases can we use with countable nouns?
1 a few, some, a bit, not many
2 lots of, not much, a little, any

13 Talk about things you used to do when you were a child.

12 Do these verbs usually describe states or activities?
1 like, play, do, believe
2 run, know, hate, work

11 HAVE A REST!

I Got You Babe   2D p19

1 Match the words that rhyme.

know ——— climb
true   talk
rent   grow
pot   ring
spring   got
clown   you
long   so
mine   spent
hand   tight
walk   wrong
goodnight   understand
go   around

2 **a)** R2.14 Listen to the song. Fill in the gaps with the words from **1**.

They say we're young and we don't ¹ _know_
Won't find out until we ² ....
Well I don't know if all that's ³ ....
'Cause you got me, and baby I got ⁴ ....

CHORUS
Babe, I got you babe
I got you babe

They say our love won't pay the ⁵ ....
Before it's earned our money's always ⁶ ....
I guess that's so, we don't have a ⁷ ....
At least I'm sure of all the things we ⁸ ....

CHORUS

I've got flowers in the ⁹ ....
I've got you to wear my ¹⁰ ....
And when I'm sad, you're a ¹¹ ....
And when I get scared, you're always ¹² ....

So let them say your hair's too ¹³ ....
I don't care, with you I can't go ¹⁴ ....
Then put your little hand in ¹⁵ ....
There ain't no hill or mountain we can't ¹⁶ ....

CHORUS

I got you to hold my ¹⁷ ....
I got you to ¹⁸ ....
I got you to ¹⁹ .... with me
I've got you to ²⁰ .... with me
I got you to kiss ²¹ ....
I got you to hold me ²² ....
I got you, I won't let ²³ ....
I got you to love me ²⁴ ....

I got you babe

b) Work in pairs. Compare answers.

3 Work in pairs. Write two more words that rhyme with each pair of words in **1**.

know   grow   *show*   *go*

Space Oddity   5D p43

1 Match words 1–7 to their meanings a)–g). Check your answers with your teacher or in a dictionary.

1 the ignition ——— a) put one foot in front of the other
2 a capsule   b) the electrical system that starts an engine
3 step   c) the part of a spaceship that you live in
4 float   d) not moving
5 peculiar   e) small points of light in the sky
6 stars   f) move slowly through the air
7 still   g) strange or unusual

2 **a)** R5.15 Listen to the song. Choose the correct words.

Ground Control to Major Tom
Ground Control to Major Tom
Take your protein pills and put your ¹*spacesuit*/*helmet* on

Ten, nine, eight, seven, six, five, four, three, two, one, lift-off

Ground Control to Major Tom
Commencing countdown, ²*engines/systems* on
³*Check/Start* ignition and may God's love be with you

This is Ground Control to Major Tom
You've ⁴*definitely/really* made the grade
And the papers want to know whose ⁵*clothes/shirts* you wear
Now it's time to ⁶*leave/open* the capsule if you dare

This is Major Tom to Ground Control
I'm ⁷*stepping/walking* through the door
And I'm floating in a most ⁸*unusual/peculiar* way
And the ⁹*stars/planets* look very different today

For here am I ¹⁰*flying/sitting* in a tin can
Far ¹¹*above/below* the world
Planet Earth is ¹²*green/blue*
And there's nothing I can ¹³*do/see*

Though I'm past ¹⁴*five/one* hundred thousand miles
I'm ¹⁵*feeling/sitting* very still
And I think my ¹⁶*capsule/spaceship* knows which way to go
Tell my ¹⁷*mum/wife* I love her very much, she knows

Ground Control to Major Tom
Your circuit's ¹⁸*dead/broken*, there's something wrong
Can you hear me, Major Tom? (x 3)
Can you ...

Here am I ¹⁹*floating/moving* in my tin can
Far above the ²⁰*sun/moon*
Planet ²¹*Mars/Earth* is blue
And there's ²²*something/nothing* I can do

b) Work in pairs. Compare answers.

3 **a)** Work in pairs. Find all the words in **1** in the song.

b) Would you like to be an astronaut? Why?/ Why not?

What the World Needs Now 9D p75

 1 Fill in the gaps in sentences 1–4 with the words in the box. Check new words with your teacher or in a dictionary.

> mountains   oceans   sunbeams   corn
> hillsides   wheat   rivers   moonbeams

1 You can **climb** _____ or _____ .
2 You can **cross** _____ or _____ .
3 You can **grow** _____ or _____ .
4 _____ or _____ can **shine**.

2 a) R9.11 Listen to the song. Cross out the extra word in each line (1–16).

CHORUS
¹ What ~~all~~ the world needs now is love, sweet love
² It's the only important thing that there's just too little of
³ What the world needs now is true love, sweet love
⁴ No, not just for some people, but for everyone

⁵ Lord, we just don't need another mountain
⁶ There are mountains and hillsides enough to climb up
⁷ There are oceans, seas and rivers enough to cross
⁸ Enough to last everyone till the end of time

CHORUS

⁹ Lord, we don't need another beautiful meadow
¹⁰ There are always cornfields and wheat fields enough to grow
¹¹ There are sunbeams and moonbeams enough to shine down
¹² Oh, listen, Lord, if you really want to know

¹³ What the world needs now, Lord, is love, sweet love
¹⁴ It's not the only thing that there's just too little of
¹⁵ What the world needs right now is love, sweet love
¹⁶ No, it's not just for some, oh, but just for every, every, everyone

Oh, what the world needs now is love, sweet love
(Oh, is love) (x 3)

b) Work in pairs. Compare answers.

3 Read the song again. What is there too little of? What are there enough of?

4 a) Write five things you need at the moment.

b) Work in groups. Compare lists. Have you got any of the same things?

You've Lost That Lovin' Feelin' 11D p91

1 Work in groups. Discuss these questions.
1 Do you like romantic films or books? If yes, which is your favourite? Why?
2 What's the best way to make yourself happy again after you break up with someone?

2 a) R11.11 Listen to the song. Match 1–12 to a)–l).

1 You never close your eyes anymore	a) not to show it (baby)
2 And there's no tenderness like before	b) when I kiss your lips
3 You're trying hard	c) I know it
4 But baby, baby	d) in your fingertips

CHORUS
You've lost that loving feeling
Oh, that loving feeling
You've lost that loving feeling
Now it's gone, gone, gone, whoa-oh

5 Now there's no welcome look in your eyes	e) something beautiful's dying
6 And girl you're starting to criticise	f) feel like crying (baby)
7 It makes me just	g) when I reach for you
8 'Cause baby	h) little things I do

CHORUS

9 Baby, baby, I'd get down	i) like you used to do, yeah
10 If you would only love me	j) let it slip away
11 We had a love, a love, a love	k) on my knees for you
12 So don't, don't, don't, don't	l) you don't find every day

Baby, baby, baby, baby, I beg you please, please, please, please
I need your love, need your love (x 2)
Bring it on back, bring it on back (x 2)
Bring back that loving feeling
Whoa, that loving feeling
Bring back that loving feeling
'Cause it's gone, gone, gone
And I can't go on, whoa-oh

Bring back that loving feeling, whoa that loving feeling

b) Work in pairs. Compare answers.

3 a) Write the top five qualities a person needs for a relationship to be successful?

being honest   having a good sense of humour

b) Work in pairs. Choose the best five qualities from both your lists.

c) Work in groups or with the whole class. Agree on a final list of five qualities.

Pair and Group Work: Student/Group A

1B 10 p7

a) You are going to ask your partner about day-to-day life in his/her home. Make subject questions with *Who … ?* and the phrases in column A.

A questions with *Who … ?*	B your answer	C your partner's answer	D follow-up questions
1 go out to work			Where?
2 leave home first			What time?
3 get home first			When?
4 do the cooking			What kind of food?
5 watch TV the most			How many hours?
6 go to bed last			What time?

b) Answer the questions for your own home (or your family/friends if you live alone) in column B.

c) Work in pairs. Take turns to ask and answer the questions. Write your partner's answers in column C. If possible, ask follow-up questions with the prompts in column D. You start.

> Who goes out to work in your home?

> My father.

> Where does he work?

> In a bank in the city centre.

d) Compare your answers to your partner's. How many are the same?

3C 9 p25

a) Work on your own. Imagine you are a tour manager for a famous singer. You organise tours to different countries. Make notes on your job. Use these ideas.

- name of the singer you work for
- why you like/don't like working for him/her
- things you have to do in your job (travel, hotels, advertising, etc.)
- good/bad things about your job
- your salary
- best/worst places you went to last year
- other singers or bands you worked for in the past
- any other interesting things about your job

b) Work with your group. Take turns to tell each other about your jobs. Ask questions to get more information.

c) Decide who has the best job and why. Tell the class which job you chose.

11A 9 p85

a) Work on your own. Pippa and her husband, Andrew, are moving house. You are Pippa. Student B is Andrew. Choose three things on your list that you have already/just done and three things you haven't done yet. Think of a different reason why you haven't done each thing.

Pippa's list
- cancel phone
- get phone connected in new house
- email new address to friends
- pack kitchen things
- empty fridge and freezer
- tell neighbours when we're moving

Andrew's list
- pack books
- tell electricity company when we're moving
- hire a removal van
- get keys for new house
- talk to lawyer
- pack clothes

b) Look at Andrew's list. Make questions with the Present Perfect and *yet*.

Have you packed the books yet?

c) Work with your partner. Ask questions to find out which things Andrew has done. If he hasn't done something, ask why.

> Have you packed the books yet?

> Yes, I've just done that.

> No, not yet.

> Why not?

> I haven't had time.

2A 7 p13

a) You are going to ask your partner the questions in column A. Write follow-up questions in the Past Simple with the prompts in column B.

A When did you last ...	B follow-up questions	
... go shopping for food?	How much / spend?	What / buy?
... have a hamburger or fried chicken?	Where / buy it?	What / be / like?
... stay up late?	What / do?	What time / go to bed?
... take a day off work/university/school?	Where / go?	What / do?
... go to the theatre?	What / see?	Who / go with?
... talk to your best friend?	What / talk about?	Where / be / you?

b) Work in pairs. Take turns to ask and answer the questions from column A and your follow-up questions. Use phrases with *ago*, *last* and *in* in your answers. Ask more questions if possible.

> When did you last go shopping for food?

> Last Friday./Three days ago.

> How much did you spend?

> About €50.

2B 9 p15

a) Work on your own. Read about how Colin and Linda met.

- Linda was teaching in China.
- They first met on a plane from Shanghai to New York.
- On their first date they went to the theatre and Linda fell asleep.
- When they first met, Colin wasn't going out with anyone else.
- They got married three and a half years ago.

b) Make questions in the Past Simple or Past Continuous with the verbs in brackets.

1 What _____ Colin _____ in China? (do)
2 How long ago _____ they _____ ? (meet)
3 _____ Linda _____ with anyone else when she met Colin? (go out)
4 What were they doing when he _____ her to marry him? (ask)
5 Where _____ they _____ married? (get)

c) Work with your partner. Take turns to ask and answer your questions. You start.

10A 10 p77

a) Work with a student from group A. Write questions with these words in the Present Simple passive or Past Simple passive.

1 Who / the Mona Lisa / paint / by ?
Who was the Mona Lisa painted by?
   a) Van Gogh   b) Picasso
   c) **Leonardo da Vinci**

2 Where / cotton / grow ?
   a) **India**   b) England   c) Canada

3 When / Taj Mahal / build ?
   a) 1316   b) **1631**   c) 1813

4 Who / the film *Titanic* / direct / by ?
   a) **James Cameron**   b) Steven Spielberg
   c) Francis Ford Coppola

5 Where / Volvo cars / manufacture ?
   a) Spain   b) **Sweden**   c) Japan

6 When / the first Harry Potter book / publish ?
   a) 1990   b) **1997**   c) 2003

b) Work with a pair from group B. Take turns to ask and answer your questions. Say the three possible answers when you ask your questions. (The correct answer is in **bold**.)

c) Which pair got more answers right?

3D 7 p27

a) Work on your own. Read about these situations and decide what you want to say in 1 and 3. You can make notes, but don't write the whole conversation.

1 You promised to go to the beach next weekend with student B, but now you can't. Think of a reason why not. Phone student B, apologise and give your reason. Promise to go another time.

2 Student B promised to meet you at a friend's party yesterday evening, but he/she didn't go. Wait for his/her phone call.

3 It's lunchtime. You promised to meet student B in town for lunch half an hour ago. Think of a reason why you're late. Phone student B, apologise and give your reason. Promise to be there in twenty minutes.

4 Student B promised to take you to the airport on Tuesday next week – you're going on holiday for two weeks. Wait for his/her phone call.

b) Work with your partner. Take turns to phone each other.

12B 8 p95

a) Work on your own. Fill in the gaps with the correct form of the verb in brackets.

1 If you .... (win) a travel competition, where would you go?

2 If you .... (can) have dinner with anyone in the world, who would you choose?

3 If there .... (be) a fire in your house, what would you take out of the house first?

4 If you .... (can) be in a TV programme, which one would you like to be in?

5 If you .... (be) a famous actor, who would you like to be?

b) Work with your partner. Take turns to ask and answer your questions.

> If you won a travel competition, where would you go?

> (I think) I'd go to Australia. What about you?

> I'd go to Mexico.

7A 7 b) p53

a) Work on your own. Read about Day 3 of the cycling tour. Then make questions to complete the information for Day 2.

Where are they travelling to on Tuesday?

New Zealand – South Island

Day 2 Tuesday 12th February
Hanmer Springs to ....

Morning
• ....
• ....

Lunch
• ....

Afternoon
• ....

Night
• ....

Day 3 Wednesday 13th February
Kaikoura to Blenheim

Morning
• Go whale watching
• Cycle or drive to Blenheim

Lunch
• Have lunch at a winery (home of New Zealand Chardonnay)

Afternoon
• Go on a tour of the winery

Night
• Stay at the Crown Hotel in Blenheim

b) Work with your partner. Ask your partner questions and complete the information for Day 2.

c) Answer your partner's questions about Day 3.

d) Which of the three days is the best, do you think? Why?

4D 7 p35

a) Take turns to ask the group what they think about these sentences. Try to continue each conversation for at least one minute. Give reasons for your opinions.

1 Women are better drivers than men.
2 People shouldn't have more than two children.
3 Money makes people happy.

> Do you think women are better drivers than men?

b) Tell the class which sentences you all agreed or disagreed with.

6D 9 p51

a) Work on your own. Read the information for phone conversations 1–4. Decide what you want to say in each conversation.

1 Phone your lawyer, Bernard Robins. If you can't speak to him, leave a message and say when you are going to leave your office. Say where he can contact you after that.

2 You are Liz Jackson's flatmate. Liz isn't in. When your partner calls, tell him/her where Liz went and when she'll be back. Offer to take a message.

3 Phone your friend, Roberto. Say who you are and ask to speak to him. If he's out, tell your partner why you're calling. Leave a message and say where/how Roberto can contact you.

4 You are the receptionist for a firm of accountants called Bradley and Wise. When your partner calls, ask him/her to wait, then try to put him/her through to Gabriela Wise. Her secretary says it's her day off today. Offer to take a message.

b) Work with your partner. Take turns to phone each other.

5A 10 p37

a) Work on your own. Write questions with *Do you think … will … ?* and these ideas. Then make two more questions of your own.

Family life in 2020

1 / families / be smaller?
   Do you think families will be smaller?
2 / people / have more free time?
3 / more people / live to be a hundred?
4 / people / be happier?
5 / more fathers / stay at home to look after the children?
6 / more people / share jobs?

b) Work with your partner. Take turns to ask and answer your questions. Continue the conversation if possible.

9A 10 p69

a) Work on your own. Your partner is going to drive from Los Angeles to Mexico City. Make questions with *you* to ask him/her about the journey.

1 What / do / if / have an accident?
   What will you do if you have an accident?
2 What / do / if / get bored with driving?
3 What / do / if / get lost?
4 Where / stay / when / arrive in Mexico City?
5 What / do / as soon as / get there?
6 Where / go / after / finish your journey?

b) Read about your journey. Make notes on your ideas.

You are going to cycle from London to Rome. Decide what you will do in these situations:

- if someone steals your bike
- if you can't find a hotel
- if you run out of money

Also decide:
- where you'll stay when you arrive in Rome
- what you'll do as soon as you get there
- where you'll go after you finish your journey

c) Work with your partner. Ask him/her the questions from **a)** about his/her journey.

d) Answer your partner's questions about your journey.

8A ⑩ p61

a) Work with a student from group A. Make questions to ask a student from group B.

1	2	3
1 What / do? *What do you do?*	How long / be / a ... ? *How long have you been a (doctor)?*	What / do / before that? *What did you do before that?*
2 Where / your best friend live?	How long / live / there?	When / last see him or her?
3 Who / be / your favourite relative?	How long / know / him or her?	When / last see him or her?
4 Have / got a car or a bicycle?	How long / have / it?	Where / buy it?
5 What / be / your most important possession?	How long / have / it?	Where / get it?

b) Work with a student from group B. Take turns to ask and answer questions from column 1. Then ask the questions from columns 2 and 3 if possible.

c) Tell the class (or other students) three things you found out about your partner.

7B ⑫ p55

a) Work with a student from group A. Describe the picture. Use *a lot of/lots of, a few, a bit, a little, not much/many, some, not any.*

There's lots of sun cream.
There's a lot of chewing gum.
There aren't many batteries.
There are a few cameras.

b) Work with a student from group B. Don't look at his/her picture. Take turns to tell your partner about your picture. Find ten differences in the pictures.

> In my picture there's lots of sun cream.

c) Work with your partner from group A. Tell him/her the differences you know. Have you got all the differences?

> In our picture there's a lot of chewing gum, but in picture B there isn't very much.

3A 🔟 p21

a) Work on your own. Tick the things you have to do in the week and at the weekend in the *you* columns.

	IN THE WEEK		AT THE WEEKEND	
	you	your partner	you	your partner
1 get up early				
2 travel a long way to get to work/ university/school				
3 wear a suit or a uniform				
4 go to meetings				
5 work in the evening				
6 look after children				

b) Make questions with *have to* and *you* for activities 1–6.

Do you have to get up early in the week?

What about at the weekend?

c) Work with your partner. Take turns to ask and answer your questions. Tick the things your partner has to do in the *your partner* columns. What do you both have to do?

d) Whose life is more stressful, do you think? Why?

10D 7️⃣ p83

a) Work on your own. Read the information for these conversations. Decide what you want to say.

1 You are a shop assistant in a department store. Your partner is a customer. He/She wants to buy a suitcase. Think about:
- the sizes and colours you have
- the price of each suitcase

2 You are a customer in a shoe shop. You want to buy some trainers. Think about:
- the size, colour and brand (*Nike, Adidas,* etc.) you want
- how much money you want to spend
- how you want to pay

b) Work with your partner. Role-play the conversations. You start conversation 1. Your partner starts conversation 2.

> Can I help you?   Yes, I'm looking for ...

3B 7️⃣ p23

a) Work on your own. Kevin has got a job as a salesman with a company called CopyRight. Read about his job.

- Every day Kevin visits other companies and tries to sell them new products.
- Kevin earns about £250 a week.
- He finishes work at about six o'clock.
- He's doing an on-the-job training course for the first two weeks.
- At the moment he's talking to a new customer.

b) Make questions in the Present Simple or Present Continuous.

1 What / the company / sell?
   What does the company sell?
2 / the company / do / well at the moment?
3 What time / Kevin / start work?
4 What / he / like about the job?
5 Where / he / work / today?

c) Work with your partner. Take turns to ask and answer your questions. You start.

d) Which job is better, do you think – Kevin's or George's? Why?

11B 10 p87

a) Work on your own. Look at these items and choose the correct words in the relative clauses. There is sometimes more than one possible answer.

1 This is the bullet *that/who/where* was taken from Jack Miller's body.

2 This is a neighbour *who/where/which* saw someone breaking into Barry Clark's house on the night of the murder.

3 This is the address of the flat *who/that/where* Adam stayed on the night of the murder. It's 30 miles away from Yately.

4 These are two people *who/that/which* were visiting Ellen on the night of the murder. They said that they all went out to dinner.

5 These are the bullets *that/who/where* were found in Barry Clark's house.

6 This is the rose *that/which/where* they found on the body.

b) Check your answers with a student from group A.

c) Remember the information. Then turn back to p87.

7D 8 p59

a) Work on your own. Read the information for phone conversations 1–4. Decide what you want to say in conversations 1 and 3 and check you understand all the receptionist's sentences.

Receptionist
I'm sorry to hear that.
I'm terribly sorry about that.
I'll send someone up straight away.
I'll send some (more) to your room.
I'll phone room service and ask them to send some more.

1 You are a guest in a hotel. Your room is very hot and the air conditioning doesn't work. Also you haven't got any soap. Phone Reception and complain politely.

2 You are the hotel receptionist. Reply to each complaint the guest makes. Use phrases from the box or your own ideas.

3 You are a guest in a hotel. You phoned room service for some coffee half an hour ago. It hasn't arrived. Also there's something wrong with the TV. Phone Reception and complain politely.

4 You are the hotel receptionist. Reply to each complaint the guest makes. Use phrases from the box or your own ideas.

b) Work with your partner. Role-play the conversations.

9C 6 p72

a) Work on your own. Fill in the gaps with the correct form of these phrasal verbs.

go back   go on   go away   give up   turn up   take off

1 Have you ever ___been back___ to your first school?
2 When was the last time you _____ for the weekend?
3 Do you always _____ your shoes before you go into your home?
4 Do you know anyone who has _____ smoking?
5 Are you planning to _____ learning English after this course?
6 Have you ever _____ at a party without an invitation?

b) Check your answers with a student from group A.

c) Work with a student from group B. Take turns to ask and answer your questions. Ask follow-up questions if possible.

4B 10 p31

a) Work on your own. You are a reporter for a local newspaper. A new rock band, Crazy Head, is playing a concert in your town. Student B is the lead singer. You are going to interview him/her. Make questions with *you* in the Present Perfect or Past Simple.

1 / ever / play / here before?
Have you ever played here before?
2 When / start / singing with Crazy Head?
When did you start singing with Crazy Head?
3 What / do / before / join / the band?
4 How many countries / go to / with Crazy Head?
5 Which country / enjoy / the most?
6 / ever / play / in the USA?
7 When / play / there?
8 / ever / work / with other musicians?
9 When / work / with them?

b) Work with your partner. Interview him/her. Ask follow-up questions if possible. Make notes on the answers.

c) Write your article about the rock singer's life for your local newspaper.

12C 10 p97

a) Work on your own. Read the trick and check you understand it.

Preparation
You need eight small pieces of paper and something to put them in (a bag or a box).

The trick
First, give your partner the bag or box. Then ask your partner to say a number with two digits. Write the number on a small piece of paper. Next, fold the piece of paper and put it in the bag. Then do this seven more times. Your partner should say a different number each time. Finally, ask him/her to take one piece of paper from the bag and look at it. While he/she is looking at the number, pretend you know what he/she is thinking. Then tell him/her the number.

The secret!
When you're writing the numbers, hold the pieces of paper in your hand so that your partner can't see what you're writing. Then write the first number your friend said on **every** piece of paper. All the pieces of paper will have the same number, so it will be easy to guess!

b) Work with your partner. Take turns to do your tricks. Which trick is better, do you think?

Pair and Group Work: Student/Group B

1B 10 p7

a) You are going to ask your partner about day-to-day life in his/her home. Make subject questions with *Who ... ?* and the phrases in column A.

A questions with *Who ... ?*	B your answer	C your partner's answer	D follow-up questions
1 go to work by public transport			How?
2 leave home last			What time?
3 get home last			When?
4 do the housework			How often?
5 use the phone the most			How many hours?
6 go to bed first			What time?

b) Answer the questions for your own home (or your family/friends, if you live alone) in column B.

c) Work in pairs. Take turns to ask and answer the questions. Write your partner's answers in column C. If possible, ask follow-up questions with the prompts in column D. Your partner starts.

> Who goes to work by public transport in your home?

> My wife.

> How does she get to work?

> By bus.

d) Compare your answers to your partner's. How many are the same?

3C 9 p25

a) Work on your own. Imagine you are a personal bodyguard. You look after famous people and protect them from danger. Make notes on your job. Use these ideas.

- the person/people you work for now
- why you like/don't like working for him/her/them
- things you have to do in your job (travel, go to parties, etc.)
- good/bad things about your job
- your salary
- best/worst places you went to last year
- other famous people you worked for in the past
- any other interesting things about your job

b) Work with your group. Take turns to tell each other about your jobs. Ask questions to get more information.

c) Decide who has the best job and why. Tell the class which job you chose.

11A 9 p85

a) Work on your own. Pippa and her husband, Andrew, are moving house. You are Andrew. Student A is Pippa. Choose three things on your list that you have already/just done and three things you haven't done yet. Think of a different reason why you haven't done each thing.

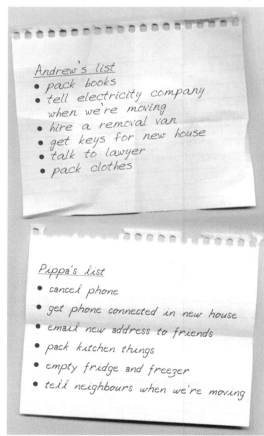

Andrew's list
- pack books
- tell electricity company when we're moving
- hire a removal van
- get keys for new house
- talk to lawyer
- pack clothes

Pippa's list
- cancel phone
- get phone connected in new house
- email new address to friends
- pack kitchen things
- empty fridge and freezer
- tell neighbours when we're moving

b) Look at Pippa's list. Make questions with the Present Perfect and *yet*.

Have you cancelled the phone yet?

c) Work with your partner. Ask questions to find out which things Pippa has done. If she hasn't done something, ask why.

> Have you cancelled the phone yet?

> Yes, I've just done that.

> No, not yet.

> Why not?

> When I call it's always busy.

2A ⑦ p13

a) You are going to ask your partner the questions in column A. Write follow-up questions in the Past Simple with the prompts in column B.

A When did you last ...	B follow-up questions	
... go to a fast food restaurant?	Which one / go to?	What / have?
... eat something unusual?	What / eat?	What / be / it like?
... have a holiday?	Where / go?	How long / go for?
... see a film at the cinema?	What / see?	Which cinema / go to?
... go shopping for clothes?	What / buy?	Where / buy (it/them)?
... stay at home all weekend?	What / do?	What time / go to bed?

b) Work in pairs. Take turns to ask and answer the questions from column A and your follow-up questions. Use phrases with *ago*, *last* and *in* in your answers. Ask more questions if possible.

> When did you last go to a fast food restaurant?

> Last weekend./Three weeks ago.

> Which one did you go to?

> McDonald's.

2B ⑨ p15

a) Work on your own. Read about how Colin and Linda met.

- Colin was working as an engineer in China.
- They first met on a plane six years ago.
- When they first met Linda had a boyfriend, but she broke up with him a week later.
- Colin asked Linda to marry him when they were waiting for a bus.
- They got married in Boston, Linda's home town.

b) Make questions in the Past Simple or Past Continuous with the verbs in brackets.

a) What _____ Linda _____ in China? (do)
b) Where _____ they _____ to when they met? (fly)
c) Where _____ they _____ on their first date? (go)
d) _____ Colin _____ with someone else when he met Linda? (go out)
e) How long ago _____ they _____ married? (get)

c) Work with your partner. Take turns to ask and answer your questions. Your partner starts.

10A ⑩ p77

a) Work with a student from group B. Write questions with these words in the Present Simple passive or Past Simple passive.

1 Where / paper / first make ?
  Where was paper first made?
  a) Egypt b) India c) **China**

2 When / *Hamlet* / write ?
  a) 1401 b) **1601** c) 1801

3 Where / first passenger jet plane / build ?
  a) **the UK** b) the USA c) Germany

4 Who / television / invent by ?
  a) Thomas Edison b) **John Logie Baird**
  c) Guglielmo Marconi

5 Where / Lada cars / manufacture ?
  a) Spain b) France c) **Russia**

6 Who / the Star Wars films / direct by ?
  a) Alfred Hitchcock b) Steven Spielberg
  c) **George Lucas**

b) Work with a pair from group A. Take turns to ask and answer your questions. Say the three possible answers when you ask your questions. (The correct answer is in **bold**.)

c) Which pair got more answers right?

3D 7 p27

a) Work on your own. Read about these situations and decide what you want to say in 2 and 4. You can make notes, but don't write the whole conversation.

1 Student A promised to go to the beach with you next weekend. Wait for his/her phone call.

2 You promised to meet student A at a friend's party yesterday evening, but you didn't go. Think of a reason why not. Phone student A, apologise and give your reason. Promise to meet him/her tomorrow for a drink.

3 It's lunchtime. Student A promised to meet you in town for lunch today. He/She is half an hour late. Wait for his/her phone call.

4 You promised to take student A to the airport on Tuesday next week, but now you can't. Think of a reason why not. Phone student A, apologise and give your reason. Promise to meet him/her at the airport when he/she comes back.

b) Work with your partner. Take turns to phone each other.

12B 8 p95

a) Work on your own. Fill in the gaps with the correct form of the verb in brackets.

a) If you _____ (can) buy any car in the world, which car would you buy?

b) If you _____ (be) a famous musician or singer, who would you like to be?

c) If you _____ (can) travel back in time, which time would you choose?

d) If you _____ (know) that the world was going to end in 24 hours, what would you do?

e) If you _____ (need) $100,000 very quickly, how would you get it?

b) Work with your partner. Take turns to ask and answer your questions.

> If you could buy any car in the world, which car would you buy?

> (I think) I'd buy a Rolls Royce. What about you?

> I'd buy a Ferrari.

7A 7 b) p53

a) Work on your own. Read about Day 2 of the cycling tour. Then make questions to complete the information for Day 3.

Where are they travelling to on Wednesday?

New Zealand – South Island

Day 2 Tuesday 12ᵗʰ February
Hanmer Springs to Kaikoura

Morning
- Go for a guided forest walk
- Cycle or drive to Kaikoura

Lunch
- Have a barbecue on the beach

Afternoon
- Go on a boat trip and swim with dolphins

Night
- Spend the night in a traditional home

Day 3 Wednesday 13ᵗʰ February
Kaikoura to _____

Morning
- _____
- _____

Lunch
- _____

Afternoon
- _____

Night
- _____

b) Work with your partner. Answer your partner's questions about Day 2.

c) Ask your partner questions and complete the information for Day 3.

d) Which of the three days is the best, do you think? Why?

4D 7 p35

a) Take turns to ask the group what they think about these sentences. Try to continue each conversation for at least one minute. Give reasons for your opinions.

1 People shouldn't smoke in restaurants or bars.
2 Everyone in the world should learn English.
3 Men are better cooks than women.

> Do you think people shouldn't smoke in restaurants or bars?

b) Tell the class which sentences you all agreed or disagreed with.

6D 9 p51

a) Work on your own. Read the information for phone conversations 1–4. Decide what you want to say in each conversation.

1 You are the receptionist for a law firm called Black and Milton. When your partner calls, ask him/her to wait, then try to put him/her through to Mr Robins. You find he is on the phone. Offer to take a message.

2 Phone your friend, Liz Jackson. Say who you are and ask to speak to her. If she's out, ask when she will be back. Then leave a message and say where/how she can contact you.

3 You are Roberto's brother/sister. He isn't at home at the moment. When your partner calls, tell him/her where Roberto went. Offer to take a message.

4 Call your accountant, Gabriela Wise. If she isn't in, leave a message and tell the receptionist two ways Gabriela can contact you.

b) Work with your partner. Take turns to phone each other.

5A 10 p37

a) Work on your own. Write questions with *Do you think … will … ?* and these ideas. Then make two more questions of your own.

The world in 2020

1 / there / be a world government?
   Do you think there will be a world government?
2 / the world / be a safer place?
3 / there / be a woman President of the USA?
4 / people / still need passports to travel?
5 / cars / use electricity?
6 / your country / win the football World Cup?

b) Work with your partner. Take turns to ask and answer your questions. Continue the conversation if possible.

9A 10 p69

a) Work on your own. Your partner is going to cycle from London to Rome. Make questions with *you* to ask him/her about the journey.

a) What / do / if / someone steals your bike?
   What will you do if someone steals your bike?
b) Where / sleep / if / can't find a hotel?
c) What / do / if / run out of money?
d) Where / stay / when / arrive in Rome?
e) What / do / as soon as / get there?
f) Where / go / after / finish your journey?

b) Read about your journey. Make notes on your ideas.

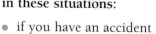

You are going to drive from Los Angeles to Mexico City. Decide what you will do in these situations:

- if you have an accident
- if you get bored with driving
- if you get lost

Also decide:
- where you'll stay when you arrive in Mexico City
- what you'll do as soon as you get there
- where you'll go after you finish your journey

c) Work with your partner. Answer his/her questions about your journey.

d) Ask your partner the questions from **a)** about his/her journey.

8A ⑩ p61

a) Work with a student from group B. Make questions to ask a student from group A.

1	2	3
1 Where / your parents live? *Where do your parents live?*	How long / live / there? *How long have they lived there?*	Where / live / before that? *Where did they live before that?*
2 be / married?	How long / be / married?	Where / go on your honeymoon?
3 What / be / your favourite possession?	How long / have / it?	Where / get it?
4 Who / be / your oldest friend?	How long / know / him or her?	Where / meet him or her?
5 What colour / be / your favourite T-shirt?	How long / have / it?	When / last wear it?

b) Work with a student from group A. Take turns to ask and answer questions from column 1. Then ask the questions from columns 2 and 3 if possible.

c) Tell the class (or other students) three things you found out about your partner.

7B ⑫ p55

a) Work with a student from group B. Describe the picture. Use *a lot of/lots of, a few, a bit, a little, not much/many, some, not any.*

There's lots of sun cream.
There isn't any perfume.
There are some rolls of film.
There are a few bottles of water.

b) Work with a student from group A. Don't look at his/her picture. Take turns to tell your partner about your picture. Find ten differences in the pictures.

> In my picture there's lots of sun cream.

c) Work with your partner from group B. Tell him/her the differences you know. Have you got all the differences?

> In our picture there isn't much chewing gum, but in picture A there's a lot.

3A ⑩ p21

a) Work on your own. Tick the things you have to do in the week and at the weekend in the *you* columns.

	IN THE WEEK		AT THE WEEKEND	
	you	your partner	you	your partner
a) go to work/ university/school				
b) get there before nine o'clock				
c) use a computer a lot				
d) do homework/ study in the evening				
e) cook for yourself or your family				
f) take children to school or other places				

b) Make questions with *have to* and *you* for activities a)–f).

Do you have to go to work in the week?

What about at the weekend?

c) Work with your partner. Take turns to ask and answer your questions. Tick the things your partner has to do in the *your partner* columns. What do you both have to do?

d) Whose life is more stressful, do you think? Why?

10D ⑦ p83

a) Work on your own. Read the information for these conversations. Decide what you want to say.

1 You are a customer in a department store. Your partner is a shop assistant. You want to buy a suitcase. Think about:
- the size and colour you want
- how much money you want to spend
- how you want to pay

2 You are a shop assistant in a shoe shop. Your partner is a customer. He/She wants to buy a pair of trainers. Think about:
- the sizes, colours and brands (*Nike*, *Adidas*, etc.) you have
- the price of each pair of trainers

b) Work with your partner. Role-play the conversations. Your partner starts conversation 1. You start conversation 2.

Can I help you?   Yes, I'm looking for ...

3B ⑦ p23

a) Work on your own. Kevin has got a job as a salesman with a company called CopyRight. Read about his job.

- CopyRight sells photocopiers and printers.
- The company is doing very well at the moment.
- Kevin starts work at half past eight every day.
- He loves having a company car.
- He's working in Liverpool today.

b) Make questions in the Present Simple or Present Continuous.

a) What / Kevin / do every day?
   What does Kevin do every day?
b) How much / he / earn every week?
c) What time / he / finish work?
d) / he / do / any training at the moment?
e) What / he / do / now?

c) Work with your partner. Take turns to ask and answer your questions. Your partner starts.

d) Which job is better, do you think – Kevin's or George's? Why?

11B 10 p87

a) Work on your own. Look at these items and choose the correct words in the relative clauses. There is sometimes more than one possible answer.

a) This is the person *where/ who/ which* says she was with Adam on the night of the murder.

b) This is the bank statement *that/which/who* Barry Clark received on the day of the murder.

c) This is the hotel *which/who/ where* Barry stayed on the night of the murder. It's 50 miles away from Yately.

d) This is the gun *where/that/who* the police found in Barry Clark's house. It's the same gun *that/which/ who* was used to kill Jack Miller.

e) This is the restaurant *where/that/ who* Ellen and her friends had dinner on the night of the murder.

f) This is a button *which/who/that* was found next to Jack's body.

b) Check your answers with a student from group B.

c) Remember the information. Then turn back to p87.

7D 8 p59

a) Work on your own. Read the information for phone conversations 1–4. Decide what you want to say in conversations 2 and 4 and check you understand all the receptionist's sentences.

> **Receptionist**
>
> I'm sorry to hear that.
> I'm terribly sorry about that.
> I'll send someone up straight away.
> I'll send some (more) to your room.
> I'll phone room service and check.

b) Work with your partner. Role-play the conversations.

1 You are the hotel receptionist. Reply to each complaint the guest makes. Use phrases from the box or your own ideas.

2 You are a guest in a hotel. You can't turn the air conditioning off and the room's very cold. Also there aren't enough towels in the bathroom. Phone Reception and complain politely. You start this conversation.

3 You are the hotel receptionist. Reply to each complaint the guest makes. Use phrases from the box or your own ideas.

4 You are a guest in a hotel. The food that room service brought you isn't hot enough. Also the TV remote control is broken. Phone Reception and complain politely. You start this conversation.

9C 6 p72

a) Work on your own. Fill in the gaps with the correct form of these phrasal verbs.

go back   sit down   put up with   go on   give up   get on with

1 Which country or city would you like to ....._go back_..... to?
2 Do you know anyone who has .... eating meat?
3 When you go to a rock concert, do you prefer to stand up or .... ?
4 Do you have to .... a lot of noise where you live?
5 What was the last party you went to? How long did it .... for?
6 Do you .... well ....the rest of your family?

b) Check your answers with a student from group B.

c) Work with a student from group A. Take turns to ask and answer your questions. Ask follow-up questions if possible.

4B 10 p31

a) Work on your own. You are the lead singer of a rock band, Crazy Head. You are playing a concert in this town. Student A is a reporter from the local newspaper. He/She is going to interview you. Look at these ideas and make notes about your life.

1 The last time you played in this town.
2 When you started singing with Crazy Head.
3 Your job before you joined Crazy Head.
4 The number of countries the band has been to.
5 The country you enjoyed the most and why.
6 Three cities in the USA you have played concerts in.
7 When you played in these cities.
8 Two other musicians you have worked with.
9 When you worked with them.

b) Work with your partner. Answer his/her questions. Give more information about your life if possible.

c) Write an article about your life for a magazine called *The Beat*.

12C 10 p97

a) Work on your own. Read the trick and check you understand it.

Preparation
Write the number 34 on a piece of paper. Fold the paper so that nobody can see the number. Then draw a big table with sixteen boxes on a different piece of paper and write the numbers 1–16 in the boxes:

1	2	3	4
5	6	7	8
9	10	11	12
13	14	15	16

The trick
First, put the piece of paper with 34 written on it on the desk between you and your partner. He/She can't open the paper yet. Next, show him/her the paper with sixteen numbers on it and ask him/her to circle any number, for example 6. Then tell him/her to cross out all the other numbers **in the same row and column**:

1	X	3	4
X	⑥	X	X
9	X	11	12
13	X	15	16

Ask him/her to do this two more times. After that, tell him/her to circle the one number that isn't crossed out. Then he/she should add up the four numbers he/she has circled. Finally, ask him/her to open the piece of paper you put on the desk. The numbers will be the same!

The secret!
The answer to this puzzle is always 34.

b) Work with your partner. Take turns to do your tricks. Which trick is better, do you think?

Pair and Group Work: Student/Group C

3C ⑨ p25

a) Work on your own. Imagine you are a personal shopper. You go shopping and buy things for famous people. Make notes on your job. Use these ideas.

- the person/people you work for now
- the easiest/most difficult person to work for
- things you have to buy for him/her/them (clothes, things for the home, etc.)
- good/bad things about your job
- your salary
- shops you usually go to
- people you worked for in the past
- any other interesting things about your job

b) Work with your group. Take turns to tell each other about your jobs. Ask questions to get more information.

c) Decide who has the best job and why. Tell the class which job you chose.

5C ⑩ p41

a) Read about this competition. What is going to be on the spaceship? Why?

Are we alone?

Next year scientists from the World Space Programme are planning to send a spaceship to faraway planets to look for alien life. On this spaceship will be eight things from Earth. If another intelligent life form finds the spaceship, these things will show them what our planet, people and culture are like. What do you think they should put on the spaceship?

Send us your list and you could win a trip to the NASA Space Centre in Florida!

Send your entries to: Space competition, P.O. Box 22

b) Work in pairs. Make a list of eight things to put on the spaceship.

c) Compare lists with another pair. Choose the eight best things from both lists.

d) Work in large groups or with the whole class. Agree on a final list of eight things.

4D ⑦ p35

a) Take turns to ask the group what they think about these sentences. Try to continue each conversation for at least one minute. Give reasons for your opinions.

1 Computer games are bad for children.
2 People shouldn't use mobile phones on public transport.
3 English is an easy language to learn.

> Do you think computer games are bad for children?

b) Tell the class which sentences you all agreed or disagreed with.

7A ③ c) p52

a) Read the list of the top 50 places from the TV programme. Tick any places you have been to and choose three places you would like to visit.

50 places to go before you die

1 The Grand Canyon, USA
2 The Great Barrier Reef, Australia
3 Disney World, Florida, USA
4 The South Island, New Zealand
5 Cape Town, South Africa
6 The Golden Temple, Amritsar, India
7 Las Vegas, USA
8 Sydney, Australia
9 New York, USA
10 The Taj Mahal, India
11 Lake Louise, The Rockies, Canada
12 Uluru (Ayers Rock), Australia
13 Chichen Itza, Mexico
14 Machu Picchu, Peru
15 Niagara Falls, Canada/USA
16 Petra, Jordan
17 The Pyramids, Egypt
18 Venice, Italy
19 The Maldives
20 The Great Wall of China
21 Victoria Falls, Zambia/Zimbabwe
22 Hong Kong
23 Yosemite National Park, USA
24 Hawaii
25 The North Island, New Zealand
26 Iguaçu Falls, Brazil/Argentina
27 Paris, France
28 Alaska, USA
29 Angkor Wat, Cambodia
30 Mount Everest, Nepal
31 Rio de Janeiro, Brazil
32 Masai Mara, Kenya
33 The Galapagos Islands
34 Luxor, Egypt
35 Rome, Italy
36 San Francisco, USA
37 Barcelona, Spain
38 Dubai
39 Singapore
40 La Digue, Seychelles
41 Sri Lanka
42 Bangkok, Thailand
43 Barbados
44 Iceland
45 The Terracotta Army, Xian, China
46 The Matterhorn, Switzerland
47 Angel Falls, Venezuela
48 Abu Simbel, Egypt
49 Bali
50 Bora Bora, Tahiti

b) Work in the same groups. Tell the other students about the places you have been to and the three places you would like to visit.

Vocabulary

V1.1 **Question words** (1A ⑤ p5)

Write these question words in the correct place in the table.

~~Who~~ ~~Which~~ Where What When Why How
How long How many How much How often How old

	question word	meaning
1	Who	a person
2		a time
3		a place
4		a reason (because ...)
5	Which	a thing (a small number of possible answers)
6		a thing (many possible answers)
7		a number
8		a period of time (for a week, etc.)
9		age
10		a way of doing something
11		an amount of money
12		the number of times you do something

TIPS! • We can often use *Which* or *What* with no difference in meaning: *Which/What newspaper do you read?*

• We use *Whose ... ?* to ask about people's possessions: *Whose coat is this? It's Tony's.*

• We use *What kind/type/sort of ... ?* to ask about which thing, activity, etc.: *What kind of food do you like?*

• We use *How far ... ?* to ask about distance: *How far is it to your house?*

V1.2 **Work** (1B ① p6)

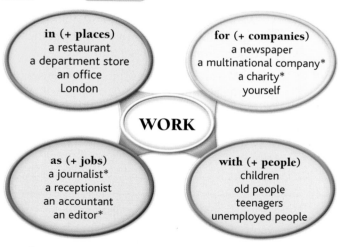

- **in (+ places)**
  a restaurant
  a department store
  an office
  London

- **for (+ companies)**
  a newspaper
  a multinational company*
  a charity*
  yourself

WORK

- **as (+ jobs)**
  a journalist*
  a receptionist
  an accountant
  an editor*

- **with (+ people)**
  children
  old people
  teenagers
  unemployed people

*a **multinational company** a large company that makes and sells things in many different countries
*a **charity** an organisation that gives money, food or help to people or animals
*a **journalist** /ˈdʒɜːnəlɪst/ a person who writes articles and reports for newspapers, TV, etc.
*an **editor** a person who prepares written text for a magazine, newspaper or book

TIPS! • We use *a* or *an* with jobs: *I work as an editor.* not ~~I work as editor~~.

• We can also say: *I work **at** home.*

V1.3 **Free time activities with *do, play, go, go to*** (1C ② p8)

do	play	go	go to
things you do in a gym or health club	sports with a ball and other games	words that end in *-ing*	places and events
judo /ˈdʒuːdəʊ/ exercise yoga /ˈjəʊgə/ aerobics /eəˈrəʊbɪks/ sport	volleyball cards basketball chess table tennis	cycling running skateboarding jogging mountain biking	concerts the theatre art galleries the gym /dʒɪm/ museums

judo   yoga   aerobics   cards

chess   skateboarding   jogging   mountain biking

TIP! • We don't usually use the verb *practise* with sports: *I play tennis.* not ~~I practise tennis~~.

V1.4 **Frequency adverbs and expressions** (1C ⑤ p9)

FREQUENCY ADVERBS

always   often   not (very) often   hardly ever
100%   0%
usually/normally/generally   sometimes   occasionally   never

- Frequency adverbs go **after** the verb *be*: *She's usually tired after work.*

- Frequency adverbs go **before** other verbs: *She always goes home at 6 p.m.*

TIPS! • *Usually, normally* and *generally* have the same meaning.

• In negative sentences we can also put *very often* at the end: *I don't play tennis very often.*

• We also use *a lot* and *all the time* to mean *often*: *He watches TV a lot/all the time.*

Language Summary 1

Vocabulary

FREQUENCY EXPRESSIONS

- To talk about frequency we use expressions with *every, once, twice, three times*, etc.: *35% normally do some gardening **every weekend**. I do yoga **twice a week***.

- Frequency expressions usually come at the end of a sentence or clause: *British people usually go on holiday **once a year***.

TIPS! • To ask about frequency, we use *How often … ?*: *How often do you do sport?*
• For plural numbers of days, weeks, etc., we use *once, twice*, etc. + *every*: *I go once every two months*.
• *a couple of weeks = two weeks*

Grammar

G1.1 Review of verb forms and questions (1A 6 p5)

POSITIVE

Present Simple: Every week millions of people **watch** him on TV.
Present Continuous: At the moment Jamie **is writing** a new book.
Past Simple: When he was only eight he **started** helping in his parents' restaurant.
be going to: He **is going to open** Fifteen restaurants in Australia and the USA.

QUESTIONS: ALL VERBS EXCEPT *BE, HAVE GOT* AND *BE GOING TO*

- We usually use an auxiliary (*do, does, did, can, is*, etc.) to make questions.

	question word	auxiliary	subject	verb	
PRESENT SIMPLE	How	does	he	travel	around London?
PAST SIMPLE	When	did	he	get	married?
can	Which instrument	can	he	play?	
PRESENT CONTINUOUS	What	is	he	writing	at the moment?

QUESTIONS: *BE, HAVE GOT* AND *BE GOING TO*

- We don't use *do, does* or *did* to make questions with *be*: *How often is Fifteen on TV? How old was he when he started college?*

- We make questions with *have got* to ask about family relationships and possessions: *How many children has he got? Have you got a car?*

- We can ask questions about future plans with *be going to*: *When is he going to open his new restaurants?*

G1.2 Subject questions (1B 7 p7)

subject	verb	object or preposition + noun
Mick Benton	made	the TV programme.
Andrea Price	lives	in Paris.

SUBJECT QUESTIONS

Who made the TV programme? Mick Benton.
Who lives in Paris? Andrea Price.

NON-SUBJECT QUESTIONS

What did Mike Benton make? The TV programme.
Where does Andrea Price live? In Paris.

- We use *Who* when we ask about the subject of a sentence and the subject is a person.

- Subject questions have the same word order as positive sentences.

- We don't use *do, does* or *did* in Present Simple and Past Simple subject questions.

- We use *do, does* or *did* in Present Simple and Past Simple questions that ask about the object or preposition + noun.

TIP! • We can also make subject questions with *What, Whose* and *Which*: *What happened? Whose journey takes two hours? Which journey costs the most?*

Real World

RW1.1 Finding things in common (1D 3 p10)

- We use *So* + auxiliary + *I* to agree with positive sentences: *I really love travelling. So do I.*

- We use *Neither* + auxiliary + *I* to agree with negative sentences: *I don't go out much. Neither do I.*

- We use a positive form of an auxiliary to disagree with a negative sentence: *I don't like cycling. Oh, I **do**.*

- We use a negative form of an auxiliary to disagree with a positive sentence: *I'm a vegetarian. Oh, I**'m not**.*

	agree	disagree
I'm a bit nervous.	Sŏ am Ĭ.	Oh, Ĭ'm nŏt.
I can't speak Turkish.	Neĭther can Ĭ.	Oh, Ĭ căn.
I've got a dog.	Sŏ have Ĭ.	Oh, Ĭ hăven't.
I don't go out much.	Neĭther do Ĭ.	Oh, Ĭ dŏ.
I had a great time.	Sŏ did Ĭ.	Oh, Ĭ dĭdn't.

TIPS! • We can also use *Me, too.* to agree with positive sentences and *Me, neither.* to agree with negative sentences.
• When we agree with positive sentences in the Present Simple and Past Simple we use *do, does* and *did*: *I **went** to Turkey last year. So **did** I.*

Vocabulary

V2.1 Past time phrases (2A 6 p13)

AGO

- We use *ago* to talk about a time in the past. We use it with the Past Simple: *We got married six months ago.* (= six months before now).

TIP! • *the day before yesterday = two days ago*

LAST

- We use *last* to say the day, week, etc. in the past that is nearest to now: *I saw Jo last Friday.* (= the Friday before now).

- We use *last* with **days**, (*last Friday*) **months** (*last May*), **seasons** (*last summer*) and in these phrases: *last night, last week, last weekend, last month, last year, last century.*

TIPS! • We say *last night*, but *yesterday morning/ afternoon/evening* not ~~last morning~~, etc.

• We don't use a preposition with *last* or *yesterday*: *last weekend* not ~~in last weekend~~, *yesterday evening* not ~~at yesterday evening~~.

• We can use *on* with **days** to mean *last*: *I bought it on Friday. = I bought it last Friday.*

IN

- We use *in* with **years** (*in 1955*) and **months** (*in July*).

- We use *in the* with **decades** (*in the sixties*) and **centuries** (*in the nineteenth century*).

V2.2 Relationships (1) (2B 5 p14)

Match phrases 1–8 to pictures a)–h).

1 go out with (someone) *e)*
2 get engaged to (someone)
3 ask (someone) out
4 go on a date
5 get married to (someone)
6 fall in love with (someone)
7 meet (someone) for the first time
8 break up with (someone)

V2.3 Connecting words (1) (2C 6 p17)

- We use **because** to give a reason why something happened:
  The King killed his wife because he found her with another man.

- We use **so** to say what the consequence of a situation is:
  The King found his wife with another man so he killed her.

- We use **until** to say something stops happening at this time:
  The King never heard the end of a story until the next evening.

- We can use **while** and **when** for things that happen at the same time:
  While the King was drinking with his friends, Shahrazad went to find her sister.
  Shahrazad was getting ready for bed when her sister came to visit her.

TIP! • We don't usually use *while* with the Past Simple: ~~Shahrazad was getting ready for bed while her sister came to visit her.~~

Grammar

G2.1 Past Simple (2A 3 p13)

- We use the Past Simple to talk about the past. We know **when** these things happened.

All verbs except *be*

POSITIVE

regular verbs: spelling rule	examples
most regular verbs: add *-ed*	need**ed** stay**ed** look**ed** work**ed**
regular verbs ending in *-e*: add *-d*	liv**ed** di**ed**
regular verbs ending in consonant + *y*: *-y* → *-i* and add *-ed*	stud**ied** marr**ied**
regular verbs ending in consonant + vowel + consonant: double the last consonant	stop**ped** travel**led**

- The Past Simple is the same for all subjects: *I/you/he/she/it/we/they closed the restaurant.*

- There are no rules for irregular verbs. There is an Irregular Verb List, p159.

- The past of *can/can't* is *could/couldn't*: *He could serve all his customers there. I couldn't understand it.*

NEGATIVE

subject	auxiliary	infinitive	
I/You/He/She/ It/We/They	didn't (= did not)	go	to work yesterday.

TIP! • We don't use the Past Simple form of the main verb in negative sentences: ~~I didn't went to work yesterday.~~

Language Summary 2

QUESTIONS

question word	auxiliary	subject	infinitive	
When	did Did	I/you/he/she/ it/we/they	learn go out	to cook? last night?

SHORT ANSWERS

Yes, I/you/he/she/it/we/they did.
No, I/you/he/she/it/we/they didn't.

TIP! • We don't use *did* when we ask about the subject of the sentence: *Who bought KFC in 1986?* not ~~Who did buy KFC in 1986?~~ (see G1.2).

The verb *be*

POSITIVE	NEGATIVE
I/he/she/it was you/we/they were	I/he/she/it wasn't (= was not) you/we/they weren't (= were not)

QUESTIONS

question word	*was/were*	subject	
When Where	was were Was Were	I/he/she/it you/we/they I/he/she/it you/we/they	in the UK? last night? late? at home?

SHORT ANSWERS

Yes, I/he/she/it was. Yes, you/we/they were.	No, I/he/she/it wasn't. No, you/we/they weren't.

G2.2 Past Continuous: positive and negative

 2B ❷ p14

● We use the Past Continuous to talk about an action that was in progress when another (shorter) action happened. The action in the Past Continuous might continue after this point:
I was travelling back from China and we met on the plane.

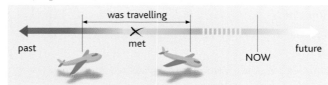

was travelling = longer action (Past Continuous)
met = short action (Past Simple)

POSITIVE

I/he/she/it + was + verb+*ing*
you/we/they + were + verb+*ing*

NEGATIVE

I/he/she/it + wasn't + verb+*ing*
you/we/they + weren't + verb+*ing*

verb+*ing*: spelling rules	examples
most verbs: add *-ing*	go → going wait → waiting
verbs ending in *-e*: take off *-e* and add *-ing*	live → living write → writing
verbs ending in consonant + vowel + consonant: double the last consonant and add *-ing*	get → getting stop → stopping travel → travelling

TIP! • We can also use the Past Continuous to talk about an activity in progress at a point of time in the past: *I was watching TV at 9 o'clock.* (= I started watching TV before 9 o'clock and continued watching after 9 o'clock).

G2.3 Past Continuous: questions 2B ❽ p15

● We make questions in the Past Continuous with: question word + *was* or *were* + subject + verb+*ing*.

question word	auxiliary	subject	verb+*ing*	
Where Who	was were	I/he/she/it you/we/they	going? talking	to?
What	were	they	doing	when Liam asked Jenny to marry him?
What	was	Liam	doing	when she said yes?

RW2.1 Starting conversations 2D ❸ p18

people you know	meeting someone in the past
How do you know David and Jane? Do you know Pam Jones? Are you a friend of David's?	Didn't we meet in Milan last year? Where did you meet David?
where people live	**people's jobs or studies**
Do you live near here?	You're a student at the English Centre, aren't you? What do you do?

TIP! • When we think the answer to a question will be yes we often use negative questions: **Didn't we meet in Milan last year?** (I think we did) or question tags: *You're a student at the English Centre,* **aren't you?** (I think you are).

RW2.2 Ending conversations 2D ❻ p19

It was nice to see you again.
I hope we meet again soon.
It was nice meeting you.
See you at school, probably.
Let's keep in touch.
See you later, maybe.

Language Summary 3

Vocabulary

V3.1 Employment 3A ① p20

Match phrases 1–12 to definitions a)–l).

I'd like ...

1	a good salary	a)	nice people to work with
2	friendly colleagues /ˈkɒliːgz/	b)	you know you'll have the job for a long time
3	my own office	c)	a good manager
4	long holidays	d)	an office only for you
5	a good boss	e)	a lot of days off a year
6	job security	f)	a lot of money for doing your job

I'd like a job with ...

7	flexible working hours	g)	the chance to get a better job in the company
8	opportunities for travel	h)	you get paid when you're ill
9	opportunities for promotion	i)	you get paid when you're on holiday
10	holiday pay	j)	you can choose when you start and finish work
11	on-the-job training	k)	the chance to travel as part of your job
12	sick pay	l)	the company you work for teaches you how to do the job

TIPS! • We use *job* to talk about a particular work activity that you do: *What's his job? He's a doctor.* It is a countable noun: *He's got a job as a cleaner.* not ~~He's got a work as a cleaner.~~
• We use *work* to talk about something you do as part of your job: *I've got a lot of work to do today.* It is an uncountable noun: *He's looking for work.* not ~~He's looking for a work.~~
• *Work* is also a verb: *I work in London.* not ~~I job in London.~~

V3.2 Looking for a job 3B ① p22

a CV /siːˈviː/ [US: a résumé /ˈrezʊmeɪ/] a document you write that describes your qualifications and the jobs you have done
apply /əˈplaɪ/ **for a job** ask a company to give you a job, usually by writing a letter or filling in a form
an application form a form from a company that you fill in when you want to apply for a job
unemployment benefit money you get from the government when you are unemployed
earn /ɜːn/ get money for doing work

V3.3 Word building: noun endings

3C ④ p24

• We can often make nouns from verbs by adding an ending (suffix) to the verb.

verb	noun	ending
collect	collection	-ion
act	actor	-or
assist	assistant	-ant
clean	cleaner	-er
advertise	advertisement	-ment
paint	paint	–

TIP! • We use the endings *-or, -ant, -er, -ist,* and *-ian* for people's jobs: *doctor, shop assistant, waiter, dentist, politician,* etc.

Grammar

G3.1 *have to/had to* (1): positive and negative 3A ③ p20

• We use **have to/has to** to say it is necessary to do this: *You have to have a degree.*

• We use **don't have to/doesn't have to** to say it is not necessary to do this, but you can if you want: *You don't have to go to university.*

• We use **had to** to say it was necessary to do this in the past: *I had to do 72 weeks' basic training.*

• We use **didn't have to** to say it wasn't necessary to do this in the past: *I didn't have to pay for it.*

		POSITIVE	NEGATIVE
PRESENT SIMPLE		I/You/We/They have to pay for it. He/She has to pay for it.	I/You/We/They don't have to pay for it. He/She doesn't have to pay for it.
PAST SIMPLE		I/You/He/She/We/They had to pay for it.	I/You/He/She/We/They didn't have to pay for it.

• We use the infinitive after *have to/had to*: *I have to* **go**. *They didn't have to* **do** *anything.*

• We also use *has to* or *had to* when the subject is *it*: *It has to be here tomorrow. It had to stop at midnight.*

TIPS! • In the present we can use *have to* or *have got to*: *I've got to work tonight.* = *I have to work tonight. Have got to* is very common in spoken English.
• We can't use *have got to* in the past: *I had to work last night.* not ~~I had got to work last night.~~
• We can't use *haven't to, hasn't to* or *hadn't to* to say something isn't or wasn't necessary: *I don't have to do that.* not ~~I haven't to do that.~~ *We didn't have to pay for it.* not ~~We hadn't to pay for it.~~

Language Summary 3

G3.2 *have to/had to* (2): questions and short answers (3A 8 p21)

QUESTIONS

	question word	auxiliary	subject	*have to*	infinitive	
PRESENT SIMPLE	When What	do does Do Does	I/you/we/they he/she/it I/you/we/they he/she/it	have to have to have to have to	go? know? have work	a degree? at night?
PAST SIMPLE	How many tests	did Did	I/you/he/she/ it/we/they I/you/he/she/ it/we/they	have to have to	do? pass	an oral test?

SHORT ANSWERS

Present Simple

Yes, I/you/we/they do.
Yes, he/she/it does.

No, I/you/we/they don't.
No, he/she/it doesn't.

Past Simple

Yes, I/you/he/she/it/we/they did. | No, I/you/he/she/it/we/they didn't.

TIPS! • In Present Simple questions we can say: *Do you have to … ?* or *Have you got to … ?*: *Do you have to work tonight?* = *Have you got to work tonight?*

• We can't use *have got to* in Past Simple questions: *Did you have to work last night?* not ~~Had you got to work last night?~~

• We can't use *Have you to … ?* or *Had you to … ?* to make questions: *Do you have to wear a suit?* not ~~Have you to wear a suit?~~ *When did you have to be there?* not ~~When had you to be there?~~

G3.3 Present Continuous and Present Simple (3B 4 p23)

• We use the **Present Continuous** for things that:
  a) are happening at the moment of speaking: *Today **he's doing** some gardening. **I'm writing** to tell you how it feels to be unemployed.*
  b) are temporary and happening around now, but maybe not at the moment of speaking: *Now **he's looking** for his first job. **I'm applying** for every job I can.*

• We use the **Present Simple** for:
  a) daily routines and things we always/sometimes/never do: *He reads the adverts in the paper every day. **I never get** an interview.*
  b) verbs that describe states (*be, want, have got, think,* etc.): *He **needs** a real job. **People think** I'm too old.*

Activity and state verbs

• Activity verbs talk about activities and actions. We can use activity verbs in the Present Simple and the Present Continuous: *He plays football every day. He's playing football now.* Typical activity verbs are: *play, work, write, eat, run* and *do.*

• State verbs talk about states, feelings and opinions. We don't usually use state verbs in the Present Continuous (or other continuous verb forms): *I like him.* not ~~I'm liking him.~~ *I think it's great.* not ~~I'm thinking it's great.~~ Learn the common state verbs in the picture.

TIP! • Some verbs can be both activity verbs and state verbs: *I'm having a shower.* (activity). *He has three children.* (state).

Common state verbs

Grammar

Present Continuous

- We make the Present Continuous with:
  subject + *be* + (not) + verb+*ing*.

POSITIVE

I'm working at the moment.
You/We/They're looking for a job.
He/She/It's waiting for you.

NEGATIVE

I'm not driving very fast.
You/We/They aren't watching TV.
He/She/It isn't working now.

WH- QUESTIONS

question word	auxiliary	subject	verb+*ing*
Where	am	I	going?
What	are	you/we/they	doing?
Who	is	he/she/it	looking at?

YES/NO QUESTIONS

Am I working today?
Are you/we/they watching TV?
Is he/she/it waiting for me?

SHORT ANSWERS

Yes, I am.	No, I'm not.
Yes, you/we/they are.	No, you/we/they aren't.
Yes, he/she/it is.	No, he/she/it isn't.

TIPS! • See G2.2 for the spelling rules for verb+*ing* forms.
• We can also make negatives and negative short answers with *'re not* and *'s not*: *They're not playing. Is she waiting? No, she's not.*
• We often use the Present Continuous with: *now, today, at the moment.*

Present Simple

- For *I/you/we/they* the Present Simple is the same as the infinitive. For *he/she/it* we add *-s* or *-es* to the infinitive: *he lives, she watches, it goes.*
- We make the Present Simple negative with: *don't* or *doesn't* + infinitive.

POSITIVE

I/You/We/They live in the UK.
He/She/It wants to go home.

NEGATIVE

I/You/We/They don't live in Germany.
He/She/It doesn't want to go out.

PRESENT SIMPLE POSITIVE: SPELLING RULES

spelling rule	examples
most verbs: add **-s**	play**s** like**s** read**s**
verbs ending in *-ch, -sh, -s, -ss, -x* or *-z*: add **-es**	watch**es** /'wɒtʃɪz/ finish**es** /'fɪnɪʃɪz/
verbs ending in consonant + *y*: *-y* → *-ies*	study → stud**ies**
the verbs *go* and *do*: add **-es**	go**es** do**es** /dʌz/
the verb *have* is irregular	ha**s**

WH- QUESTIONS

question word	auxiliary	subject	infinitive
Where	do	I/you/we/they	live?
What	does	he/she/it	do?

YES/NO QUESTIONS

Do I/you/we/they live here?
Does he/she/it come from England?

SHORT ANSWERS

Yes, I/you/we/they do.	No, I/you/we/they don't.
Yes, he/she/it does.	No, he/she/it doesn't.

Real World

RW3.1 Apologies, reasons and promises (3D ③ p26)

- For **apologies** we often use: *I'm (really) sorry, (but) I can't/couldn't* + infinitive.
  I'm really sorry, but I can't see you tonight.
  I'm sorry, I couldn't finish it yesterday.
- For **reasons** we often use: *I have to/had to* + infinitive.
  I have to take a client out to dinner.
  I had to help Kate.
- For **promises** we often use: *I'll* + infinitive.
  I'll do it now.
  I'll see you on Friday, I promise.

TIPS! • There is often a pattern in this type of conversation: we apologise → we give a reason → we make a promise.
• To respond to an apology we often use these phrases:
Oh, don't worry. Another time, maybe.
Oh, dear. What happened?
Oh, right. Why not?

Language Summary 4

V4.1 Types of film (4A ❷ p28)

a love story   a comedy   a cartoon   a war film   a thriller   an action film

a horror film   a western   a historical drama   a musical   a science-fiction (sci-fi) /ˈsaɪfaɪ/ film   a romantic comedy

TIP! • The American English word for *film* is *movie*: *a horror movie, a war movie*, etc.

V4.2 Music (4B ❶ p30)

jazz   classical music

blues   rock music

rap   country music

opera   pop music

rock'n'roll   dance music

traditional folk music   reggae

V4.3 TV nouns and verbs (4C ❶ p32)

TV EQUIPMENT

Cable or satellite TV is a system of sending television programmes into your house along cables in the ground (cable TV) or to a satellite dish on your house (satellite TV).

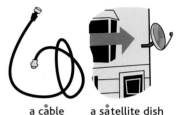

a cable   a satellite dish

A **DVD player** is a machine that plays DVDs so you can watch them on TV.

The **remote control** is something you hold in your hand and use it to turn on/off the TV and change channel from your chair.

A **video recorder** [US: **a VCR**] is a machine that records and plays videos so you can watch them on TV.

TV PROGRAMMES

The news tells you about important things happening in the world.

On **chat shows** a presenter interviews famous people.

Soap operas are invented stories about the lives of a group of people living in one area. They are usually on TV three or four times a week.

Documentaries give information and facts about real situations or people.

Reality /riˈælɪti/ **TV programmes** have ordinary people in them, not actors, for example, *Big Brother*.

On **game shows** people try to win prizes or money by answering questions or doing unusual things.

Dramas are serious plays for TV, the theatre, radio, etc.

Current affairs programmes have reports and discussions about things that are happening in the news.

Sports programmes show popular sports: football, tennis, etc.

TV VERBS

You **turn on** the TV when you want to watch something.

You can **record a programme** on a video or a DVD and watch it later.

You **turn off** the TV before you go to bed.

You **turn over** when you want to watch a different channel.

TIPS! • We say *the news is*, not ~~the news are~~: *The news is on at six o'clock.*

• We often use *on* to mean *on TV*: *What time is the football on?*

Vocabulary

V4.4 **-ed and -ing adjectives** (4C **8** p33)

- We use **-ed** adjectives to describe how people feel: *Many people are worried about how much TV children watch.*

- We use **-ing** adjectives to describe the thing, situation, place or person that causes the feeling: *TV can sometimes be fun and exciting.*

She's excited.   He's worried.   She's surprised.   He's frightened.   She's tired.

TIP! • People can be *bored* or *boring* and *interested* or *interesting*. Look at the picture. **A** is *bored* and **B** is *boring*. **C** is *interested* and **D** is *interesting*.

Grammar

G4.1 **Present Perfect for life experiences (1): positive and negative** (4A **6** p29)

- We use the **Present Perfect** for experiences that happened sometime before now. We don't know or don't say when they happened: *He's been to Star Wars conferences all over the world.*

- We use the **Past Simple** if we say exactly when something happened: *He met his wife, Holly, in 1994.*

POSITIVE

subject	auxiliary	past participle	
I/You/We/They	've (= have)	seen	the first Star Wars film.
He/She/It	's (= has)	met	some of the actors.

NEGATIVE

subject	auxiliary + *not*	past participle	
I/You/We/They	haven't (= have not)	seen	the new Star Wars film.
He/She/It	hasn't (= has not)	met	the director.

TIPS! • To make past participles of regular verbs, add *-ed* or *-d* to the infinitive: *play → played*, *watch → watched*, etc. The Past Simple and past participles of regular verbs are the same. See G2.1 for spelling rules.

• There are no rules for irregular past participles. There is an Irregular Verb List, p159.

G4.2 **Present Perfect for life experiences (2): questions with *ever*** (4B **5** p30)

- We use the **Present Perfect** to ask about people's experiences. We don't ask about when these experiences happened.

- We use the **Past Simple** to ask for more information about these experiences.

auxiliary	subject	*(ever)*	past participle	
Have	I/you/we/they	ever	met	anyone famous?
Has	he/she/it	ever	been	to a concert?
Have	you	ever	been	to a rock festival?
Have	they	ever	seen	U2 in concert?
Has	Julie	ever	heard	of Miles Davis?

SHORT ANSWERS

Yes, I/you/we/they have.	No, I/you/we/they haven't.
Yes, he/she/it has.	No, he/she/it hasn't.

TIP! • *ever* + Present Perfect = any time in your life until now.

• *go* has two past participles, *been* and *gone*. When we use the Present Perfect to talk about experiences, we usually use *been*: *I've been to the USA* (I'm back in my country now).

Real World

RW4.1 **Agreeing, disagreeing and asking for opinions** (4D **3** p34)

agreeing	disagreeing	asking for opinions
Yes, maybe you're right.	I'm sorry, I don't agree.	What do you think?
Yes, definitely.	I'm not sure about that.	What about you, (Jackie)?
I agree (with Jackie).	No, definitely not.	Do you think ... ?
Yes, I think so.	No, I don't think so.	Do you agree (with that)?

TIPS! • We often use *I'm not sure about that.* as a polite way of disagreeing.

• We can also agree and disagree with *Do you think ... ?* questions with *Yes, I do.* and *No, I don't.*

Language Summary 5

Vocabulary

V5.1 **Verb-noun collocations (1)** (5A **2** p36)

look after* old people
build cars
recognise* (someone's) face
take over* the world
look like* (someone)

move around easily
do the housework
feed* the cat
clean the carpets

look after take care of someone or something by keeping them safe and healthy. You can look after old people, other people's children, pets, plants, etc.: *Sally's looking after my cat while I'm on holiday.*

recognise know someone or something because you have seen or heard them before: *I haven't seen him for years but I recognised him immediately.*

take over get control of something you didn't control before, for example, a company: *Donna took over the company when her father retired.*

look like have a similar face to another person: *My brother, Jake, looks like Tom Cruise.*

feed give food to a baby, an animal, etc.: *Can you feed the baby?*

V5.2 **Verb-noun collocations (2)** (5B **2** p38)

have a great time
spend time doing (something)
do a degree (in biology)
spend time with (someone)

live abroad*
take photos
learn how to do (something)
get a suntan*

abroad /əˈbrɔːd/ in or to a foreign country: *John lives abroad. We went abroad for our holiday this year.*

a suntan when your skin is brown after you have been in the sun: *I got a really good suntan on holiday.*

V5.3 **Verbs and prepositions** (5C **4** p40)

verb + preposition	example
travel to a place **by** a method of transport	He travels to London by train.
go on a trip	She's going on a trip to Amsterdam.
return to the place you started	When did he return to England?
pay an amount of money **for** something	He paid £8,000 for his car.
look for something you want to find	I'm looking for my mobile.
sell something **to** people **for** an amount of money	She sold her car to Max for £500.
look out of a window	Look out of the window – it's snowing!
spend an amount of money **on** something	They spend £100 on food every week.
fly to a place	I'm going to fly to Moscow tomorrow.
talk about a topic	He always talks about his job.

Grammar

G5.1 ***will* for prediction; *might*; *will be able to*** (5A **4** p37)

- We use *will* + infinitive to predict the future: *Robots will take over the world.*
- The negative form of *will* is *won't*: *Domestic robots won't look like humans.*
- We use *might* to say 'will possibly': *By 2050 robots might win the World Cup.*

TIPS! • *Will* and *might* are the same for all subjects (*I/you/he/she/it/we/they*).

• We usually write *'ll* after pronouns and *will* after names: *I'll speak English fluently. Gary will be famous one day.*

• We also use *will* for offers: *I'll help you with the shopping.* and promises: *I'll do it tomorrow.*

Grammar

QUESTIONS

question word	will	subject	infinitive	
Where	will	I/you/he/she/it/we/they	live	in 2020?
	Will	I/you/he/she/it/we/they	get	the job?
When	will	robots	be able to	run?
	Will	domestic robots	look like	humans?

SHORT ANSWERS

Yes, I/you/he/she/it/we/they will.
No, I/you/he/she/it/we/they won't.

TIPS! • We often use *Do you think ... ?* to make questions with *will*: *Do you think robots will take over the world?*

• The short answers to all *Do you think ... ?* questions are: *Yes, I do.* and *No, I don't.*

• We can also use *might* in short answers: *(Yes,) I might. (Yes,) he might.*, etc.

will be able to

● To talk about ability in the **present** we use *can/can't* + infinitive: *At the moment robots can't move around easily.*

● To talk about ability in the **future** we use *will/won't be able to* + infinitive: *By 2020 robots will be able to walk and run.*

TIP! • We can also use *be able to* to talk about ability in the present: *At the moment robots aren't able to move around easily.* But *can* is more common.

G5.2 Future plans and ambitions: *be going to* (5B 4 p38)

● We use *be going to* + infinitive to talk about future plans: *We're going to drive around Australia.*

● We use *will* + infinitive to talk about future predictions: *I'm sure we'll have a great time.* (see G5.1).

POSITIVE AND NEGATIVE

subject	auxiliary (+ *not*)	*going to*	infinitive	
I	'm/'m not	going to	work	after that.
You/We/They	're/aren't	going to	drive	around Australia.
He/She/It	's/isn't	going to	study	history of art.

QUESTIONS

question word	auxiliary	subject	*going to*	infinitive	
When	am	I	going to	see	you again?
What	are	you/we/they	going to	do	tomorrow?
	Is	he/she/it	going to	retire	soon?

TIPS! • We don't usually use *going to* in short answers: *Yes, she is.* not ~~*Yes, she's going to.*~~

• With the verb *go*, we usually say: *I'm going to Italy.* not *I'm going to go to Italy.* but both are correct.

G5.3 Future plans and ambitions: other phrases (5B 5 p38)

● We can also use these phrases to talk about future plans and ambitions:
be planning + infinitive with *to*: *I'm planning to retire early.*
be hoping + infinitive with *to*: *We're hoping to spend about a year travelling.*
be looking forward to + verb+ing: *I'm looking forward to spending more time doing the things I enjoy.*
would like + infinitive with *to*: *I'd like to live abroad.*
be thinking of + verb+ing: *I'm thinking of doing a degree in history of art.*

● *I'm looking forward to ...* = I'm excited about this and I'm going to enjoy it when it happens.

● *I'm planning to ...* is more certain than *I'm thinking of ...* .

● *I'm hoping to ...* is less certain than *I'm going to ...* .

TIPS! • We can also use a pronoun or a noun after *I'm looking forward to*: *I'm looking forward to it/my* **holiday**.

• We can also use *I want* and *I'd love to* to talk about future plans and ambitions: *I want to be famous.* **I'd love to** *travel around the world.*

Real World

RW5.1 Offers, suggestions and requests

(5D 3 p42)

making offers	responding to offers
Shall I make some posters? **Can I** give you a hand? **I'll** help you, if you like.	Yes, that'd be great. Great, thanks a lot. Yes, why not? No, don't worry. Thanks anyway.

making requests	making suggestions
Will you organise that? **Could you** give me a hand? **Can you** do that?	**Shall we** start? **Let's** decide who does what. **Why don't we** ask Steve?

TIPS! • After all the phrases in **bold** we use the infinitive: *Shall I* **make** *some posters?*

• *Could you ... ?* is more polite than *Can you ... ?*

Language Summary 6

V6.1 Character adjectives 6A ① p44

Shy /ʃaɪ/ people aren't very confident, especially about meeting or talking to new people.

Bright /braɪt/ people are intelligent and can learn things quickly.

Noisy people make a lot of noise.

Stubborn /'stʌbən/ people won't change their ideas or plans when other people want them to.

Helpful people like helping other people.

Moody people are often unfriendly because they're angry or unhappy.

Patient /'peɪʃənt/ people don't get angry when they have to wait a long time for something to happen.

Lazy people don't want to work or do anything that's difficult.

Honest /'ɒnɪst/ people always tell the truth and don't lie.

Selfish people usually only think about themselves, not other people.

Mature /mə'tʃʊə/ people behave like adults, not children.

Polite people show respect for other people and aren't rude to them.

Aggressive people behave in an angry or violent way to other people.

Ambitious people want to be very successful or powerful.

Organised people plan things well and don't waste time.

Considerate people are very kind and helpful.

Easy-going people are very relaxed and don't worry about things.

She's bright.

He's polite.

He's aggressive.   She's organised.

V6.2 Relationships (2) 6B ① p46

FAMILY RELATIONSHIPS

my grandfather   my grandmother

my father   my mother   my uncle   my aunt

my brother   my sister-in-law   ME   my cousins

my niece /niːs/   my nephew

● Your **stepfather** is your mother's husband, but he isn't your father. Your mother married again.

● A **relative** is a person in your family (an aunt, a cousin, a grandparent, etc.). Your *parents* are your mother and father only.

OTHER RELATIONSHIPS

Your **boss** is your manager at work.

Your **flatmate** is the person you share a flat with.

A **close friend** is a very good friend.

Your **ex-girlfriend** is a woman you went out with in the past. She isn't your girlfriend now.

A **neighbour** /'neɪbə/ is a person who lives near you in the same street or building.

A **colleague** /'kɒliːg/ is a person who works with you in the same company.

Your **employer** is the person or company you work for.

An **employee** is a person who works for a company.

TIPS! • We use *cousin* for both girls/women and boys/men.

• We can use *ex-*, *step-*, *grand-*, and *-in-law* with other family words: *ex-wife*, *stepsister*, *granddaughter*, *mother-in-law*, etc.

• We always use hyphens (-) with *ex-* and *-in-law*, and we don't usually use hyphens with *step* or *grand*.

V6.3 Prefixes and opposites of adjectives: *un-, in-, im-, dis-*
  6C ③ p49

● We often use prefixes (*un-*, *in-*, etc.) to make opposites of adjectives.

un-	unemployed unhelpful unreliable unselfish unhappy unintelligent unambitious unfriendly unattractive unsure unhealthy
in-	inconsiderate incorrect
im-	impatient immature impolite impossible
dis-	dishonest disorganised

TIPS! • Adjectives beginning with **c** usually take the prefix *in-*: *correct* → *incorrect*.

• Adjectives beginning with **p** usually take the prefix *im-*: *patient* → *impatient*.

• We can't use prefixes with all adjectives: *moody* → ~~immoody~~; *shy* → ~~unshy~~.

• We can use *un-* to make opposites of some verbs: *pack* → *unpack*; *do* → *undo*; *dress* → *undress*; *lock* → *unlock*.

G6.1 Making comparisons 6A 5 p45

COMPARATIVES

type of adjective	spelling rule	comparative
most **1**-syllable adjectives	add -*er*	older brigh**ter** but! dry → drier
1-syllable adjectives ending in -*e*	add -*r*	nicer safer
1-syllable adjectives ending in consonant + vowel + consonant	double the last consonant and add -*er*	big**ger** fat**ter** but! new → newer
2-syllable adjectives ending in -*y*	-*y* → -*i* and add -*er*	easi**er** noisi**er**
2-syllable adjectives <u>not</u> ending in -*y*	put *more* before the adjective	**more** mature **more** patient
adjectives with **3** syllables or more	put *more* before the adjective	**more** aggressive **more** organised
irregular adjectives	*good* *bad* *far*	better worse further/farther

- We use comparatives to compare two people or things that are different: *Harry's more aggressive than Tom.*
- The opposite of *more* is *less*: *He's less stubborn than his brother.*
- When we compare two things in the same sentence we use *than* after the comparative: *Tom is two years older than Harry.*
- We use *a lot* or *much* before the comparative to say there's a big difference: *He's a lot noisier. He's much lazier.*
- We use *a bit* before the comparative to say there's a small difference: *He's also a bit more patient.*

TIP! • We can also use *more* with nouns: *He's got more money than her. I've got more free time than my brother.*

(NOT) AS + ADJECTIVE + AS

- We can also use *not as* + **adjective** + *as* to compare two people or things that are **different**: *Harry isn't as happy as Tom.* (= Tom is happier than Harry).
- We use *as* + **adjective** + *as* to say that two people or things are **the same**: *Tom's as intelligent as Harry.* (= they are both equally intelligent).
- We use the adjective with *(not) as ... as*, not the comparative form: *He's as old as me.* not ~~He's as older as me.~~
- We don't use *than* with *(not) as ... as*: *She isn't as shy as her sister.* not ~~She isn't as shy than her sister.~~

G6.2 Superlatives 6B 5 p47

type of adjective	spelling rule	superlative
most **1**-syllable adjectives	add -*est*	rich**est** old**est** but! dry → driest
1-syllable adjectives ending in -*e*	add -*st*	nicest safest
1-syllable adjectives ending in consonant + vowel + consonant	double the last consonant and add -*est*	big**gest** thin**nest** but! new → newest
2-syllable adjectives ending in -*y*	-*y* to -*i* and add -*est*	happi**est** funni**est**
2-syllable adjectives <u>not</u> ending in -*y*	put *most* before the adjective	**most** boring **most** patient
adjectives with **3** syllables or more	put *most* before the adjective	**most** popular **most** attractive
irregular adjectives	*good* *bad* *far*	best worst furthest/farthest

- We use superlatives to compare three or more things: *Eric is the most boring man Dom has ever met.*
- The superlative form of *less* is *least*: *He's my least favourite relative.*

TIPS! • Before superlatives in sentences we use:

the

*She's **the** happiest person Dom knows.*

possessive *'s*

*He's **Jake's** best friend.*

possessive adjectives

*She's **our** richest relative.*

• *the* + superlative is the most common form.

RW6.1 Leaving phone messages 6D 5 p50

asking to speak to someone

Can I speak to (Peter Parker), please?
Is (Peter) there, please?
Could I speak to (Jim Moore), please?

leaving a message

Could you ask him/her to phone me tomorrow?
Could you ask him/her to phone me back?
Just tell him (Peter Parker) called.

saying where people can contact you

He/she can ring me at the office.
He/she can get me on my mobile.
He/she can call me at home this evening.

TIP! • When we tell people who we are on the phone, we say: *This is Jim.* or *It's Jim.* not ~~I'm Jim.~~ *This is* is more formal than *It's*.

Language Summary 7

V7.1 Travel (7A ❶ p52)

tràvel go from one place to another by car, plane, bus, etc.: *He travelled over 100 miles to be there.*

a jòurney /'dʒɜːni/ when you travel from one place to another place: *Did you have a good journey?*

a trip when you go to a place for a short time and then come back: *How was your trip to Paris?*

a tour when you visit lots of places in the same city or country: *My parents are on a tour of Europe.*

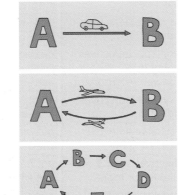

TIPS! • *Travel* is usually a verb. When we want to use a noun, we usually use *journey* or *trip*: *How was your journey/trip?* not *How was your travel?*

• We usually use *go on* with *journey, trip* and *tour*: *I went on a tour of London.* not *I made a tour of London.*

• A *package tour* is a holiday where everything is included in the price – hotel, food, trips to famous places, etc.

• When we say goodbye to people we often say: *Have a good journey/trip.* not *Have a good travel/tour.*

V7.3 Quantity phrases (7B ❼ p55)

• We often use the phrases in **bold** to talk about quantity. We can use these phrases with countable nouns, uncountable nouns and plural nouns.

a piece of chèwing gum   **a bar of** soap
a bottle of pèrfume   **a pair of** shorts
a packet of tèa   **a tube of** tòothpaste
a roll of film

TIP! • *Piece, bottle, packet,* etc. are all countable nouns and can be plural: *She's got three bottles of perfume. I bought two pairs of shorts.*

V7.4 Expressions with *go* (7C ❼ p57)

• We use *go to* + place: *You can also go to local villages.*
• We use *go with* + person: *I went with an excellent guide.*
• We use *go* + activity (verb+ing): *You can go diving or snorkelling.*
• We use *go for* + activity (noun): *I went for a walk in the rainforest.*
• We use *go on* + travel words (*a tour, holiday,* etc.): *You should go on a tour of the shipwreck.*

TIPS! • We also use *go on* with *trip* and *journey*: *He went on a business trip to Spain.*

• We often use *go for a* + noun or *go* + verb+ing to mean the same thing: *go for a swim/run/walk = go swimming/running/walking.*

V7.2 Things we take on holiday (7B ❷ p54)

 a sùitcase /'suːtkeɪs/

sùn cream

shorts

a T-shirt

soap

a swìmsuit /'swɪmsuːt/

film

 màke-up

chèwing gum

shàving foam

a towel

tòothpaste

pèrfume

sàndals

a ràzor

sùnglasses

shampòo

swìmming trunks

tea

wàlking boots

a càmera

TIPS! • To talk about clothes you wear for swimming in general, we often use *swimming costume*: *Don't forget to bring your swimming costumes.*

• The word *film* can be countable or uncountable: *How much film have you got? = How many films have you got?*

Grammar

G7.1 Present Continuous for future arrangements

 7A 5 p53

- We usually use the Present Continuous for definite future arrangements: *They're going on holiday for two weeks.*

- We usually know exactly when the arrangements are happening. They are often the type of arrangements we can write in a diary: *We're leaving on Saturday.*

- We make the Present Continuous with: subject + *be* + verb+ing (see G3.3).

TIPS! • When we use the Present Continuous for future arrangements we usually use a future time phrase (*next weekend, on Saturday*, etc.), or both people know from the situation that we are talking about the future.

• We often use the Present Continuous to ask about people's arrangements: *What are you doing this evening/weekend?*

• The arrangement doesn't have to be in the near future. The important thing is how certain we are about it: *We're getting married in July next year* (we've decided on a date and booked the church).

G7.2 Quantifiers   7B 5 p55

SOME AND *ANY*

- We usually use *some* in positive sentences: *There's some tea. There are some towels.*

- We usually use *any* in questions: *Is there any sun cream? Are there any T-shirts?*

- We usually use *any* in negative sentences: *There isn't any coffee. There aren't any jackets.*

TIPS! • We use *some* and *any* with uncountable nouns (*soap, chewing gum, shampoo*, etc.) and plural countable nouns (*cameras, suitcases, razors*, etc.).

• We often use *some* in questions with *Would you like ... ?*: *Would you like some tea?*

• We can use *no* to mean *not any*: *There's no coffee.*

OTHER QUANTIFIERS

countable nouns	uncountable nouns	both
a few not many	a bit of a little not much	a lot of/lots of some any

- With countable nouns we use *a few* and *not many* to mean a small quantity: *There are a few CDs = There aren't many CDs.*

- With uncountable nouns we use *a bit of*, *a little* and *not much* to mean a small quantity: *There's a bit of toothpaste = There's a little toothpaste = There isn't much toothpaste.*

- With both countable and uncountable nouns we use *a lot of/lots of* to mean a large quantity: *There are a lot of T-shirts. There's lots of make-up.*

TIPS! • We don't usually use *much* or *many* in positive sentences: *I've got lots of free time.* not ~~I've got much free time~~. *There are a lot of chairs.* not ~~There are many chairs~~.

• We use *How much ... ?* to ask about uncountable nouns and *How many ... ?* to ask about countable nouns: *How much soap have we got? How many towels are there?*

G7.3 Possessive pronouns   7B 10 p55

- We use possessive pronouns for possessive adjective + noun or possessive 's + noun: *That's **my bag**.* → *That's **mine**. Those are **Jane's shoes**.* → *Those are **hers**.*

- We often use possessive pronouns when we know what thing we are talking about: *Is this your camera? No, it's his.* (= his camera).

subject pronouns	object pronouns	possessive adjectives	possessive pronouns
I	me	my	mine
you	you	your	yours
he	him	his	his
she	her	her	hers
it	it	its	–
we	us	our	ours
they	them	their	theirs

Real World

RW7.1 Complaints and requests   7D 4 p58

complaints	requests
I'm sorry, but I've got a bit of a problem. I'm afraid I've got a complaint. I'm sorry, but I think there's something wrong with the TV.	I wonder if you could check for me? I wonder if I could have some more towels, please? Could I speak to the manager, please? Could you help me? Would you mind sending someone to look at it?

- After *I wonder if I/you could* and *Could I/you* we use the infinitive: *I wonder if you could **help** me? Could you **help** me?*

- After *Would you mind* we use verb+ing: *Would you mind **helping** me?*

TIP! • *I wonder if I/you could ... ?* and *Would you mind ... ?* are more polite than *Can/Could I ... ?*

Language Summary 8

V8.1 Describing your home (8A 2 p60)

unusual /ʌn'juːʒʊəl/ different to what is normal: *His house is very unusual – there are no windows!*

typical similar to all the others: *Our house is typical for the area.*

spacious /'speɪʃəs/ with lots of space: *It's a very spacious flat.*

air conditioning a machine in a building or a car that keeps the air cool: *In hot countries most offices have air conditioning.*

central heating a system of heating in a building: *Has your flat got central heating?*

busy /'bɪzi/ full of activity and people: *I live in a very busy street.*

close to near: *My house is close to the shops.*

fashionable popular at a particular time: *This is quite a fashionable part of town these days.*

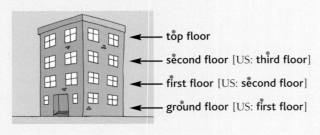

→ top floor
→ second floor [US: third floor]
→ first floor [US: second floor]
→ ground floor [US: first floor]

V8.2 Going to dinner (8B 1 p62)

Match words/phrases 1–10 to the pictures a)–j).

1	the host *d)*	6	shake hands
2	the hostess	7	kiss
3	a guest /gest/	8	a starter
4	invite (someone)	9	a main course
5	arrive on time	10	a dessert /də'zɜːt/

V8.3 Traveller's tips (8C 1 p64)

a doorway

point at someone

blow your nose

a plate

take off

admire /əd'maɪə/

V8.4 Verb patterns (8C 3 p64)

- When we use two verbs together, the form of the second verb usually depends on the first verb. This is called a verb pattern: *If you **plan to go** abroad, … . Things you **should** and **shouldn't do** around the world. Travellers **enjoy meeting** new people.*

+ infinitive (do)	+ infinitive with *to* (to do)	+ verb+*ing* (doing)
should	plan	enjoy
can	would like	like
must	need	start
might	try	finish
will	forget	prefer
	decide	

TIPS! • Some verbs have more than one verb pattern. We can say *start/like/prefer doing* or *start/like/prefer to do*. For these verbs the meaning is the same: *I started to write a book.* = *I started writing a book.*

• A few verbs change their meaning with different verb patterns, for example, *try* and *need*. But the verb patterns in the table are the most common.

• In British English, *like/love* + verb+*ing* is more common than *like/love* + infinitive with *to*: *I like watching TV.* In American English, *like/love* + infinitive with *to* is more common: *I like to watch TV.*

Vocabulary

V8.5 Adjectives to describe places (8D ❶ p66)

towns/cities	people	weather	food
industrial*	welcoming*	wet	delicious*
polluted*	helpful	freezing*	spicy*
crowded	relaxed*	changeable*	bland*
touristy*	reserved*	windy	healthy
cosmopolitan*	(dangerous)		
dangerous	(healthy)		
(welcoming)			

*industrial with a lot of factories and other industry: *Detroit is an industrial city.*

*polluted /pə'lutɪd/ the air and water are dirty and dangerous to people's health: *Cities are often very polluted.*

*touristy with a lot of tourists and things for tourists to buy or do (usually negative): *It was a nice place, but a bit touristy.*

*cosmopolitan full of people, restaurants, shops, etc. from different countries: *London's a very cosmopolitan city.*

*welcoming friendly to you when you arrive in a place: *The people were very welcoming when I arrived.*

*relaxed /rə'lækst/ not worried or stressed: *People who live in the country are usually more relaxed.*

*reserved /rə'zɜːvd/ you don't show your feelings to other people: *People often say the British are quite reserved.*

*freezing extremely cold: *It's freezing here in winter.*

*changeable the weather changes quickly and often: *In April the weather is quite changeable.*

*delicious /də'lɪʃəs/ with a very nice taste: *This food is delicious!*

*spicy /'spaɪsi/ with strong flavours from spices: *Indian food is very spicy.*

*bland with very little flavour (usually negative): *I liked the hotel, but the food was a bit bland.*

TIP! ● We can also use *hot* to mean *spicy*: *That chilli sauce is really hot!*

Grammar

G8.1 Present Perfect for unfinished past with *for* and *since* (8A ❹ p60)

● We use the **Past Simple** to talk about something that happened in the past but does not continue in the present: *I lived in Adelaide for seven years before I moved to Coober Pedy* (I don't live in Adelaide now).

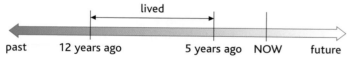

● We use the **Present Perfect** to talk about something that started in the past and continues in the present: *My family and I have lived in this house for five years* (we started living there five years ago and we still live there now).

TIPS! ● For how to make the Present Perfect positive and negative, see G4.1.
● For how to make past participles of regular verbs, see G4.1.
● For past participles of irregular verbs, see the Irregular Verb List, p159.

FOR AND *SINCE*

● We use *for* with a period of time (how long): *We've been married for six years.*

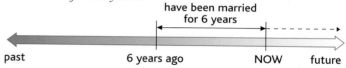

● We use *since* with a point in time (when something started): *Alain's lived on this boat since 1995.*

TIPS! ● We can also use *for* with the Past Simple: *I lived in Germany for two years* (but I don't live there now).
● We don't use *ago* with the Present Perfect: *I've been married for two years.* not ~~I've been married since two years ago~~.

Language Summary 8

Grammar

G8.2 *How long ... ?* (8A **7** p61)

- We use *How long ... ?* to ask about a period of time.

- We use questions with *How long ... ?* and the Past Simple to ask about something that started and finished in the past:
  How long did Luke live in Adelaide? (he doesn't live in Adelaide now).

- We use questions with *How long ... ?* and the Present Perfect to ask about something that started in the past and is still happening now:
  How long has he lived in his underground house? (he lives there now).

- We can answer both Past Simple and Present Perfect questions with *for* (*for two years*, etc.), but we can't answer Past Simple questions with *since*:
  How long did you live there?
  For ten years. not ~~Since 1995~~.

PAST SIMPLE QUESTIONS WITH *HOW LONG ... ?*

How long	auxiliary	subject	infinitive	
How long	did	I/you/he/she/it/ we/they	live	there?

PRESENT PERFECT QUESTIONS WITH *HOW LONG ... ?*

How long	auxiliary	subject	past participle	
How long	have	I/you/we/they	lived	there?
How long	has	he/she/it	been	in Australia?

TIPS! • We often answer *How long ... ?* questions with short phrases, not complete sentences:
How long have you lived here?
Since 2001./For five years.

• We can also make questions in the Past Simple with *How long ago ... ?*:
How long ago did you see him?
About three months ago.

G8.3 *should, shouldn't, must* (8B **4** p62)

- We use *should, shouldn't* and *must* to give advice.

- We use *should* to say we think something is a **good** thing to do: *You should wait for the hostess to start eating first.*

- We use *shouldn't* to say we think something is a **bad** thing to do: *You shouldn't ask people how much they earn.*

- We use **must** to give very strong advice: *You must ask the hostess if you can smoke.*

- After *should, shouldn't* and *must* we use the **infinitive**.

QUESTIONS WITH *SHOULD*

question word	*should*	subject	infinitive	
What	should	I/you/he/she/ we/they	do?	
What time	should	I	arrive?	
	Should	I	take	something to eat?

SHORT ANSWERS
Yes, I/you/he/she/we/they should.
No, I/you/he/she/we/they shouldn't.

TIPS! • We often use *I (don't) think* with *should*: *I (don't) think you should go to work.*

• We often use *Do you think I should ... ?* to ask for advice: *Do you think I should take some food?*

• The word *advice* is uncountable: *Could you give me some advice?* not ~~Could you give me an advice?~~ We can also say *a piece of advice*: *Let me give you a piece of advice.*

G8.4 *Infinitive of purpose* (8B **10** p63)

- To say why we do something, we often use the **infinitive with *to***: *I came here **to study** English.* = *I came here because I wanted to study English.*

TIPS! • We don't say: ~~I came here for study English.~~ or ~~I came here for to study English.~~

• We can also use *for* + noun to say why we do something: *I went to the shops for some coffee.*

Real World

RW8.1 *Asking about places* (8D **4** p66)

- We use questions with *What's/What are ... like?* to ask what you know about a place:
  What's Edinburgh like? (= Tell me what you know about Edinburgh.)
  It's very cosmopolitan.

- Questions with *Do you like ... ?* ask how you feel about a place:
  Do you like Edinburgh? Yes, I love it.

- We can also use *What's/What are ... like?* to ask what you know about other things in a place:
  What's the city like?
  What are the people like?
  What's the weather like?
  What's the food like?, etc.

TIP! • We don't use *like* in the answers to *What's/What are ... like?* questions: *What are the people like? They're very friendly.* not ~~They're like very friendly.~~

Vocabulary

V9.1 **Everyday problems** (9A 1 p68)

oversleep* on Monday mornings
get lost*
leave your wallet at home
miss* a plane/a train
lose your keys

run out of* money/time
forget (someone's) birthday
have an accident*
get stuck* in traffic

*oversleep sleep longer than you planned to in the morning: *He overslept and was late for work.*

*run out of use all of something so there is no more left: *She's run out of coffee.*

*get lost you don't know where you are or where to go: *She got lost and couldn't find the hotel.*

*an accident something bad that happens and often hurts people: *He had a car accident on his way to work.*

*miss arrive too late to do something: *He missed the train because he overslept.*

*get stuck not be able to move: *We got stuck in traffic and missed the plane.*

TIP! • In American English you can say: *I forgot my wallet at home.*

V9.2 **Adjectives to describe feelings** (9B 1 p70)

stressed worried and not able to relax: *He's very stressed about work.*

depressed very unhappy, often for a long time: *He was very depressed when his wife left him.*

angry a strong negative feeling you have which makes you want to shout at someone: *I'm really angry with my husband. He forgot my birthday!*

pleased happy about something that happened: *I'm pleased you enjoyed it.*

embarrassed /im'bærəst/ feel stupid because of something you did or something that happened: *I couldn't remember your father's name! I was so embarrassed.*

satisfied pleased because you have got what you wanted: *He's very satisfied with his new car.*

guilty /'gɪlti/ feel very bad about something you did wrong: *He felt guilty about leaving them on their own.*

upset unhappy or worried because something bad has happened: *She got very upset when I told her the bad news.*

lonely unhappy because you don't have any friends or anyone to talk to: *I was quite lonely when I was a child.*

nervous /'nɜːvəs/ worried because of something that's going to happen: *I always get nervous before exams.*

confident certain that you can do things well: *You have to be confident to be a salesman.*

fed up annoyed or bored because you have done something for too long: *I'm fed up with my job.*

sad unhappy: *I was sad to hear you lost you job.*

calm /kɑːm/ relaxed and peaceful: *I always feel very calm after yoga.*

annoyed a bit angry: *I get annoyed when people talk at the cinema.*

bored, worried, excited, tired see V4.4.

TIPS! • We can also use these *-ing* adjectives to describe things, situations, places or people: *depressing, pleasing, embarrassing, satisfying, annoying, boring, worrying, exciting, tiring.* For the difference between *-ed* and *-ing* adjectives, see V4.4.

• We say a situation is *stressful* not ~~stressing~~.

V9.3 **Phrasal verbs** (9C 4 p72)

• There are a lot of common verbs in English with two or three words: *get up, eat out, stay in, look after, go out with, run out of,* etc. These are called phrasal verbs. They are very common in spoken English.

• Phrasal verbs have two or three parts: a verb and one or two particles.

verb	particle(s)
move	in
get	on with
sit	down
put	up with

• Some phrasal verbs are literal. We can understand the meaning from the verb and the particle(s): *move in, sit down, go away, take off, go back.*

• Some phrasal verbs are non-literal. We can't usually understand the meaning from the verb and the particle(s): *get on with, put up with, give up, go on, turn up.*

TIP! • We often use *well* with *get on with*: *I get on well with my all my other neighbours.*

Language Summary 9

G9.1 First conditional 9A **4** p68

- We use the first conditional to talk about the result of a possible event or situation in the future.

- The **if clause** talks about things that are possible, but not certain: *If I'm late again, I'll lose my job* (maybe I'll be late again). The **main clause** says what we think the result will be in this situation. (I'm sure I'll lose my job).

if clause (if + Present Simple)	main clause (will/won't + infinitive)
If I'm late again,	I'll lose my job.
If we don't get there by five,	we'll miss the plane.

TIPS! • The *if* clause can be first or second in the sentence. When we start with the *if* clause we use a comma (,) after this clause. When we start with the main clause we don't use a comma: *You'll be OK if you get a taxi.*
• We don't usually use *will/won't* in the *if* clause: ~~If I'll be late again, I'll lose my job~~.

G9.2 Future time clauses with *when, as soon as, before, after, until*

9A **8** p69

- We can use sentences with *when, as soon as, before, after* and *until* to talk about the future: *I'll pack before I go to bed.*

- After these words we use the Present Simple: *I'll call Frank when I **get** home.* not ~~I'll call Frank when I'll get home~~.

- In the main clause we use *will/won't* + infinitive: *As soon as I finish this report, **I'll go** to the bank.*

- We use **when** to say we are certain something will happen.

- We use **if** to say something is possible, but it isn't certain.

- We use **as soon as** to say something will happen immediately after something else.

- We use **until** to say something stops happening at this time.

TIP! • As in first conditional sentences, the future time clause with *when, as soon as*, etc. can come first or second in the sentence: *After I talk to him, I'll phone the hotel. = I'll phone the hotel after I talk to him.*

G9.3 *too, too much, too many, (not) enough* 9B **6** p71

- We use *too, too much* and *too many* to say something is <u>more</u> than we want.
  too + adjective: *I try not to get home too late.*
  too much + uncountable noun: *He's got too much work to do.*
  too many + countable noun: *I've always got too many things to do.*

- We use *not enough* to say something is <u>less</u> than we want.
  not + adjective + enough: *She's not old enough to talk.*
  not + verb + enough + noun: *I don't have enough energy to do anything in the day.*

- We use *enough* to say something is the <u>correct</u> number or amount.
  enough + noun: *I earn enough money for the whole family.*
  adjective + enough: *I think this place is big enough for us.*

TIPS! • We often use the infinitive with *to* after these phrases: *I've got too many things **to do** today.*
• We don't use *too* to mean *very very*: *It was really beautiful.* not ~~It was too beautiful~~.

RW9.1 Invitations and making arrangements 9D **4** p74

asking about people's arrangements	inviting someone to do something
Are you doing anything next Friday? Are you free on Wednesday? What are you doing on Tuesday?	Would you like to come? Why don't we meet for a drink?
saying yes or no	**arranging a time and place**
Yes, I'd love to. I'd love to, but I can't. Yes, that'd be great.	Where/What time shall we meet? How about six thirty?

TIPS! • We use the Present Continuous to ask about arrangements: *What **are you doing** on Tuesday?* (see G7.1).
• We use the infinitive after *Why don't we ... ?*: *Why don't we **meet** for a drink?*
• We use the infinitive with *to* after *Would you like ... ?*: *Would you like **to come**?*
• We can say *Yes, I'd love to.* and *Yes, I'd love to come.* but not ~~Yes, I'd love~~.

Vocabulary

V10.1 Verbs often used in the passive (10A 8 p77)

Match the verbs to the nouns.

manufacture	newspapers, magazines, books, etc.
publish	machines
invent	cars
paint	crops (rice, cotton, etc.)
write	pictures
grow	books, plays, etc.
direct	films
build	products (phones, shoes, etc.)
make	houses

V10.2 *anything, someone, no one, everywhere,* etc.
(10B 7 p79)

	1	2	3	4
people	someone	anyone	no one	everyone
places	somewhere	anywhere	nowhere	everywhere
things	something	anything	nothing	everything

- We usually use *someone, somewhere* and *something* in positive sentences to mean one person/place/thing: *Someone bought their clothes for them.*

- We usually use *anyone, anywhere* and *anything* in negative sentences and questions to mean one person/place/thing: *Men didn't use to do anything like that.*

- *No one, nowhere* and *nothing* mean not one person/place/thing: *No one's surprised anymore.*

- *Everyone, everywhere* and *everything* mean all the people/places/things: *Now you can buy them everywhere.*

TIPS! • We can use *-body* or *-one* for people: *somebody = someone, anybody = anyone, nobody = no one, everybody = everyone.*

• *No one, nowhere* and *nothing* are negative words. We use them with a positive verb: *No one **likes** it.* not ~~No one doesn't like it.~~

• *Everyone, everywhere* and *everything* have a plural meaning, but we use these words with a singular verb: *Everyone **is** watching TV.* not ~~Everyone are watching TV.~~

V10.3 Use of articles: *a, an, the,* no article (10C 4 p81)

- We use *a* or *an*:
  a) with jobs. *He was **a** designer.*
  b) to talk about a person or a thing for the first time. *He had **a** small shop in Florence.*

- We use *the*:
  c) to talk about a person or a thing for the second/third/fourth, etc. time. ***The** shop was the beginning of the family business.*
  d) when there is only one (or one in a particular place). *In **the** world.*
  e) with superlative adjectives. *Gucci is one of **the** most famous fashion houses.*

- We don't use an article:
  f) to talk about people or things in general. *Lots of people love buying clothes.* not ~~Lots of people love buying the clothes~~.
  g) for most cities and countries. *It was started in Italy.* not ~~It was started in the Italy~~.

TIPS! • We use *the* with some countries: *the UK, the USA, the Czech Republic,* etc.

• We use *the* in some fixed phrases: *go to the cinema/shops, in the morning/afternoon, at the weekend, the news,* etc.

V10.4 Shopping (10D 1 p82)

Match words/phrases 1–12 to pictures a)–l).

1 size *h)*	7 try on
2 small	8 it doesn't fit
3 medium /'mi:dɪəm/	9 sign /saɪn/ here
4 large	10 a receipt /rə'si:t/
5 extra large	11 cash
6 a fitting room *b)*	12 here's your change

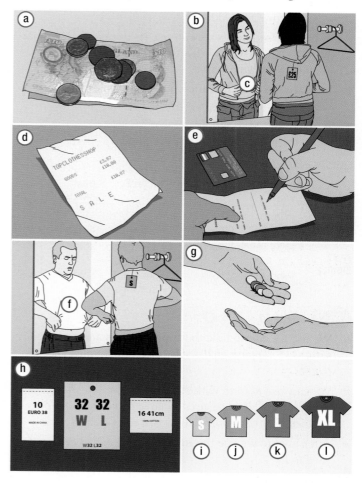

TIP! • We can say *pay cash* or *pay by cash* not ~~pay with cash~~: *How did you pay for your new sofa? We paid cash. Would you like to pay by cash or credit card?*

Language Summary 10

G10.1 Present Simple passive; Past Simple passive

10A ④ p77

- In English the main topic usually comes at the beginning of the sentence.

	subject	verb	object
active	Ian Fleming	used	this typewriter.
	subject	verb	by + agent
passive	This typewriter	was used	by Ian Fleming.

- In the **active** sentence we are more interested in Ian Fleming, so we make him the subject.
- In the **passive** sentence we are more interested in the typewriter, so we make it the subject.
- The person or thing doing the action is the subject of **active** sentences: *These auction houses make a lot of money selling memorabilia.*
- We often use the **passive** when we are more interested in what happened to someone or something than in who did the action: *One of George Harrison's guitars was sold for £117,000.*
- In **passive** sentences we can use *by* to say who or what did the action (we call this the agent): *This dress was worn by Marilyn Monroe.*
- To make the Present Simple passive we use: subject + *am, is* or *are* + past participle.
- To make the Past Simple passive we use: subject + *was* or *were* + past participle.

QUESTIONS

	question word	auxiliary	subject	past participle	
PRESENT SIMPLE	Where	is	rice	grown?	
	Where	are	Audi cars	made?	
PAST SIMPLE	How much	was	the Picasso painting	sold	for?
	Who	were	Elvis's hair cuttings	sold	by?

G10.2 *used to* 10B ③ p78

- We use *used to* to talk about **past** habits and repeated actions: *'Shopping girlfriends' used to help men choose clothes.*
- We **can** use *used to* with state verbs (*be, like, have, want,* etc.): *Selfridges used to have a special room only for men.* For common state verbs, see G3.3.
- After *used to* we use the **infinitive**: *It's not as bad as it used to be.*
- We **can't** use *used to* for an action that only happened once: *Selfridges opened in 1909.* not ~~Selfridges used to open in 1909.~~

POSITIVE AND NEGATIVE

- We make positive sentences with: subject + *used to* + infinitive. *I/You/He/She/It/We/They used to do the shopping.*
- We make negative sentences with: subject + *didn't use to* + infinitive. *I/You/He/She/It/We/They didn't use to buy the food.*

QUESTIONS

question word	*did*	subject	*use to*	infinitive	
Where	did	I/you/he/she/it/we/they	use to	live	when you were a child?
What	did	single men	use to	do?	
	Did	single men	use to	buy	skincare products?

SHORT ANSWERS
Yes, I/you/he/she/it/we/they did.
No, I/you/he/she/it/we/they didn't.

TIPS! • We can only use *used to* to talk about the past. When we want to talk about the present, we use *usually* + Present Simple: *I used to get up early* (but I don't get up early now). *I usually get up early* (I get up early now).

• Notice the spelling of *use to* in negatives and questions: *Did you use to know him?* not ~~Did you used to know him?~~

• In the negative we can use *didn't use to* or *never used to*: *Most married men never used to do the food shopping.*

RW10.1 In a shop 10D ④ p82

WHAT SHOP ASSISTANTS SAY
Can I help you?
What size do you want?
What size is that one?
I'll have a look ... yes, here's a medium.
The fitting room's over there.
Does it fit?
Here you are. That's £10 altogether.
How would you like to pay?
Check the amount and sign here, please.
Here's your change and your receipt.

WHAT CUSTOMERS SAY
I'm just looking, thanks.
Excuse me.
Have you got this T-shirt in a smaller size?
Can I try this on, please?
OK, I'll take it.
Could I have this map, please?
Do you sell batteries?

Vocabulary

V11.1 Verb-noun collocations (3) (11A ❶ p84)

get

sacked*   lost

promoted*

have

an accident   a problem

an operation*

lose/find

a job   your keys

a wallet

pass/fail

a driving test   a course

an exam

*get sacked lose your job, usually because you did something wrong: *Mark got sacked because he was always late.*

*get promoted get a better job in the same company: *Gary's got promoted to sales manager.*

*have an operation when a doctor cuts open your body to repair something: *He's had an operation on his knee.*

*a driving test an exam you take to get a driving licence: *I passed my driving test last week.*

V11.2 Crime (1) (11B ❷ p86)

Fill in the gaps with the words in the boxes.

| rob   steal   burgle /bɜːgəl/ |

1 You can .... money and things, but not people or banks.

2 You can .... people and banks, but not money or things.

3 You can .... houses and flats, but not banks or cars.

| murder   break into   shoot   bullets |

4 If you .... someone, you kill him/her deliberately.

5 If you .... a building or a car, you enter it by breaking something (e.g. a window, a lock, etc.).

6 You put .... in a gun.

7 You use a gun to .... people, animals or things.

| arrest   a victim   a suspect |

8 If a crime happens to you, you are ....

9 If the police think you stole something or murdered someone, you are ....

10 If the police .... you, they catch you and take you to the police station for questioning.

TIPS! • *Rob*, *steal* and *burgle* all mean 'take something that isn't yours'. We use them with different objects in a sentence: *rob a bank*, *steal money*, *burgle houses*, etc.

• You can also say *I was burgled.* to mean *My house/flat was burgled.*

• *Steal*, *break* and *shoot* are irregular verbs. See the Irregular Verb List, p159.

• We often use 'crime verbs' in the passive: *My car was stolen. A man was arrested.*

• We often use the verb *commit* with the word *crime*: *Have you ever committed a crime?*

V11.3 Crime (2) (11B ❸ p86)

verb	criminal	crime
rob	robber	robbery
steal	thief /θiːf/	theft
burgle	burglar	burglary
murder	murderer	murder

verb	*I was robbed* outside the station last night.
criminal	*The robber* ran away.
crime	There was *a robbery* at the station.

TIP! • The plural of *thief* is *thieves* /θiːvz/.

V11.4 Guessing meaning from context (11C ❻ p89)

● Sometimes you can guess the meaning of a word by:
  a) knowing what type of word it is (noun, verb, adjective, etc.).
  b) understanding the general meaning of the word and the rest of the sentence.

1 **severe** /sə'vɪə/ (adjective) very bad: *It was a severe storm.*

2 **damage** /'dæmɪdʒ / (noun) when things are broken: *He walked around looking at the damage.*

3 **branch** (noun) the 'arms' of a tree: *A large branch fell on his head.*

4 **barked** (verb – infinitive: *bark*) made a noise like a dog: *Lulu barked like a dog to get help.*

5 **weird** /wɪəd/ (adjective) unusual: *She made this weird noise for about 15 minutes.*

6 **blind** (adjective) you can't see: *Lulu is blind in one eye.*

TIP! • Sometimes you don't have to know the exact meaning of every word to understand the complete article or story.

Language Summary 11

G11.1 Present Perfect for giving news with *just, yet* and *already* (11A ❸ p85)

- We use the **Present Perfect** for giving news about things that happened in the past, but are connected to now. We don't say the exact time they happened: *He's had a car accident. Pippa's just lost her job!*

- We use the **Past Simple** when we say the exact time something happened: *He hasn't received the money for the work he did for you **last month**.*

- We use *yet* to say something hasn't happened, but we think it will happen in the future: *I don't know all the details yet.*

- We use *just* to say something happened a short time ago, but we don't know exactly when: *I've just heard that Tim's in hospital.*

- We use *already* to say something happened some time in the past (perhaps sooner than we expected): *He's already had an operation.*

- We usually use *just* and *already* in positive sentences. These words go between the auxiliary and the past participle: *Robin Hall's just phoned. Ted's already done three dives.*

- We usually use *yet* in negative sentences and questions. *Yet* usually goes at the end of the sentence or clause: *I haven't done any yet. Have you sent him the cheque yet?*

TIPS! • For how to make the Past Simple, see G2.1.
• For how to make the Present Perfect, see G4.1 and G4.2.
• In American English we often use the Past Simple with *just, yet* and *already*: *Did you do it yet?* [US] = *Have you done it yet?* [UK].

- *go* has two past participles, *been* and *gone*. We often use *been* to mean 'go and come back', and *gone* to mean 'go, but not come back yet'. Compare these two sentences: *He's just been to the shops* (he's back home now). *He's just gone to the shops* (he's at the shops now).

- We can use the Present Perfect with *this morning, this afternoon*, etc. when it is still that time of day: *I've seen him this morning* (it is still morning). *I saw him this morning* (it is now afternoon).

G11.2 Relative clauses with *who, which, that* and *where* (11B ❼ p87)

- We use relative clauses to say which person/place/thing we are talking about.

- To introduce relative clauses we use:
  a) *who* or *that* for people. *He's the man **who/that** was murdered*.
  b) *which* or *that* for things. *Her marriage is the only thing **which/that** makes her happy*.
  c) *where* for places. *That's the place **where** they found the body*.

TIPS! • We usually use *who* for people (but *that* is also correct): *He's the man who lives next door.*
• We usually use *that* for things (but *which* is also correct): *Here's the article that I was talking about.*
• We don't use *what* in relative clauses: *This is the letter that I got today.* not ~~This is the letter what I got today~~.

RW11.1 Echo questions (11D ❸ p90)

- We use echo questions (*Didn't you? Are you?*, etc.) when we are interested or surprised.

- We usually use the **auxiliary** in echo questions: *Hannah's had twins. Has she?* not ~~Has she had?~~

- We only use **subject pronouns** in echo questions: *Max doesn't want to sell his computer. Doesn't he?* not ~~Doesn't Max?~~

- If the sentence is positive, the echo question is **positive**: *I'm going to Rome next month. Are you?*

- If the sentence is negative, the echo question is **negative**: *I didn't go to work today. Didn't you?*

TIPS! • To respond to a positive sentence in the Present Simple or Past Simple, we use *do, does* or *did* in the echo question:
I work for a TV company. Do you?
His mother really likes it here. Does she?
They went to Sydney last week. Did they?
• To respond to a sentence with the verb *have got*, we use *have/haven't* or *has/hasn't* in the echo question:
She's got four sisters. Has she?
• To respond to a sentence with the verb *be*, we use *am, is/isn't* or *are/aren't* in the echo question:
My car's twenty years old. Is it?
• We say *Aren't I?* not ~~Amn't I?~~:
You aren't in this class. Aren't I?

Vocabulary

V12.1 Money (12A 1 p92)

lend money (to someone) give money to someone for a period of time: *I lent Mark £50 last week.*

borrow money (from someone) take money from someone for a period of time: *Can I borrow £20 until Friday?*

owe /əʊ/ **money (to someone)** when you borrow money from a person or a bank and have to give it back in the future: *I owe the bank a lot of money.*

pay money back give money back to the person you borrowed it from: *I'll pay you back tomorrow.*

spend money use money to buy things: *I spend £70 on food every week.*

save money keep money so that you can use it in the future: *I'm saving £100 a month for a holiday.*

earn /ɜːn/ **money** get money for doing work: *He earns about £50,000 a year.*

win money get money from a lottery, a competition, a horse race, etc.: *I won £10 on the lottery last Saturday.*

lose money a) you can't find some money that you had: *I've lost £50 – I can't find it anywhere.* **b)** opposite of *win money*: *He lost all his money in Las Vegas.*

waste money (on something) spend money on something you don't need or want, or isn't very good: *I've wasted a lot of money on my car. It still doesn't work!*

cost a lot of money pay a lot of money to buy something: *Our new kitchen's beautiful, but it cost a lot of money.*

get money out (of the bank) take money out of your own bank account: *I have to get some money out of the bank tomorrow.*

TIPS! • The verbs *lend* and *borrow* are very similar. Look at the picture. *Chris is lending money to Mark. Mark is borrowing money from Chris.*

Chris   Mark

• When you want to borrow money you can say: *Can I borrow £20?* or *Can you lend me £20?*

• We say *It's a waste of money.* when we think something isn't very good or is too expensive: *Don't buy that – it's a waste of money.*

• The verbs *lend, spend, win, lose, cost* and *get* are irregular. See the Irregular Verb List, p159.

V12.2 Unusual activities (12B 2 p94)

hypnotise /'hɪpnətaɪz/ put someone into a state where they are nearly asleep, but can hear what you are saying and respond to things that you say to them.

a karaoke /kæri'əʊki/ **machine** a machine in a bar or a club which plays music and shows the words of the song at the same time. People sing the songs for the other people in the bar.

dye your hair change the colour of your hair: *I dyed my hair black last night.*

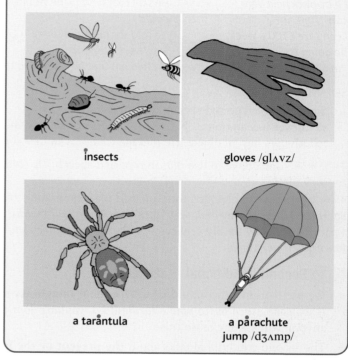

insects   gloves /glʌvz/

a tarantula   a parachute
                     jump /dʒʌmp/

TIPS! • A *tarantula* is a type of *spider*.

• A person who hypnotises other people is called *a hypnotist* /'hɪpnətɪst/.

V12.3 Connecting words (2) (12C 3 p97)

• We use *while* and *when* to connect things that are happening at the same time.

• We use *first, next, then, after, after that* and *finally* to show the order of events.

TIPS! • We usually use *while* with continuous verb forms: *While he **was studying** to be an actor, he used to do magic tricks.*

• *After* can be followed by subject + verb or a noun: *He became famous after **he made** a TV show. They left after **breakfast**.*

• *After that* is always followed by subject + verb: *After that **he lived** without food for 44 days.*

Language Summary 12

G12.1 Reported speech 12A ④ p93

- We use reported speech when we want to tell someone what another person said.

- We usually change the verb forms in reported speech.

verb form in direct speech	verb form in reported speech
Present Simple	Past Simple
I want to work abroad.	*He said that he wanted to work abroad.*
Present Continuous	Past Continuous
I'm working in a restaurant.	*He said he was working in a restaurant.*
will	*would*
I'll be back next year.	*He said that he'd (= he would) be back next June.*
can	*could*
I can save £100 a week.	*He told me he could save £100 a week.*
be going to	*was/were going to*
I'm going to work for a charity.	*He told me that he was going to work for a charity.*

SAY AND TELL

- To introduce reported speech we can use *say* or *tell*:
  say **never** has an object. *He said (that) … not ~~He said me (that)~~ … .*
  tell **always** has an object. *He told me (that) … not ~~He told (that)~~ … .*

TIPS! • We don't have to use *that* in reported speech: *He said (that) he wanted to work abroad.*

• We often have to change pronouns and possessive adjectives in reported speech. "*I don't see **my** aunt very often.*" → *Philip said that **he** didn't see **his** aunt very often.* "*I don't see **my** nephew very often.*" → *Maureen said that **she** didn't see **her** nephew very often.*

G12.2 Second conditional 12B ④ p95

- We use the second conditional to talk about **imaginary** situations:
  If someone asked me to hold a tarantula, I wouldn't do it (I don't think anyone will ask me to do this).

- The second conditional talks about **the present or the future**. It often talks about the opposite of what is true or real: *If I had enough money, I'd buy that jacket* (I haven't got enough money now). *If I had some free time, I'd go with you* (I don't have any free time).

POSITIVE AND NEGATIVE

If	subject	Past Simple		subject	*'d/wouldn't*	infinitive	
If	I	won	a parachute jump,	I	'd (= would)	do	it.
If	someone	asked	me to hold a tarantula,	I	wouldn't	do	it.

TIPS! • The *if* clause can be first or second in the sentence. We only use a comma when the *if* clause is first: *If I had enough time, I'd help you. I'd help you if I had enough time.*

• We don't usually use *would* in the *if* clause: *If I won the lottery, I'd leave my job.* not ~~If I would win the lottery, I'd leave my job.~~

• We can say *If I/he/she/it was … or If I/he/she/it were … in the second conditional: If I was/were younger, I'd come with you. If she was/were rich, she'd move to the Caribbean.*

WHAT WOULD YOU DO … ? QUESTIONS

- We often make questions in the second conditional with *What would you do … ?*. This phrase can come at the beginning or the end of the question: *What would you do if you won a parachute jump? If someone asked you to hold a tarantula, what would you do?*

- We can answer these questions with: *(I think) I'd … or I wouldn't … : I think I'd do it. I wouldn't hold it.* We don't usually repeat the *if* clause in the answer.

First conditional or second conditional?

- We use the first conditional to talk about **possible** situations (see G9.1). We use the second conditional to talk about **imaginary** situations. Compare these two sentences:

First conditional
If she studies hard, she'll pass the exam (she's a good student and I think she might pass the exam = possible situation).

Second conditional
If she studied hard, she'd pass the exam (she's not a good student and she never studies, so I don't think she will pass the exam = imaginary situation).

Recording Scripts

Who worked in Bangkok?
Where did Mick work?
Who lives in Spain?
Where does Ian live?
Who works for a newspaper?
What time does the programme start?

MICK Tony, you spend 6 hours a day commuting from Liverpool to London.
TONY That's right.
M And it costs you £8,000 a year. Why do you do it?
T Well, my wife works in a department store in Liverpool and the children are very happy at school there. My family don't want to move down to London and I don't either.
M So tell me about your journey.
T Well, I leave the house at quarter past 6 and drive to the station. Then I catch the 7 o'clock train. I'm at my desk at 9.15 and I'm back home again at 8.45. And I do this 5 times a week.

M Andrea, why do you work in London, but live in Paris?
ANDREA Well, I know it sounds crazy, but my husband and I really love living in Paris. It's a much nicer city than London *and* the food is better.
M So tell me about your journey.
A Well, I work from 3.30 p.m. to 2 a.m., 4 days a week. I leave home at 11.30, catch the 12 o'clock train to London – you know, the Eurostar – and get to the office at about 3.25.
M So that's nearly 4 hours' travelling.
A Yes, but I only go there and back once a week. I stay with a friend when I'm in London.

M Ian, it's nearly 1,000 km from Santander to London. Why do you live so far away from your job?
IAN Well, my wife's Spanish. We lived in London for a few years, but flats are really expensive, so 2 years ago we moved to Santander and bought a flat there instead. Now I live there and work in London 4 days a week.
M And how long does the journey take?
I 4 hours, door to door.
M And how much does it cost?
I I buy cheap flights in advance. A return ticket costs between £30 and £60.

ANSWERS b) 35% c) 17% d) 16% e) 32%
f) the theatre g) four h) 47% i) men
j) women k) Spain l) 30% m) 46% n) tea
o) coffee p) 16

INTERVIEWER Excuse me?
LOUISE Yes?
I We're doing a survey on the free time habits of British people. Can I ask you a few questions?
L Er ... sure.
I Thanks very much. Right, first question. How often do you go to a bar or a pub?
L Oh, not very often. Probably about once a month. I don't drink, you see, but I sometimes go with friends.
I OK. Do you do any sport?
L Yes, I go swimming three times a week, at lunchtimes.
I Three times a week.
L Uh-huh.
I Right. And how often do you go to the theatre?
L Oh, hardly ever. About once a year, perhaps. I go to the cinema quite a lot, but not the theatre.
I OK. And do you ever do any gardening?
L No, I don't. I haven't got a garden – I live in a flat.
I And what about holidays? How often do you go on holiday?
L I normally have two holidays a year. One in the summer and one around Christmas.
I And where do you usually go?
L I usually go somewhere in Asia.
I Oh.
L Thailand, India, places like that. Somewhere hot!
I Right, last one. How much TV do you watch a week?
L Hmm, let me think. Probably about an hour a day.
I So that's seven hours a week.
L Yeah.
I OK, that's all the questions. Thanks very much. Now if you could tick one of the age boxes ...

CHRIS Hi, my name's Chris.
BECKY Hello, I'm Becky.
C Nice to meet you. I'm a bit nervous, actually.
B Yes, so am I. Everyone is, I think.
C Yes, probably.
B So, Chris, what are you interested in?
C Well, I really love travelling.
B Oh, so do I.
C Yes, last year I went to Turkey for 3 weeks.
B So did I! Where did you go?
C I stayed in a place called Fethiye. And you?
B I was in Istanbul, visiting friends. I had a great time.
C Me, too. Can you speak any Turkish?

B Er, no, I can't.
C No, neither can I. But lots of people spoke English and they were really friendly.
B And what do you do in the evenings?
C Well, I don't go out much ...
B Neither do I.
C ... but I really like going to the cinema.
B Oh, me, too. What kind of films do you like?
C Well, I really like horror films, you know, vampires and that kind of thing ...

MARCUS Hi, I'm Marcus.
BECKY Hello, I'm Becky.
M Nice to meet you. Can I ask the first question?
B Er, yes, of course.
M Have you got any children?
B No, I haven't.
M Oh good. Neither have I. I'm not looking for someone with children, you see.
B No, er, me neither. So what do you do in your free time, Marcus?
M I play football and tennis, and I go to the gym a lot.
B Do you ever go cycling?
M No, I don't. I don't like cycling.
B Oh, I do. I love it ... er ... have you got any pets?
M Yes, I've got a dog.
B So have I. I really love animals.
M Yes, so do I. I eat them every day. They're delicious.
B Oh ...
M What's the matter?
B Well, I'm a vegetarian.
M Oh, I'm not. I think animals are for eating.
B Oh, I don't.
M Well, everybody's different, I suppose. So ... what's your favourite football team?
B Er ...

BECKY Right, so let's think. Who did I talk to? Well, there's Chris ... yes, definitely, he was nice. I'd like to see him again. We had a lot in common. So a tick for him. And Marcus ... oh no, definitely not! He was the most boring man I met all evening! I never want to see him again!

So am I. | Neither am I. | So can I. | Neither can I. | So have I. | Neither have I. | So do I. | Neither do I. | So did I. | Neither did I. | Oh, I do. | Oh, I don't. | Oh, I did. | Oh, I didn't.

I'm not married. | I've got a car. | I didn't study English last year. | I haven't got any pets. | I usually get up before seven. | I can't drive. | I went to the cinema last weekend. | I don't watch TV very often.

R2.2

A

WOMAN How did you meet your wife, Liam?

LIAM When we first met, she was going out with my best friend.

B

MAN Where did you first meet your husband, Hilary?

HILARY We were standing in a queue at the supermarket and he said hello.

C

WOMAN Where did you meet your wife, Colin?

COLIN I was travelling back from China and we met on the plane.

R2.3

travelling back from China → I was /wəz/ travelling back from China → I was /wəz/ travelling back from China and we met on the plane. | standing in a queue at the supermarket → We were /wə/ standing in a queue at the supermarket → We were /wə/ standing in a queue at the supermarket and he said hello. | going out with my best friend → she was /wəz/ going out with my best friend → When we first met she was /wəz/ going out with my best friend.

R2.4

ANSWERS 1 met, were waiting 2 was raining, offered 3 were driving, gave 4 saw 5 was talking, didn't see 6 left, were waiting 7 was walking, stopped 8 invited, was

R2.5

WOMAN How did you meet your wife, Liam?

LIAM When we first met she was /wəz/ going out with my best friend, Ben. That was /wəz/ 2 years ago.

W Did you like her the first time you met her?

L Yes, of course. She was /wəz/ very beautiful and really funny.

W So what happened?

L Well, I went to Ben's birthday party and Jenny wasn't there. Apparently, they broke up in January and Ben was /wəz/ already going out with someone else.

W Did you call Jenny straight away?

L No, not straight away. I waited until the day after the party.

W And then?

L Well, I asked her out and she said yes. We went on our first date the next weekend. I took her to the cinema and then to my favourite restaurant.

W Was /wəz/ it a good first date?

L Er, no, not exactly. She was /wəz/ very ill after the meal. Food poisoning. She was /wəz/ ill for a week!

W Oh, no!

L Yes, it wasn't a very good start. Anyway, we started going out in March and I fell in love with her very quickly. Then,

about 8 months later, we were /wə/ having a drink in a bar and she was /wəz/ laughing a lot. I just thought – I want to hear that laugh forever. So I asked her to marry me.

W And she said yes.

L Well, not immediately. She was /wəz/ very surprised and didn't know what to say. Then a few days later I was /wəz/ cooking dinner and she just said, "OK, let's get married." And so we got engaged that day.

W And when did you get married?

L 6 months after that.

W Were /wə/ there lots of people at the wedding?

L Yes, there were /wɜ:/. About 200.

W And was /wəz/ Ben there?

L Yes, he was /wɒz/. He was /wəz/ my best man.

W Nice!

R2.8

So that night, Shahrazad was /wəz/ getting ready for bed when her sister came to /tə/ visit her. She began telling her sister a story called *The /ðə/ Fisherman and the /ən ðə/ Genie*. While she was /wəz/ telling the /ðə/ story, the /ðə/ King came into the /ðə/ room. He started listening to /tə/ her story too, and /ən/ became more and /ən/ more interested.

Shahrazad continued telling the /ðə/ story all night, but she stopped just before the end and /ən/ said, "The /ðə/ morning's here, husband. Am I going to /tə/ die now?" "No, no," said the /ðə/ King. "Tell me the end of the /əv ðə/ story." "I'll tell you this evening, but not before," said Shahrazad with a smile.

That night Shahrazad finished the /ðə/ story – and then immediately began another. This continued night after night. The /ðə/ King never heard the end of /əv/ a story until the /ðə/ next evening. He couldn't kill his wife because he always wanted to /tə/ know how each story ended.

As time passed, the /ðə/ King fell in love with Shahrazad. He knew he could never kill her because he couldn't live without her and her stories. To show Shahrazad he really loved her, the /ðə/ King married her again.

The /ðə/ stories Shahrazad told the /ðə/ King became the /ðə/ stories of *The /əv ðə/ Thousand and /ən/ One Nights*.

R2.10

1

CELIA Hello, I'm Celia.

SAMI Hello, Celia. I'm Sami.

C Nice to meet you. Are you enjoying the party?

S Yes, it's great.

C How do you know David and Jane?

S I met them when I was travelling in

Africa last year.

C Oh really? I'd love to go there. One day, maybe.

S And what about you, how do you know them?

C Oh, I live next door.

S Right.

C Do you live near here?

S No, actually I live in Manchester, but I'm down here because ...

2

DAVID Simon, I'd like you to meet my sister, Paula.

SIMON Nice to meet you, Paula.

PAULA Hello. Er ... didn't we meet in Milan last year?

S You mean at the film festival?

P Yes, that's right. You were talking to a friend of mine, Sally Brigg.

S Oh yes, I remember. How is Sally, anyway?

P Oh, she's fine. Working hard, as usual.

S Right.

P Where did you meet David?

S We went to school together.

P Really? Do you see each other often?

S No, not very often. The last time was when I went to ...

3

STEPHEN Hello, you're a student at The English Centre, aren't you?

CARLOS Yes, I am. Sorry, have we met before?

S No, I don't think so. I'm Stephen Black. I work with David and Jane at the Centre.

C Nice to meet you. My name's Carlos.

S Are you a friend of David's?

C No, I'm a friend of Jane's. Well, actually, she's my English teacher. She invited the whole class to the party and ...

R2.12

ANSWERS 1C 2B 3A

R2.14

They say we're young and we don't know
Won't find out until we grow
Well I don't know if all that's true
'Cause you got me, and baby I got you

CHORUS
Babe, I got you babe
I got you babe

They say our love won't pay the rent
Before it's earned our money's always spent
I guess that's so, we don't have a pot
At least I'm sure of all the things we got

CHORUS

I've got flowers in the spring
I've got you to wear my ring
And when I'm sad, you're a clown
And when I get scared, you're always around

So let them say your hair's too long
I don't care, with you I can't go wrong

Then put your little hand in mine
There ain't no hill or mountain we can't climb

CHORUS

I got you to hold my hand
I got you to understand
I got you to walk with me
I've got you to talk with me
I got you to kiss goodnight
I got you to hold me tight
I got you, I won't let go
I got you to love me so
I got you babe

R3.1

NIGEL I became a pilot about 20 years ago. I had to do 72 weeks' basic training, but I didn't have to pay for it – the company did. I was lucky, I suppose, and now I have a job that I love. But these days most pilots have to pay a lot of money to do their training.

GARY You don't have to go to university, but you probably learn more facts than a university student – at least that's what people say! A London taxi driver has to know 25,000 streets and all the important places in the city.

MELISSA It's not easy to become a vet. You have to have a degree and the training takes 5 years. And you don't have much free time when you're a student vet – you have to work very hard.

R3.3

1 You don't have to /hæftə/ go to university.
2 A London taxi driver has to /hæstə/ know twenty-five thousand streets.
3 I had to /hædtə/ do seventy-two weeks' basic training.
4 I didn't have to /hæftə/ pay for it.
5 Most pilots have to /hæftə/ pay a lot of money.
6 Now I have /hæv/ a job that I love.

R3.4

MELISSA It's not easy to become a vet. You have to have a degree and the training takes 5 years. And you don't have much free time when you're a student vet – you have to work very hard. To get my practical experience I had to work with vets or farmers every weekend and in the holidays. As I said, the degree course is 5 years and in the final year students have to do a written exam, a practical exam and an oral exam. And the cost? Well, I had to pay about £13,000 a year for my training. It's much more now, I think. But I'm pleased I did it – I love my job.

NIGEL I became a pilot about 20 years ago. I had to do 72 weeks' basic training, but I didn't have to pay for it – the company did. I was lucky, I suppose, and now I have a job that I love. But these days most pilots have to pay a lot of money

to do their training. I think it costs about £80,000 to get a pilot's licence now. Anyway, to get my licence I had to do 200 hours of flying and I had to pass 12 written exams. Then I started working for a major airline and I had to do another 10-week training course with them. So pilots are very well trained, you'll be pleased to know!

R3.5

He's doing some gardening. | I'm writing to tell you how it feels. | I'm applying for every job I can. | He reads the adverts every day. | I never get an interview. | He needs a real job. | I want to work.

R3.6

INTERVIEWER Daniel Ash, your new book is a collection of articles about people with strange jobs.

DANIEL Yes, I collected stories about unusual jobs from all over the world.

I So you're not talking about actors or shop assistants.

D No, all the people in the book have very strange jobs.

I I see it's organised into different industries, like the cleaning industry. But isn't cleaning a normal job?

D Normally, yes. But did you know there's a man in America called Brad Fields and he cleans chewing gum off the Statue of Liberty? Well, actually, now he's got a company called Gumbusters. But that's all they do – they clean gum off the streets and famous buildings of New York.

I Oh, what a horrible job!

D Yes, apparently Americans chew 56 billion pieces of chewing gum a year. Then they throw most of it onto the street. That's a lot of cleaning.

I OK, that job is quite unusual. But what about in the food industry?

D Well, when a company wants to advertise food they sometimes need a food stylist. Their job is to make food look good in advertisements.

I I've never heard of that job before.

D Well, there are only about 20 food stylists in Britain. For example, when we look at a picture of strawberries and cream we're really looking at strawberries and white paint.

I Really?

D Yes, and they paint sausages with washing-up liquid, then coffee, to make them look natural.

I So what's the strangest job in your book, do you think?

D Well, how about a vermiculturalist?

I What's that?

D A vermiculturalist is a worm farmer. These people manage farms that only have worms. No other animals, only worms.

I But why?

D Well, worms like eating rubbish and that's good for the environment. So companies pay a worm farmer to clean up their rubbish.

I Fascinating, but ugh, not a job for me. I see there's also a chapter about artists. What strange jobs did you find in …

R3.7

1

JOANNE Hello?

RITA Hi, Joanne. It's Rita.

J Oh, hi. How are things?

R Oh, er, fine, thanks. Look, I'm really sorry, but I can't come to the cinema tonight. My boss is ill and I have to take a client out for dinner.

J Oh, don't worry. Another time, maybe.

R Yes, that would be nice. And I'll buy you dinner afterwards.

J Oh, lovely!

R Anyway, I have to go. I'll call you at the weekend.

J OK, speak soon. Have a nice dinner. Bye.

R Bye.

2

MR BUTLER Wayne, where's the Morgan report?

WAYNE I'm sorry, I couldn't finish it yesterday.

B Oh, dear. What happened?

W I had to help Katie. Her computer crashed.

B But I need that report for the meeting this afternoon.

W Yeah, I know. I'll do it now and email it to you. Don't worry, I'll finish it before lunch.

B I hope so.

3

TAMMY Hello?

PAUL Hi, Tammy, it's me.

T Hi, Paul. Where are you?

P I'm at work. Look, I'm really sorry, but I can't see you tonight.

T Oh, right. Why not?

P I have to take my parents to the airport.

T Can't they get a taxi?

P You know my mum doesn't like getting taxis at night. I'll see you on Friday, I promise. We can go out somewhere nice.

T Sure, if you're paying.

P I'll phone you tomorrow. Love you.

T Love you too. Bye.

R4.3

SCOTT Have you ever been to a rock festival, Julie?

JULIE Yes, I have. I've been to lots, actually. The last one was in Germany.

S Oh, right. Who did you see there?

J I saw David Bowie and U2. They were great! Have you ever seen them in concert?

S No, I haven't. I'm not a big rock fan. I prefer classical music or jazz.

J Hmm. I like bits of classical music. I quite like Mozart.

S Have you ever been to a classical concert?

J No, never.

Recording Scripts

S Oh, listening to an orchestra playing live is a fantastic experience. You don't know what you're missing. And how about a jazz concert?

J Yes, I've been to one. It was OK.

S Oh, I've been to hundreds. Live jazz is just amazing. Have you heard of Miles Davis?

J No, I haven't. Who's he?

S Seriously, you've never heard of him? He was a brilliant jazz musician. You've never heard of his 'Kind of Blue' album?

J Er, no, never.

S You're joking! It's only *the* best-selling jazz record of all time! You don't know anything about *real* music. Right. Your musical education starts with Miles Davis.

J And yours starts with ... er ... Radiohead.

S Radio what?

J Radiohead. They're a rock band. Don't you know *anything*?

R4.4

Have you ever been to a rock festival? | Yes, I have. | No, I haven't. | Have they ever seen U2 in concert? | Yes, they have. | No, they haven't. | Has Julie ever heard of Miles Davis? | Yes, she has. | No, she hasn't.

R4.5

1

JULIE Have you /w/ ever met anyone famous?

SCOTT Yes, I have, actually. When I was in Mexico /w/ on vacation.

J Really? Who did you meet?

S Mick Jagger. He was in the same restaurant as me.

2

S Has your mother ever been to /w/ a rock concert?

J Yes, she has. She went to /w/ one or two when she was young.

S Who did she see?

J Well, I know she saw David Bowie before he became famous.

3

S Have you /w/ ever learned to play an instrument?

J No, /w/ I haven't. What about you?

S Well, I tried to learn the piano /w/ at school.

J Were you /w/ any good?

S No, I had no /w/ idea what I was doing!

R4.6

JO Where /r/ are my glasses?

TOBY They're /r/ over there /r/ on the table.

J Hey, here's a quiz for you. It's about telly /j/ addicts.

T What, me? I don't watch TV very /j/ often.

J Yeah, right. OK, here's the first question. Do you watch TV for more than twenty /j/ hours a week?

T Er ... well ... I /j/ always watch football

and the news, and I /j/ enjoy watching films.

J And do you watch at least one soap opera /r/ every day?

T Yeah, OK. So /w/ I probably do watch TV for twenty /j/ hours a week.

J Twenty /j/ hours a day, more like ... OK, question 2. Have you /w/ ever watched TV all night?

T No, /w/ I don't think I have ... not *all* night, anyway!

J OK, next question – do you /w/ ever work or study with the TV /j/ on?

T No, never. I can't work when there's any noise. I have to have complete quiet.

J And question 4 – have you got a TV /j/ in your bedroom or the kitchen?

T No, I haven't – you know that.

J And do you /w/ always have to have the remote control?

T Er ... yes, I do /w/ actually.

J Yes, you do, don't you? Men always have to have the remote. It's a power thing.

T Oh, I don't know /w/ about that. I /j/ usually can't find it!

J OK, on to the next one. Do you sometimes have dinner in front of the TV?

T If I'm on my /j/ own, then yes, of course. Doesn't everyone?

J Hmm, you're not doing very well, are you? Question 7. Do you know /w/ exactly when all your favourite programmes are /r/ on?

T Er ... yes, I do /w/ actually.

J OK, last one. Have you /w/ ever missed something important because you wanted to watch TV?

T Er, yes, once. I missed my cousin's wedding because I wanted to watch the football.

J Toby!

T But it was the World Cup quarter-final!

J Right. I see.

T So how did I do?

J Well, you get one point for /r/ each tick, so that's ... er ... let's see ...

R4.8

excited | exciting | worried | worrying | surprised | surprising | tired | tiring | frightened | frightening | bored | boring | interested | interesting

R4.9 R4.10

CHAIRPERSON Welcome to Q and A. With me are Jackie Nash from the National Union of Students, Penny Little, Head of Bingham University, and Stuart Downs from the Ministry of Education. And the first question, please.

MR DAVIS Hello. My name's Jon Davis and my question is "Do you think university education should be free?" **[end of R4.9]**

C Stuart Downs, what do you think?

STUART I'm sorry, I don't agree. Universities need more money, as we know, and students get good jobs when they leave university. So they should all pay.

PENNY I'm not sure about that. I don't think everyone should pay. I didn't have to pay for my university education and neither did you, Stuart.

S But there are many more students now than there were 20 years ago, Penny. It's impossible for the government to pay for everyone.

P Yes, maybe you're right. But I think the government should help people who haven't got the money to pay.

C What about you, Jackie? Do you think students should pay?

JACKIE No, definitely not. The government can always find money to pay for wars, so why can't they find money to educate the young people of Britain?

C So do you think that universities in the future will only be for rich people?

J Yes, definitely. That's what's happening now.

P I agree with Jackie. That's why we have to help students from poor families to go to university.

C Do you agree with that, Stuart?

S Yes, I think so. We can help them, certainly. But I don't think the government should pay for everything. The students should pay something too.

C What do you think, Mr Davis? Should universities be free for everyone?

D No, I don't think so. I didn't go to university and I don't earn much money. Why should I pay for someone to become a doctor or a lawyer and watch them get rich?

C Thank you, Mr Davis. And the next question. Yes, the lady in the front row ...

R5.1

INTERVIEWER Today my guest is Dr Dylan Evans, head of the robotics department at the University of the West of England. Welcome to the programme, Dylan.

DYLAN Thank you.

I Firstly, what kind of things can robots do now?

D Well, today robots can't do very much. They can build cars and other machines very quickly, but they can't move around easily.

I And what will robots be able to do in 5 or 10 years' time?

D By 2020, robots will be able to learn a language, recognise your face and understand what you say. They'll also be able to walk and run, just like humans.

I Really?

D Yes, but they won't be able to do more complicated things, like, er, play football. That won't happen for another

20 or 30 years. But by 2050 a team of robots might win the World Cup!

I Hmm, that *is* an interesting thought! And what about at home? Will a lot of people have robots in their houses?

D Oh, yes, I think so. In 2020 most homes in Japan will have 2 or 3 domestic robots. Old people will have robot friends to look after them and rich people will have lots of robot servants.

I That's amazing! What will these domestic robots be able to do?

D They'll be able to do the housework, clean the carpets – and even feed the cat! They'll also be able to talk to other machines in your house, like your computer and your fridge. But they won't look like humans, they'll still look like machines.

I So will robots ever be able to think like humans?

D Yes, definitely. There will certainly be intelligent robots before the end of the century.

I And finally, do you think robots will take over the world, like in the movies?

D No, I don't think so. Humans and robots will have to work together, because they'll need each other.

I Thank you very much. That was Dr Dylan Evans, who ...

R5.3

I'll stay at home all day. | They'll have their own lives. | We have two children. | I'll speak English fluently. | We won't be in England. | I want to have children.

R5.4

1

In 2020 ... well, I'll probably be married. And I want to have children, but I only want girls. I don't like boys very much, they're stupid. My husband will go out to work and I'll stay at home all day and watch TV. And we'll have lots of horses.

2

Well, we won't be in England, that's for sure. In 2020 we'll have a house somewhere hot, like Spain or France. We have 2 children, you see, so we can't move now. But they'll have their own lives by then, so we'll be able to live wherever we want.

3

At the moment I'm doing a degree in engineering. So in 2020 I'll probably be an engineer for a big company or something like that. Or I might be a teacher, but at a university, not a school. And maybe I'll speak English fluently by then.

4

HUSBAND Well, I'll be 67, so I'll be a bit fatter perhaps and I won't have much hair.

WIFE I think I'll be old and grey. I'll probably look like my mother.

H You look like your mother now.

W Hey! Oh, and I'll have a new husband, too ...

R5.5

I'll /aɪl/ stay at home all day. | We'll /wiːl/ have lots of horses. | They'll /θeɪjl/ have their own lives. | We'll /wiːl/ be able to live wherever we want. | I might be a teacher. | We won't be in England. | I won't have much hair.

R5.6

ANSWERS 1C 2A 3B

R5.7

ANSWERS 1b) drive 1c) writing 1d) take 2a) learn 2b) go 2c) visit 2d) spending 3a) live 3b) spending 3c) getting 3d) learn

R5.8

buy a camper van → We're going to buy a camper van. | thinking of writing a book → Kelly's thinking of writing a book. | take lots of photographs → I'm going to take lots of photographs. | learn Italian → I'm hoping to learn Italian. | go to Italy → I'd like to go to Italy. | spending more time with my grandchildren → I'm looking forward to spending more time with my grandchildren.

R5.10

ANSWERS 2b) 3a) 4a) 5a) 6b)

R5.11

GARY You're listening to *Talk Talk*, with Martina Webb and me, Gary Baker.

MARTINA Welcome back.

G Now joining Martina /r/ and me /j/ in the studio /w/ is Anthony Shuster, who's written a new book on Mars called *The Red Planet*. Welcome to *Talk Talk*, Anthony.

ANTHONY Thank you.

G Firstly, what's the weather like on Mars?

A Well, Earth is about 78 million km nearer the sun than Mars and so Mars is much colder than here. Actually, the /j/ average temperature /r/ on Mars is minus 55 degrees.

M So you need to take a jumper, then.

A Yes, probably.

G Is Mars bigger than Earth?

A No, /w/ it's a lot smaller. And there's no /w/ oxygen on Mars, of course.

G So does that mean there's no life there /r/ either?

A No, not necessarily. In the 1970s scientists thought there was no life there. But now they think differently.

G Why's that?

A Well, photographs taken by the /j/ European Space Agency /j/ in 2004 show that there /r/ is definitely water /r/ on Mars. And where there's water, there's probably life.

M But we're not talking about little green men, are we?

A No, we're not. As I said, scientists now think that there might be life on Mars, but it will be very small organisms like bacteria, not aliens or spacemen.

G And will we /j/ ever see people walking on Mars, do you think?

A Oh, yes, I think so. The /j/ Americans and Europeans are talking about the /j/ Aurora Programme, which is hoping to fly people to Mars before 2030.

M So /w/ in 50 years there'll probably be /j/ a McDonald's on Mars.

A Yes, maybe.

G Thanks for talking to /w/ us, Anthony.

A My pleasure.

M On the subject of space, a new /w/ exhibition opened in London yesterday which ...

R5.12

ALEX OK everyone, shall we start? OK, we haven't got long, so let's decide who does what. Who's going to organise the tickets?

JANET I'll do that. How many do you think we'll need?

A Oh, about 100.

J Fine. Shall I make some posters too?

A Yes, that'd be great. Where shall we put them?

J Well, we can put them up in all the offices and maybe in some local pubs.

KIM Yes, that's a good idea. Can I give you a hand with that?

J Great. Thanks a lot.

A Fine ... right. And we need lots of tables and chairs. Ray, will you organise that?

RAY Er ... yes, of course. I know someone who does weddings. I'll ask him.

A Great. And what about the food and drink?

GLORIA I'll do all the food. We don't want Ray to do it – everyone will be ill!

R Hey!

G Kim, could you give me a hand with the shopping?

K Sure. Just tell me when you want to do it.

A OK. What else? What about music?

R Why don't we ask Steve? He's in a really good jazz band. They could play while people are eating.

A Yes, why not? Oh, but remember, we can't pay anyone. It's for charity. Right, anything else?

G Who's going to write the questions?

A Ah, yes. Can you do that, Ray?

R Sure, no problem. I've got lots of general knowledge books at home and I love quizzes.

J I'll help you, if you like.

R No, don't worry. Thanks anyway.

A Right. That's it. Thanks for coming, everyone.

Recording Scripts

G Just one more question, Alex.
A What's that?
G What are *you* going to do?
A Er … well … someone has to be the boss.
ALL Yeah … Right … Typical …

R5.14

ANSWERS 2 why not 3 why don't 4 Could you 5 I'll 6 thanks 8 Shall I 9 that'd be 10 Can I 11 don't worry 12 Let's

R5.15

Ground Control to Major Tom
Ground Control to Major Tom
Take your protein pills and put your helmet on

Ten, nine, eight, seven, six, five, four, three, two, one, lift-off

Ground Control to Major Tom
Commencing countdown, engines on
Check ignition and may God's love be with you

This is Ground Control to Major Tom
You've really made the grade
And the papers want to know whose shirts you wear
Now it's time to leave the capsule if you dare

This is Major Tom to Ground Control
I'm stepping through the door
And I'm floating in a most peculiar way
And the stars look very different today

For here am I sitting in a tin can
Far above the world
Planet Earth is blue
And there's nothing I can do

Though I'm past one hundred thousand miles
I'm feeling very still
And I think my spaceship knows which way to go
Tell my wife I love her very much, she knows

Ground Control to Major Tom
Your circuit's dead, there's something wrong
Can you hear me, Major Tom? (x 3)
Can you …

Here am I floating in my tin can
Far above the moon
Planet Earth is blue
And there's nothing I can do

R6.1

Tom's easier to live with than Harry. | He's a lot noisier than Tom. | He's more aggressive than Tom. | He's much harder to live with. | He's also a bit more patient. | Harry isn't as considerate as Tom. | Harry isn't as happy as Tom. | Tom's as intelligent as Harry.

R6.2

CHARLIE Hello, Dom.
DOM Oh hi, Charlie. Are you enjoying yourself?

C Yes, thanks. But I don't know anyone here apart from you, Jake and Diana.
D Well, who do you want to know about?
C Who's the woman in the red dress?
D Ah. That's Naomi. She's Diana's best friend from university.
C She's gorgeous.
D Yes, she is. And she's the happiest person I know.
C Really?
D And she's married.
C Oh.
D That's her husband next to her – the one in the blue suit. His name's Eric. He's a colleague of Jake's.
C What's he like?
D Actually, he's the most boring person I've ever met in my life. All he talks about is work, work, work.
C And he's got the worst haircut ever.
D Yes, you're right. Why she married him I'll never know.
C Who's he talking to?
D Oh, that's Aunt Harriet. She's our richest relative. It's quite sad really – she never got married because she thought men only wanted her for her money. No one knows how much she has, but she's got the biggest house you've ever seen and she lives there on her own. She's a bit strange.
C Yes, she looks it.
D And the guy talking to my brother is Rupert. He's Jake's best friend. Do you know a place called The Bug Bar in Market Street?
C Yes, I've been there once or twice.
D Well, he owns it. Apparently it's the most popular bar in town at the moment. You have to queue to get in.
C Look, someone's waving at you.
D Oh no. It's my least favourite relative. Hello, Uncle Patrick! How are you? That's my great-uncle Patrick. He's 90 next birthday.
C Wow! He doesn't look that old.
D Yes, well, he's married to a much younger woman. She's only 76! Anyway, come with me and I'll introduce you to Naomi's sister. I don't think *she's* married …

R6.3

She's the happiest person I know. | He's the most boring person I've ever met. | He's got the worst haircut here. | She's got the biggest house you've ever seen. | He's Jake's best friend. | It's the most popular bar in town. | He's my least favourite relative.

R6.4

employed | unemployed | reliable | unreliable | intelligent | unintelligent | ambitious | unambitious | friendly | unfriendly | healthy | unhealthy | considerate | inconsiderate | patient | impatient | mature | immature |

honest | dishonest

R6.5

CLIVE Hello, Lydia. What happened at the bank this afternoon?
LYDIA Bank managers. They're all idiots.
C Oh, dear. We can't borrow any more money, is that what you're saying?
L Of course that's what I'm saying. And if we don't start paying them back soon, they're going to close this restaurant.
C Oh, no. They can't do that!
L Yes, they can. And they will. In 2 weeks.
DARREN Hi, Mum.
L Hello, Darren.
D How did it go at the bank?
L Oh, don't ask.
D Don't worry, things'll get better. And soon.
L I hope so. How many customers have we got in today?
C Er … 6.
L 6? Is that all? I bet The Angel has more than 6 customers.
D Yes, it's full. I walked past a few minutes ago. There were people waiting outside.
L Oh, dear. If we don't get our customers back, we're going to have to close the restaurant.
D That won't happen, Mum, I promise you.
C Darren, these are for table 2. And they want a bottle of house red. Come on, hurry up, we still have *some* people to look after …
D OK, I'm going.
TRUDY Hi, Dad.
C Hello, Trudy. How are you?
T Yeah, not bad. Hey, guess what? I've got a job!
L For how long, we wonder …
C Well done, darling! What kind of job is it?
T I'm a waitress … at that new restaurant down the street.
L What?! You mean The Angel?
T Yeah, that's right. I'm starting on Monday.
C But if you want to be a waitress, why don't you work here?
T Because you haven't got any customers, that's why. And anyway, I live with you people. I don't want to work with you as well. I have to go … bye!
L I don't believe it … that … *woman*!
C Calm down … at least she's got a job.
L Not *her* … Eve King, the woman at The Angel. How could she take my daughter away from me?
C Yes, I know … but what can you do?
L I'll show you what I can do …
C Lydia … Lydia … where are you going?

R6.6

KATHY Hello, darling. [Are] You OK?
DARREN Hi, Kathy. Yeah, [I'm] fine.
K Darren, I'm worried. Elizabeth's not very well.

D Oh, dear.

K Shouldn't you be at work?

D [I'm] Having a break.

K [Are] You going out?

D Yeah. [Have you] Seen my cigarettes?

K [They're] Over there, on the table. Where are you going, anyway?

D [I'm going] Out. And where's my lighter?

K [It's] On the table. Darren, what's going on?

D [I've] Got some things to do, that's all.

K You never spend time with us anymore.

D See you later, Kathy. Bye.

K Bye. Oh, Elizabeth, I'm so sorry your Dad's not here with us. But I am ... I'll always be here for you. Now do you want to play with your toys ... do you?

CLIVE And here's your receipt. (Thanks) Thanks very much. Come again. (Thank you. Goodnight.) Right, that's the last customer. How much have we made tonight? ... £126 ... oh, dear ... Sorry, we're closed ... oh, it's you, Darren. Where did you go?

DARREN [I went] Out. [I] Had things to do.

C But we had customers.

D [I] Thought you could look after them. There were only 6. Where's Mum?

C She's ... er ... I don't know ... There you are, Lydia. Where have you been?

LYDIA [I] Went for a walk. [I] Needed some time to think. Is Trudy home?

C Yes, [she's] in her room.

L Oh, good. Now I think we all need to talk about things. Darren, can you go and get ...

C Sorry, we're ... Oh, my ...

L Nick!

NICK Hi, everyone! How's business?

L Nick, darling, I can't believe it's you. Where have you been? Why didn't you call?

D And why have you come back?

N There's only one reason I'm back.

C What's that, son?

N To see my daughter.

C Your daughter?

N Yes, Elizabeth. She's my daughter, not Darren's. Ask Kathy. She'll tell you. I'm Elizabeth's father.

L What?!

C What's happening outside?

N There's a fire down the street. A restaurant, I think. It looked quite bad too. So, how is everyone?

R6.7

ANSWERS 1 off 2 message 3 called 4 line 5 meeting 6 leave

R6.8

1

RECEPTIONIST Good afternoon, Acton Film Centre. Can I help you?

JIM Yes, can I speak to Peter Parker, please?

R I'm afraid he's taken the afternoon off.

Can I take a message?

J Yes, please. Could you ask him to phone me tomorrow? My name's Jim Moore. He can ring me at the office.

R Yes, of course.

J Actually, don't worry. I'll call him on his mobile. Thanks anyway. Bye.

R Goodbye.

2

CLARE Hello?

JIM Hi, Clare, it's Jim. Is Peter there, please?

C No, he isn't. He's at work.

J Oh, OK. He er wasn't in his office. Ah well.

C Have you tried his mobile?

J Yes. There was no answer, but I left a message.

C Oh, OK. Shall I tell him you called?

J Yes, thanks. And can you ask him to call me back? I need to talk to him about our golf weekend.

C Sure.

J He can get me on my mobile or he can call me at home this evening.

C OK. I'll tell him. Bye, Jim.

J Bye, Clare.

3

RECEPTIONIST Good afternoon, RTL Limited. Can I help you?

PETER Hello. Could I speak to Jim Moore, please?

R Hold the line, please, I'll put you through ... I'm sorry, he's in a meeting. Would you like to leave a message?

P Er, no. Just tell him Peter Parker called. I'll call back later.

R OK, I'll give him the message. Goodbye.

P Bye.

R6.10

JIM Hello, Jim Moore.

PETER Hello, Jim. It's Peter. I got your message.

J At last! Where are you? Your receptionist thinks you're at home and your wife thinks you're at work.

P Er, well, you see, I'm ... er ...

J Are you on a golf course?

P Yes, I am. I just wanted to get a bit of practice before our golf weekend.

J Peter! You should be at work, not playing golf!

P But I'm going to beat you this time. You just wait.

J Well, we'll see at the weekend.

P Anyway, what did you want to talk to me about?

J I just wanted to check that you've booked the hotel for Saturday night.

P Of course.

J Fine. What time do you think we should leave?

R6.11

Listening Test (see Teacher's Book)

R7.1

KEITH Did you see that programme on BBC1 last night? It was called *50 places to go before you die*.

SOPHIE No, I didn't. Sounds interesting.

K Yes, it was.

S So, what was number 1?

K Number 1 was the Grand Canyon, which isn't surprising really. Number 2 was the Great Barrier Reef, then Disney World was third ... and I think the South Island in New Zealand was fourth.

S Was it? That's where Rob and I are going on holiday.

K Wow, lucky you!

S Yeah, we're leaving on Saturday. The tickets arrived this morning. We're really excited!

K I'm sure. How long are you going for?

S 2 weeks. And of course, it's summer over there now. 2 weeks of sunshine. I can't wait!

K Nice. Where are you staying?

S We're staying with friends for a week – they live in Christchurch. Then we're going on a package cycling tour for 3 days.

K Cycling for 3 days. Wow, that sounds like hard work!

S Well, it's not all cycling. Sometimes we're driving to places in a tour bus and then cycling when we get there.

K Oh, right.

S What about you? Are you having a holiday this year?

K No, I'm not going anywhere. But I've videoed that programme so I'll watch it again instead!

R7.2

We're leaving on Saturday. | How long are you going for? | Where are you staying? | We're staying with friends for a week. | We're driving to places in a tour bus. | Are you having a holiday this year? | No, I'm not going anywhere.

R7.4

ANSWERS 1 a piece of chewing gum 2 a bottle of perfume 3 a packet of tea 4 a roll of film 5 a bar of soap 6 a pair of shorts 7 a tube of toothpaste

R7.5

ROB OK. I'm ready, I think.

SOPHIE Wow, that was quick.

R Well, we don't need many clothes. It's summer over there, remember.

S Are you taking any sun cream?

R No, I'm not. We can get that there. I suppose you're taking lots of pairs of shoes.

S Yes. Is that a problem?

R Well, only because I'll probably have to carry them.

S No you won't. I can carry my own suitcase.

Recording Scripts

R Oh, yeah. I've heard that one before. By the way, I'm taking some CDs. Have you got any requests?

S Well, let's just say I don't want to take any of yours! Anyway, I'm taking a few books. I like reading when I'm on holiday.

R Books are heavy. How many are you taking?

S Oh, just one or two. Rob?

R Yes?

S Have you got any room in your suitcase?

R Maybe. Why?

S Oh, there are just some things I can't get in mine.

R Such as?

S Um, let's see. There's my camera and some rolls of film. My walking boots. A few T-shirts. Oh, and a packet of tea.

R Tea!?

S Well, I can't live without tea. And you can't get good tea outside the UK.

R OK. Where are all these things, anyway?

S There, on the chair.

R What? All that! What's in that bag?

S Oh, just a bit of make-up.

R Do you need all that?

S Well, you know what I look like without any make-up.

R True. You should definitely take the make-up.

S Hey!

R But maybe you can leave the tea.

R7.8

1

RECEPTIONIST Hello. Reception.

MR LINTON This is John Linton, room 28. I'm sorry, but I've got a bit of a problem. My breakfast hasn't arrived and I ordered it for 7 o'clock. I wonder if you could check for me.

R Oh, I'm terribly sorry about that, Mr Linton. I'll call the kitchen immediately.

L Oh, and I wonder if I could have some more towels, please. I dropped mine in the bath last night.

R Right, I'll send some up.

L Thank you very much.

R You're welcome.

2

RECEPTIONIST Can I help you, sir?

MR KELLY I certainly hope so. I'm afraid I've got a complaint. I'm in room 102 and it's much too noisy. It's right next to the lift and I didn't sleep at all last night.

R I'm very sorry, but I'm afraid there isn't another room available today. We're fully booked.

K Right. Could I speak to the manager, please?

R If you take a seat, I'll tell him you'd like to see him.

K Thank you.

3

MRS GIBSON Excuse me. Could you help me?

RECEPTIONIST Oh, hello, Mrs Gibson. What's the problem?

G I'm sorry, but I think there's something wrong with the TV. Would you mind sending someone to look at it, please?

R Of course. I'll send someone up straight away. It's room 12, isn't it?

G Yes. Thank you very much.

R Not at all.

G Oh, and er we're leaving today, of course.

R Yes, that's fine. Check-out is at 12 o'clock.

MR KELLY So there is a room available today.

R Yes, but it's already booked, I'm afraid. Ah, here's the manager, Mr Jones. I'm sure he'll be able to help you.

K Are you the manager?

MANAGER Er, yes, I am.

K Well, I've never stayed in such a terrible hotel in my life …

R7.9

1 I'm sorry, but I've got a bit of a problem. **a)**
2 I wonder if you could check for me. **b)**
3 I wonder if I could have some more towels, please. **b)**
4 I'm afraid I've got a complaint. **a)**
5 Could I speak to the manager, please? **a)**
6 Could you help me? **b)**

R8.2

ANSWERS 2 have you known **3** did you first meet **5** has he lived **6** did he live **8** has he been **9** did you last see

R8.3

ANTONIA You know Richard, my new boyfriend?

POLLY Yes.

A Well, his parents have invited us to dinner this evening …

P Oh, how lovely!

A … And I don'[t] wan[t] to do anything wrong. Could you give me some advice?

P Yes, of course. Wha[t] do you wan[t] to know?

A OK, the firs[t] thing, wha[t] time should I arrive?

P Well, you shouldn't arrive late. British people are usually on time, as you know.

A Not even a few minutes?

P Well, a few minutes is OK, but it's a bi[t] rude to arrive more than fifteen minutes late.

A Right. Should I take something to ea[t], like cake or ice cream?

P We don't often take food, bu[t] we usually take something for the hostess, like flowers or a bottle of wine, or some chocolates.

A Hmm, that's good to know.

P And when you mee[t] someone you don'[t] know, it's polite to shake hands. British people often kiss their friends, bu[t] no[t] people they don'[t] know.

A Oh, yes, I knew that.

P Oh, another thing – you must ask the hostess if you can smoke. Mos[t] British people don'[t] smoke and think it's rude to smoke a[t] the dinner table.

A Right.

P Oh, and you should wai[t] for the hostess to start eating first. And you mus[t] say you like the food – even if it's terrible! Er … anything else? Oh, yes, British people like to sit and talk for an hour or two after they've had dessert, so you shouldn'[t] leave immediately after the meal.

A Right. And is there anything I shouldn'[t] talk about?

P No, no[t] really, you can talk about anything – places you've been to, work, family and the weather, of course. Bu[t] you shouldn't ask people how much they earn.

A OK, thanks a lot. That's really useful.

P No problem. I'm sure you'll have a grea[t] time! So, what are you going to wear …

R8.4

ANSWERS 1a) 2a) 3a)

R8.5

ANTONIA Mmm, this is delicious!

MOTHER Thank you, Antonia.

RICHARD Yes, Mum's food is always delicious.

FATHER Have you been to England before, Antonia?

A Yes, when I was 16 I came here to study English. I went to a language school in Bath.

M And where have you been this time?

A Well, last week I went back to Bath to visit some friends. That was really nice.

F And what are you planning to do with the rest of your time here?

A I don't know, really.

M Well, you should go to Cambridge to see the university. It's really beautiful. We've got some friends there. I'm sure you can stay with them, if you like.

A That sounds good. Thank you.

F And Richard should take you to London to see the sights, of course.

R Yes, maybe.

M Oh, yes. And you must go on the London Eye while you're there.

A What's that?

M It's a big wheel, about 150 metres high. You can see the whole city from the top. It's wonderful.

A That sounds amazing! And I want to go to Oxford Street to do some shopping.

R Oh, no!

A I need to buy some presents for my family back in Italy and I want to get some new clothes. Maybe we can go next Saturday, Richard?

R Clothes shopping in London on a Saturday afternoon? You're joking!

M Richard!

R8.6

INTERVIEWER On *Around the World* this week we're looking at giving presents in differen[t] cultures. With me is travel writer, Neil Palmer. Welcome to the programme, Neil.

NEIL Thank you.

I Now everyone gives presents, of course. But it isn't as easy /j/ as that, is it?

N No, /w/ i[t] certainly /j/ isn't. In some places, like China, for /r/ example, it's polite to refuse a presen[t] once or twice before /r/ accepting it. If you /w/ accept it immediately, people migh[t] think you're greedy. And you should give the presen[t] with both hands, no[t] jus[t] one hand.

I Oh, that's interesting.

N And even opening presents can be /j/ a problem. In mos[t] Western countries, like England or the USA, people wan[t] you to /w/ open the presen[t] when they give it to you. But in places like Thailand and Vietnam it's very rude to /w/ open a present immediately. You should keep the present and open i[t] when you ge[t] home.

I And is there /r/ anything you shouldn'[t] give as a present?

N Well, tha[t] depends on the country. In Japan you mus[t] never give anything you can cu[t] with, like knives or scissors, as these are /r/ a symbol of death.

I Oh, dear. Tha[t] could be /j/ embarrassing.

N Yes, and in both Japanese and Chinese the word for 4 means 'death' – so you shouldn'[t] give anyone an even number /r/ of things. That's why /j/ in Japanese departmen[t] stores you /w/ always buy glasses in sets of 5 or 7.

I In the /j/ UK we /j/ often give flowers. Is tha[t] the same all over the world?

N Yes, bu[t] you still need to be careful. In countries like Turkey, for /r/ example, you shouldn'[t] give your hostess whi[te] flowers – people only give whi[te] flowers a[t] funerals. And you mus[t] give an odd number /r/ of flowers – an even number /r/ is unlucky.

I I never knew giving presents was so difficult! Neil Palmer, thank you for coming in to talk to /w/ us today.

N It was a pleasure.

R8.8

It's very rude to open a present immediately. You shouldn't give anyone an even number of things.
You always buy glasses in sets of 5 or 7.
And you must give an odd number of flowers.

R8.9

MARLEN Whereabouts in Scotland are you from, Bruce?

BRUCE The capital, Edinburgh.

M Oh, I'm going there next month on business. So what's Edinburgh like?

B Fantastic – it's very cosmopolitan and the city itself is very beautiful. The centre's a bit touristy, but the city still has lots of tradition. And of course there's Edinburgh Castle, which is amazing.

M Is Scotland similar to England?

B No, it's quite different. We have the same currency as England but we have our own bank notes. And we have our own language, Gaelic. But don't worry, everybody speaks English – with a Scottish accent, of course.

M I must admit I don't know much about Scotland.

B Most people don't. They know that men sometimes wear a kilt, which is like a skirt, but for men, and that we play a musical instrument called the bagpipes. And of course Scottish whisky is one of the most famous drinks in the world. But Scotland's much more than that.

M So what are the people like?

B Well, they're quite reserved, but they really like foreign visitors and they're always very welcoming and friendly.

M Hmm. And what's the weather like?

B It can be quite wet and windy and the winters are freezing. But on a warm sunny day there's nowhere better in the world.

M And what's the food like?

B Ah. Delicious. Have you heard of haggis?

M Yes, but I don't know what it is.

B Basically it's a sheep's heart, cut up and cooked in the sheep's stomach.

M Ugh. It sounds horrible.

B I know, but it's really good. Er … when did you say you were going?

M In August.

B Brilliant, you'll be there for the Edinburgh Festival. Now that *is* an experience. Lots of street theatre, comedy and music. It goes on for nearly a month.

M That sounds great! Is it easy to get tickets for things?

R9.1

1

REBECCA Morning. Do you want some coffee?

NATALIE No thanks. I overslept … again.

R Oh, dear. A late night, was it?

N Yes, a bit. Look, I have to go. If I'm late again, I'll lose my job.

R Don't worry. You'll be OK if you get a taxi.

N Yes, good idea.

R Right, have a good day.

N You too. Bye.

2

ALAN Where are the car keys? I can't find them anywhere.

KATHRYN I don't know, Alan. Where did you put them last?

A That's a stupid question, isn't it?

K Well, we'll miss the film if we don't find them soon.

A Yes, I know.

K Maybe they're in your coat pocket.

A No, they're not. I've looked.

K OK, I'm just trying to help.

3

BRIAN Oh, no, more traffic. Why didn't we leave sooner?

ELEANOR We'll be fine. We've still got an hour.

B If we don't get there by 5, we'll miss the plane.

E Don't worry. We'll get there.

B What will we do if we're too late?

E Well, we'll have to get the next one. Just relax, all right?

R9.2

I'll lose my job → If I'm late again, I'll lose my job. | OK if you get a taxi → You'll be OK if you get a taxi. | get there by five, we'll miss the plane → If we don't get there by five, we'll miss the plane. | if we're too late → What will we do if we're too late? | if we don't find them soon → We'll miss the film if we don't find them soon.

R9.3

ALAN Now, where's my list? OK. I won't leave the office until I finish this report. I need that for the meeting in Zurich. Right, what's next? Oh, yes, I need some euros. OK, as soon as I finish the report I'll go to the bank. They'll still be open, I think. If not, I'll get some at the airport. Right – tickets … Frank's got the tickets … I'll call him when I get home, just to check. And I'll phone the hotel to check our reservations after I talk to him. Hmm … what time do I have to be at the airport? Wow, that's early – I think I'll pack before I go to bed. OK, that's everything, I think. Now, where's that report?

R9.4

VICKY Well, my life has changed completely, of course – looking after a child is a full-time job. After Meg was born I was quite depressed for a few weeks, but I'm less stressed about things now, I think. Martin helps when he's home, but I get upset when he says he's got too much work to do. I have to work 24 hours a day! Meg isn't sleeping well at the moment, so I never get enough sleep and then I don't have enough energy to do anything in the day. Also, I miss work and my adult friends. Now I'm at home all the time with the baby, it can be quite lonely. I haven't been out with my friends since Meg was born so I don't really have a social life. But I'm never bored – I've always got too many things to do and there aren't enough hours in the day to do them all. But of course there are lots of good things too. I was very excited when she smiled for the first time and I love watching her sleep. Yes, I'm very happy being a mother, but I don't want to have any more children – I think one child is enough.

MARTIN Life's changed a lot since Meg was born, but I don't mind – I'm just pleased that she's a healthy baby. The change has been a lot harder for Vicky, I think, but Meg wakes up a lot in the night so neither of us is getting much sleep. Also, we don't really have a social life together anymore, because Vicky's usually too tired to go out in the evening. When I get home we normally just have dinner and watch TV. I sometimes go out with friends from work, but I feel a bit guilty, so I try not to get home too late. At least I earn enough money for the whole family, so we don't have to worry about paying the bills or anything. Vicky would like to move to a bigger house, but I think this place is big enough for us, for now anyway. And the good things? Well, I love watching Meg's face. She's not old enough to talk, but she makes some funny faces! Yes, I'm really pleased I'm a dad – I think she's beautiful.

R9.5

get home too late → I try not to get home too late. | too much work to do → He's got too much work to do. | too many things to do → I've always got too many things to do. | not old enough to talk → She's not old enough to talk. | enough energy → I don't have enough energy. | enough money for the whole family → I earn enough money for the whole family. | big enough → This place is big enough.

R9.6

A new couple have moved /in next door. | Their parties go /w/ on all night. | Their friends turn /up at two /w/ in the morning. | They told me to go /w/ away. | I've had to give them /up. | I take off my coat. | I sit down /in front /of the TV. | I can't put /up with the noise any longer. | I get /on well with /all my /j/ other neighbours. | I don't want to go back to my parents' house.

R9.7

PRESENTER … And we'll have more about that story later in the programme. A new report out today says that one of the biggest causes of stress is our neighbours. So we sent our reporter, Mandy Stevens, to find out what the public think.

MANDY Excuse me, can I ask you if you get on well with your neighbours?

FIRST PERSON Oh, yes, definitely. I've got fantastic neighbours – well, they're friends really, not just neighbours. We often, you know, go round to visit each other for er coffee and um just talk about the day. And when I um go away for the weekend they, you know, always look after my cats, which is really useful.

SECOND PERSON Well, I kind of get on with all my neighbours er except one. They've er got a teenage son, you see, and he's, like, learning to play the drums. They're really loud and er it drives us crazy! I've, like, talked to his parents, but you know, they just don't care. We're thinking of moving house to get away from them.

THIRD PERSON Well, I don't um have any neighbours, actually. I live in a big house in the country and er there's nobody near me. The nearest house is about um 4 miles away. And, you know, that's um just the way I want it. I like the quiet, you see.

FOURTH PERSON Well, *most* of my neighbours are, you know, OK, but um it's the *kids* that are the problem. There aren't enough places for them to play, you see, so they just get into trouble. It's er it's not really their fault, they're kind of … just bored really and you know there's not much to do round here.

FIFTH PERSON Well, in our street there're, like, not enough places to park. So you know, people just um park anywhere. So sometimes I er have to leave my car a long way from my house, which is, you know, really annoying. I've got 2 kids under the age of 2, you see, and sometimes I um have to carry them quite a long way. So, yeah, my neighbours are a bit of a problem.

R9.8

1

LUCY Hello?

MARTIN Hello, Lucy. It's Martin.

L Hello, Martin. How are you?

M I'm fine, thanks.

L And how are Vicky and Meg?

M Oh, they're very well. But being a parent is hard work!

L Yes, so I've heard.

M Anyway, um are you doing anything next Friday?

L Um … I don't think so, no. Why?

M Well, we haven't seen anyone since Meg was born. So we er decided to invite a few friends round for dinner. Would you like to come?

L Yes, I'd love to. What time?

M Oh, er about 8?

L Great! Do you want me to bring anything?

M No, it's OK. See you Friday, then.

L I'm really looking forward to it. Bye.

M Goodbye.

2

DAVE Hello?

MARTIN Hello, Dave, it's Martin.

D Martin! I haven't heard from you for ages.

M Yeah, well, you know – new baby and all that.

D Yeah, I remember what that's like. How are Vicky and Meg?

M They're both very well, thanks. Anyway, the reason I'm calling is er do you fancy coming round for a meal on Friday?

D Oh, I'd love to, but I can't. I'm really sorry! I'm going away this weekend.

M Oh, what a shame.

D Look er why don't we meet for a drink after work instead?

M Yes, that'd be great.

D Are you free on Wednesday?

M No, um Vicky's out on Wednesday so I'm babysitting.

D Well er what are you doing on Tuesday?

M Nothing special. Yes, Tuesday's good. Where shall we meet?

D Er … let's meet at The Green Man.

M Is that the pub on the High Street? It's been so long.

D Yes, that's right. What time shall we meet?

M How about 6.30?

D Yeah, that's fine.

M Right. I'll see you there at 6.30. Bye.

D Bye.

R9.9

1 Yes, I'd love to. **a)**
2 I'm really looking forward to it. **b)**
3 I haven't heard from you for ages. **a)**
4 I'd love to, but I can't. **a)**
5 Yes, that'd be great. **b)**
6 I'll see you there at 6.30. **a)**

R9.11

CHORUS
What the world needs now is love, sweet love
It's the only thing that there's just too little of
What the world needs now is love, sweet love
No, not just for some, but for everyone

Lord, we don't need another mountain
There are mountains and hillsides enough to climb
There are oceans and rivers enough to cross
Enough to last till the end of time

CHORUS

Lord, we don't need another meadow
There are cornfields and wheat fields enough to grow
There are sunbeams and moonbeams enough to shine
Oh, listen, Lord, if you want to know

What the world needs now, is love, sweet love
It's the only thing that there's just too little of
What the world needs now is love, sweet love
No, not just for some, oh, but just for every, every, everyone

Oh, what the world needs now is love, sweet love (Oh, is love) (x 3)

R10.1

ANSWERS 1 £58,000,000 2 £117,000
3 £56,000 4 £700,000 5 £73,000
6 £1,770,000 7 £157,000

R10.2

Christie's and Sotheby's are known all over the world. | Thousands of items are bought and sold every day. | This typewriter was used by Ian Fleming. | Cuttings from Elvis Presley's hair were sold by his hairdresser. | This Rolls Royce was owned by John Lennon.

R10.3

INTERVIEWER My next guest is Sam Bennett, whose programme *Real Men Shop!* is on Radio 10 tonight at 6.30. Sam, why did you make a programme about the history of men and shopping?

SAM Well, men's attitudes to shopping have changed a lot over the years in Britain. For example, let's take Selfridges, which opened in 1909. Selfridges was actually London's first department store and they used to /juːstə/ have a special room only for men. The husbands used to /juːstə/ go to this room, sit in comfortable chairs and read their newspapers while their wives did the shopping. It used to /juːstə/ be very popular.

I I'm sure it was. And what about the food shopping?

S Oh, men didn't use to /juːstə/ do anything like that, of course. Everyone knows that the women did all the food shopping.

I They still do mostly, don't they?

S Yes, but it's not as bad as it used to /juːstə/ be. Even as recently as the 1970s, married men never used to /juːstə/ do the food shopping and some of them didn't even buy their own clothes – their wives did.

I What did single men use to /juːstə/ do?

S Often someone bought their clothes for them – their mothers or sisters, probably. Interestingly, the men's clothes shop, Austin Reed, used to /juːstə/ have a "shopping girlfriend" service for single men.

I What was that exactly?

S Well, these "shopping girlfriends" used to /juːstə/ go round the shop with the man and help him buy his clothes.

I Really?

S Mmm. But nowadays most men buy their own clothes, of course, and you see husbands doing the weekly shopping in the supermarket all the time – no one's surprised anymore.

I But the wife had to write the list!

S Yes, probably. And of course products have changed too. 40 years ago, you didn't use to /juːstə/ see perfumes and skincare products for men. But now you can buy them everywhere. So things have changed quite a lot, really.

I Well, thanks for coming in to talk to us today, Sam. You can hear *Real Men Shop!*, the history of men's shopping habits, tonight on Radio 10 at 6.30.

R10.5

ANSWERS 2 used to open 3 used to eat
4 didn't used to sell 5 didn't use to be
6 used to buy 7 didn't used to have
8 used to take

R10.6

ANSWERS 2 a 3 – 4 – 5 a 6 the 7 – 8 a 9 a
10 – 11 the 12 the 13 the 14 – 15 the
Extra information:
… in 1984. In September 1988 he opened the first Versace shop in Madrid, Spain.
… was killed. But 9 days later a man was found dead on Miami beach. The police believe that he was Versace's murderer.

R10.7

1

SHOP ASSISTANT Can I help you?
CUSTOMER 1 I'm just looking, thanks. … Excuse me. Have you got this T-shirt in a smaller size?
SA What size is that one?
C1 Large.
SA I'll have a look. … Yes, here's a medium.
C1 OK. Can I try it on, please?
SA Yes, sure. The fitting room's over there.
C1 Thank you. …
SA Does it fit?
C1 Yes, it's fine, I think. How much is it?
SA It's £15.
C1 OK, I'll take it.
SA Thank you. Here's your change and your receipt.
C1 Thanks very much. Bye.
SA Bye.

2

SHOP ASSISTANT Who's next, please?
CUSTOMER 2 Hi. Could I have this map, please?
SA Sure. That's er £5.20.
C2 And do you sell batteries?
SA Yes, we do. What size do you want?
C2 Double A, I think.
SA Here you are. That's £10.75 altogether.
C2 OK.
SA How would you like to pay?
C2 Credit card, if that's OK.
SA That's fine. Check the amount and sign

here, please. … Thank you.
C2 Thanks a lot. Goodbye.
SA Bye.

R11.1

I've just heard that Tim's in hospital. | He's already had an operation. | I don't know all the details yet. | Robin Hall's just phoned. | Have you sent him the cheque yet? | Ted's already done three dives. | I haven't done any yet. | Pippa's just lost her job!

R11.2

SHARON Pippa, **I've jus[t] got your message.** I'm so sorry.
PIPPA Thanks.
S When are you leaving?
P Today. I've already told them I'm no[t] staying to the end of the month. Actually, I've jus[t] finished clearing my desk.
S Have they paid you for this month?
P Yes, they have. I've already checked my bank account.
S **And what_about_Andrew?** Have you told him yet?
P No, I haven'[t]. **He isn'[t] back from Germany until Friday.** I don'[t] wan[t] to tell him over the phone.
S No, of course no[t], I understand.
P And guess what? **I've just_opened an email from Ed Burrows** in Cardiff …
S Oh, yes?
P … He wants me to call him – he says he might have a job for me.
S Wow, news travels fast. Have you phoned him ye[t]?
P No, no[t] yet. I need some time to think abou[t] what I wan[t] to do. I've jus[t] been on the Interne[t] looking for a cheap holiday. I haven'[t] found anything ye[t], but I'll have another look when I ge[t] home. Uh-oh, here comes the boss. I have to go. I'll call you later, Sharon. Bye.
S Bye.

R11.4

ALICE Excuse me, are you er the new person who's just moved in across the street?
MARY Yes, I am.
A Hello, my name's Alice. I own the flower shop on the corner.
M Nice to meet you. I'm Mary.
A Have you heard the news?
M No, what's happened?
A Well, the man who lives in the big house at the end of the village was murdered last night.
M What?!
A Yes, at the, um, new Garden Centre.
M The Garden Centre?
A Yes, that's the place where they found the body. Jack Miller – he's the man who was murdered – is the owner. And it, um, only opened 2 weeks ago.
M How … how was he killed?

A They said on the radio he was shot.

M Oh, dear, that's terrible. So, um, you probably know everyone who lives in the village. Who do you think did it?

A Well, um I shouldn't be saying this, but er do you know Barry Clark?

M Um, no ...

A He's Jack's business partner. Apparently they had a big argument yesterday at the Garden Centre.

M What were they arguing about?

A Money. Barry said Jack was stealing from him. And you don't want to steal from Barry Clark – he's a bit crazy, if you know what I mean.

M Right.

A And then of course there's um ... Ellen, Jack's wife. Last month she told me Jack um wanted to leave her – you know, get divorced.

M Oh, dear.

A Yes, she was very upset, obviously. Her marriage is the only thing which makes her happy. Especially after um ... after what happened to their son.

M Why, what happened?

A Well, 4 years ago their son, Adam, was sent to prison.

M Oh, no. What for?

A He robbed the local post office and um shot a policeman while he was trying to escape.

M That's terrible. So he's still in prison, then.

A No, he came out 2 weeks ago. And they never found the money that was stolen.

M Hmm ... and I thought Yately was a sleepy village where nothing ever happened ...

R11.5

PRESENTER ... has promised more money for schools in the coming year ... And I hear that the Miller murder trial has just ended. Here's our reporter, Alexander Harris.

ALEXANDER Well, a few minutes ago 47-year-old flower-shop owner, Alice White, was found guilty of the murder of Yately businessman, Jack Miller. During the trial we heard how she broke into the home of Mr Miller's business partner, Barry Clark. She stole his gun and went to the Yately Garden Centre, where Mr Miller was working late. She shot him once in the heart, killing him instantly and then left a single red rose on his body. Then she returned to Mr Clark's house and put the gun back.

P So how did the police catch her?

A They found a button near Mr Miller's body. When a photo of the button appeared in the evening paper, a local woman, Mary Barnes, called the police. She said she was talking to Mrs White the morning after the murder and

noticed that a button was missing on her coat. The police visited Mrs White's home and found the coat, with the button still missing.

P And why did she murder Mr Miller?

A Well, during the trial we heard that Mrs White's flower shop was losing business to the new garden centre. She thought that if she killed Mr Miller and his business partner was arrested, the garden centre would have to close.

P That was Alexander Harris at the Miller murder trial. And now sport. Wolverhampton Wanderers have beaten Manchester United 5–1 in the ...

R11.6

ANNOUNCER It's six o'clock. And here with a summary of today's news is James Humphrey.

JAMES Protesters fought with police outside today's meeting of the World Trade Organisation in Frankfurt. Angry **demonstrators** sat in the road to try and **prevent** world leaders from travelling to the conference hall. Several people were **injured** and were taken to nearby hospitals, and there were over forty arrests.

An English animal rights worker was murdered on the island of St Lucia yesterday. Barbara Devlin was found dead in her car after she was shot twice. Ms Devlin was trying to stop the opening of swim-with-dolphin centres in the Caribbean, which she believed were **cruel** to the animals.

A painting by Van Gogh was stolen from a private collection in New York this morning. The robbers, who were dressed as gas inspectors, told **residents** of an exclusive Manhattan **apartment block** to leave the building because of a gas **leak**. They then broke into the apartment of seventy-year-old art collector, Mrs Dorothy Stone, and stole the Van Gogh. The painting is **worth** over twenty million dollars.

Doctors in America have developed a cream to help stop skin cancer. The magic ingredient in the cream is green tea. Dr Ruth Baxter from the British Medical Association welcomed the news.

DR BAXTER This is a very interesting product, but it's important that we do our own tests on anything that's sold in this country. So unfortunately this cream won't be available in Britain for at least 2 years.

R11.7

A

MAN 3 I'm going to Rome next month.

WOMAN 3 Are you? Who with?

M3 Some friends from my Italian class.

We're going to study over there.

W3 Wow, that's great. How long are you going for?

M3 2 weeks.

B

MAN 1 You know Max doesn't want to sell the company.

MAN 2 Doesn't he?

M1 No, he hates the idea.

M2 Why's that?

M1 Well, the company's been in the family for 80 years.

M2 Oh, right.

C

MAN 4 So, Angus, how are you?

ANGUS I'm really tired. I didn't go to work today.

M4 Didn't you? Why not?

A Well, an old friend came to visit and we stayed up all night talking.

M4 Really? Who's the friend?

A His name's Josh. We used to work together. But his life's changed quite a lot since we last met ...

D

WOMAN 1 Have you heard? Hannah's had twins!

WOMAN 2 Has she? What did she have?

W1 2 girls.

W2 Wow, fantastic! Did everything go OK?

W1 Yes, they're all well.

W2 Oh, good.

R11.8

1

A Gregory's got a new girlfriend.

B Has he? (I)

2

A They don't know where he lives.

B Don't they? (NI)

3

A I can't ride a bike.

B Can't you? (I)

4

A Sonya and Felix are getting married.

B Are they? (I)

5

A I've seen this film before.

B Have you? (NI)

6

A My wife didn't leave the house last week.

B Didn't she? (I)

R11.9

Has she? | Doesn't he? | Didn't you? | Are you? | Has he? | Don't they? | Can't you? | Are they? | Have you? | Didn't she?

R11.10

ANGUS His name's Josh. We used to work together. But his life's changed quite a lot since we last met ... He's a millionaire now ... Yes, he made over 10 million pounds last year ... But he still hasn't got a car ... Anyway, he's got a new girlfriend now ...

Yes, and she's a really famous actress …
They met on a yoga holiday in Spain …
She lives in a great big house in
Hollywood … Julia Roberts used to live
there … And he's invited me to go and
meet her … Yes, I'm leaving on Sunday …

R11.11

You never close your eyes anymore when
  I kiss your lips
And there's no tenderness like before in
  your fingertips
You're trying hard not to show it (baby)
But baby, baby I know it

CHORUS

You've lost that loving feeling
Oh, that loving feeling
You've lost that loving feeling
Now it's gone, gone, gone
Whoa-oh

Now there's no welcome look in your eyes
  when I reach for you
And girl you're starting to criticise little
  things I do
It makes me just feel like crying (baby)
'Cause baby something beautiful's dying

CHORUS

Baby, baby, I'd get down on my knees for
  you
If you would only love me like you used to
  do, yeah
We had a love, a love, a love you don't find
  every day
So don't, don't, don't, don't let it slip away

Baby, baby, baby, baby, I beg you please,
  please, please, please
I need your love, need your love
I need your love, I need your love
Bring it on back, bring it on back
Bring it on back, bring it on back
Bring back that loving feeling
Whoa, that loving feeling
Bring back that loving feeling
'Cause it's gone, gone, gone
And I can't go on, whoa-oh

Bring back that loving feeling, whoa that
  loving feeling

R12.1

MAUREEN Philip. How nice to see you!
PHILIP Oh, hi, Aunt Maureen.
M Great news! Congratulations – a degree
   in medicine!
P Ah, you've heard.
M Of course I've heard. First doctor in the
   family! I'm so proud. Now what's next?
   Are you looking for a job?
P Um … I've already got a job.
M So quickly! Which hospital are you
   working in?
P Actually, I'm working in a restaurant.
M A restaurant?
P Yes. I've decided to take a year off before
   I start my career. I want to work abroad

so I need to save some money.
M Work abroad?
P Yes, I'm going to work for a charity. It's
   called Eyes Worldwide.
M Oh, I see. Helping people around the
   world. Hmm. What a good boy you are.
P Well, I want to do something different
   for a few months. But don't worry, I'll be
   back next June – and you'll still have
   a doctor in the family.
M And who's paying for all this?
P The charity pays for everything when
   I'm there, but I have to pay for my own
   flight.
M So that's why you're working at the
   restaurant – to buy your plane ticket.
P Yes, that's right. I can save £100 a week,
   I think. So I can leave in a couple of
   months.
M How much is the flight going to cost?

R12.2

MAUREEN Guess who I saw in town this
   morning?
ARTHUR Who?
M Philip. He's a qualified doctor now,
   you know.
A Yes, I know. Has he got a job yet?
M Yes, he has.
A Oh, that's good.
M Yes, he said he was working in
   a restaurant.
A Hmm, funny job for a doctor. Or is the
   food really bad there?
M No, silly. He's saving money. He told me
   that he was going to work for a charity.
A What, in the restaurant?
M No, he said that he wanted to work
   abroad. He wants to help people, Arthur.
   Isn't that wonderful? But he said that
   he'd be back next June. Then he'll start
   working as a proper doctor.
A Hmm.
M He told me he could save £100 a week,
   but I don't think he can, do you? Not
   working in a restaurant …
A Hmm.
M Are you listening to me, Arthur?
A Sorry, what? Yes, of course I am.
M Anyway, he said that the flight was about
   £700 …

R12.3

he wanted to work abroad → He said that
/ðət/ he wanted to work abroad. | he was
going to work for a charity → He told me
that /ðət/ he was going to work for a charity.
| he was working in a restaurant → He said
he was working in a restaurant. | he could
save a hundred pounds a week → He told
me he could save a hundred pounds a
week. | he'd be back next June → He said
that /ðət/ he'd be back next June.

R12.4

MAUREEN Are you listening to me, Arthur?
ARTHUR Sorry, what? Yes, of course I am.

M Anyway, he said that the flight was about
   seven hundred pounds. Which is a lot of
   money, I think.
A Yes, it is.
M And [h]e told me that [h]e didn't earn
   very much – only a hundred and eighty
   pounds a week.
A Hmm.
M Well, I said that it was going to take
   [h]im ages to save enough money …
A Years, probably …
M Exactly. And then [h]e said that [h]e
   was working 7 days a week. Well, I don't
   think [h]e should have to work that
   hard, do you?
A Yes … er … I mean no.
M Good. I'm so glad you agree. Because
   I told [h]im we'd pay for his ticket.
A What?!
M Yes, he was very happy, I can tell you.
   So I got the money out of the bank this
   afternoon and gave it to him. He said
   [h]e could pay me back next year, but
   I told [h]im that it was a present from
   us both.
A And you didn't want to discuss this with
   me first?
M What's the point? You never listen to a
   word I say anyway … Right, I'm just
   going to phone Mrs Jenkins and tell
   [h]er … oh, and Mrs Lindsay and
   Dorothy Black and …

R12.5

ANSWERS See R12.4.

R12.6

I'd do it → If I won a parachute jump, I'd do
it. | I wouldn't do it → If I won a parachute
jump, I wouldn't do it. | if you won a
parachute jump → What would you do if
you won a parachute jump? | I'd do it. | I
wouldn't do it. | would you do it? → If
someone asked you to hold a tarantula,
would you do it? | Yes, I would. | No, I
wouldn't.

R12.7

INTERVIEWER I'm talking to film-maker, Oliver
   Fuller, who's making a new
   documentary /j/ about the great
   magician, Harry Houdini.
OLIVER Hello.
I Oliver, what can you tell us about
   Houdini's early life?
O Well, his real name was Erich Weiss and
   he was born in Budapest, in Hungary, in
   1874. His family moved to the USA
   when he was 4.
I And when did he start doing magic?
O He became interested in magic when he
   was a boy and started working as a
   professional magician when he was 17.
I Did he become famous very quickly?
O No, he didn't. In the /j/ early days
   Houdini and his wife Bess used to do
   magic shows all over New York,

157

sometimes 20 shows_a day. But_after 5 years_of trying, he wanted to give_up magic. He put_an advert_in the newspaper offering to sell_all his magic secrets for $20. Luckily for him, nobody_/j/_answered the_/j/_ad.

I What was his greatest trick, do you think?

O Well, the /j/_underwater /r/_escape, I suppose. He was put_into /w/_a tank_of water in handcuffs and chains, then Bess pulled_a curtain_around_it. When she_/j/_opened the curtain_a few minutes later, Houdini was standing next to the tank. It was really_/j/_amazing to watch!

I So how did he do his tricks?

O Well, he used to practise_opening handcuffs for 10 hours_a day. He also used to hide pieces_of wire in his hair_/r/_and between his toes. And he was very fit – he could stay_/j/_underwater for 3 minutes_or more.

I How did he die?

O Well, many people think he died_onstage, but that_isn't true. What really happened was that he had bad stomach problems while he was doing_a show in 1926. He refused to go to hospital until he finished the show. He died_a week later.

I Well, that was_Oliver Fuller, whose new documentary …

R12.8

Listening Test (see Teacher's Book)

Answer Key

4C ③ b) p32

Are you a telly addict?

1–2 ticks:
You don't have a problem with TV. You probably do more interesting things in your free time and prefer reading to watching television.

3–4 ticks:
You like watching television, but it doesn't control your life. You probably only watch the programmes you really like and turn off the TV when they finish.

5–6 ticks:
You probably watch too much television. Why don't you go for a walk instead – when your favourite programme isn't on, of course!

7–8 ticks:
You are totally addicted to TV! You probably love your TV more than your friends! Why not turn it off and do something more interesting?

10C ⑦ c) p81

Are you a fashion victim?

1 a) 3 points	b) 2 points	c) 1 point
2 a) 2 points	b) 1 point	c) 3 points
3 a) 1 point	b) 2 points	c) 3 points
4 a) 3 points	b) 2 points	c) 1 point
5 a) 2 points	b) 1 point	c) 3 points
6 a) 2 points	b) 3 points	c) 1 point

6–9 points:
You're definitely not a fashion victim. Clothes aren't very important to you and you probably wear the first thing you see in the morning. Perhaps you should go shopping next weekend and buy some new clothes.

10–12 points:
You don't worry about clothes very much, but you like looking good and probably enjoy getting dressed up for parties and weddings. You like shopping but probably don't buy things that you don't need.

13–15 points:
What you wear is important to you. You go shopping because you want to, not because you need to, and you probably like buying fashionable clothes. You're not a fashion victim – but you might be soon!

16–18 points:
You're definitely a fashion victim! What you wear is very important to you and you love buying new clothes. Maybe you don't need to go shopping for a while – you've probably got lots of beautiful clothes at home that you never wear!

10 Review ① p83

1 Pablo Picasso
2 Switzerland
3 radium
4 Germany
5 Brazil
6 Mary Shelley

12B ③ d) p94

RISK-TAKER!

1 a) 1 point	b) 3 points	c) 2 points
2 a) 3 points	b) 2 points	c) 1 point
3 a) 1 point	b) 3 points	c) 2 points
4 a) 3 points	b) 1 point	c) 2 points
5 a) 3 points	b) 2 points	c) 1 point
6 a) 2 points	b) 3 points	c) 1 point
7 a) 3 points	b) 2 points	c) 1 point

7–11 points:
You like things the way they are and probably don't do new things very often. Perhaps you're not having as much fun as you could. Go on, take a few more risks!

12–16 points:
You like the idea of taking risks and you're probably ready to be a bit more adventurous. Maybe it's time to do all those things you've always wanted to do!

17–21 points:
You'll try anything, any time, anywhere! You should probably get some extra insurance because you're a real risk-taker!

Phonemic Symbols

Vowel sounds

/ə/	/æ/	/ʊ/	/ɒ/	/ɪ/	/i/	/e/	/ʌ/
father ago	apple cat	book could	on got	in swim	happy easy	bed any	cup under

/ɜː/	/ɑː/	/uː/	/ɔː/	/iː/			
her shirt	arm car	blue too	born walk	eat meet			

/eə/	/ɪə/	/ʊə/	/ɔɪ/	/aɪ/	/eɪ/	/əʊ/	/aʊ/
chair where	near we're	tour mature	boy noisy	nine eye	eight day	go over	out brown

Consonant sounds

/p/	/b/	/f/	/v/	/t/	/d/	/k/	/g/
park soup	be rob	face laugh	very live	time white	dog red	cold look	girl bag

/θ/	/ð/	/tʃ/	/dʒ/	/s/	/z/	/ʃ/	/ʒ/
think both	mother the	chips teach	job page	see rice	zoo days	shoe action	television

/m/	/n/	/ŋ/	/h/	/l/	/r/	/w/	/j/
me name	now rain	sing think	hot hand	late hello	marry write	we white	you yes

Irregular Verb List

infinitive	Past Simple	past participle
be	was/were	been
become	became	become
begin	began	begun
bet	bet	bet
blow	blew	blown
break	broke	broken
bring	brought /brɔːt/	brought /brɔːt/
build /bɪld/	built /bɪlt/	built /bɪlt/
buy	bought /bɔːt/	bought /bɔːt/
can	could /kʊd/	been able
catch	caught /kɔːt/	caught /kɔːt/
choose	chose /tʃəʊz/	chosen
come	came	come
cost	cost	cost
cut	cut	cut
do	did	done /dʌn/
draw /drɔː/	drew /druː/	drawn /drɔːn/
drink	drank	drunk /drʌŋk/
drive	drove	driven
eat	ate	eaten
fall	fell	fallen
feed	fed	fed
feel	felt	felt
find	found	found
fly	flew /fluː/	flown /fləʊn/
forget	forgot	forgotten
get	got	got [US: gotten]
give	gave	given
go	went	been/gone
grow /grəʊ/	grew /gruː/	grown /grəʊn/
have	had	had
hear	heard /hɜːd/	heard /hɜːd/
hide	hid	hidden
hit	hit	hit
hold	held	held
keep	kept	kept
know	knew /njuː/	known /nəʊn/
learn	learned/learnt	learned/learnt

infinitive	Past Simple	past participle
leave	left	left
lend	lent	lent
let	let	let
lose /luːz/	lost	lost
make	made	made
meet	met	met
pay	paid /peɪd/	paid /peɪd/
put	put	put
read /riːd/	read /red/	read /red/
ride	rode	ridden
ring	rang	rung /rʌŋ/
run	ran	run
say	said /sed/	said /sed/
see	saw /sɔː/	seen
sell	sold	sold
send	sent	sent
shake	shook /ʃʊk/	shaken
shoot	shot	shot
show	showed	shown
sing	sang	sung /sʌŋ/
sit	sat	sat
sleep	slept	slept
speak	spoke	spoken
spell	spelled/spelt	spelt
spend	spent	spent
stand	stood	stood
steal	stole	stolen
swim	swam	swum /swʌm/
take	took /tʊk/	taken
teach	taught /tɔːt/	taught /tɔːt/
tell	told	told
think	thought /θɔːt/	thought /θɔːt/
throw /θrəʊ/	threw /θruː/	thrown /θrəʊn/
understand	understood	understood
wake	woke	woken
wear	wore	worn
win	won /wʌn/	won /wʌn/
write	wrote	written

CD-ROM/Audio CD instructions

Start the CD-ROM

- Insert the *face2face* CD-ROM into your CD-ROM drive.
- If Autorun is enabled, the CD-ROM will start automatically.
- If Autorun is not enabled, open **My Computer** and then **D:** (where D is the letter of your CD-ROM drive). Then double-click on the *face2face* icon.

Install the CD-ROM to your hard disk (recommended)

- Go to **My Computer** and then **D:** (where D is the letter of your CD-ROM drive).
- Right-click on *Explore*.
- Double-click on *Install face2face to hard disk*.
- Follow the installation instructions on your screen.

Listen and practise on your CD player

You can listen to and practise language from the Student's Book Real World lessons on your CD player at home or in the car:

R1.11	R1.12	R2.11	R2.13	R3.8	R4.11
R5.13	R6.7	R6.9	R7.10	R8.9	R8.10
R9.10	R10.8	R11.9	R11.10		

What's on the CD-ROM?

- **Interactive practice activities**

Extra practice of Grammar, Vocabulary, Real World situations and English pronunciation. Click on one of the unit numbers (1–12) at the top of the screen. Then choose an activity and click on it to start.

- **My Activities**

Create your own lesson. Click on *My Activities* at the top of the screen. Drag activities from the unit menus into the *My Activities* panel on the right of the screen. Then click on *Start*.

- **My Portfolio**

This is a unique and customisable reference tool. Click on *Grammar, Word List, Real World* or *Phonemes* at any time for extra help and information. You can also add your own notes, check your progress and create your own English tests!

Practice activities   My Activities

My Portfolio

System specification
- Windows 98, NT4 with (Service Pack 6), ME, 2000 or XP
- 128Mb RAM
- 500Mb hard disk space (if installing to hard disk)

Support

If you experience difficulties with this CD-ROM, please visit:
www.cambridge.org/elt/cdrom

Acknowledgements

The authors would like to thank all the team at Cambridge University Press for the continuing devotion to the *face2face* project. We would particularly like to thank the following people for their support, enthusiasm and inspiration: Sue Ullstein (Commissioning Editor); Laurie Harrison (Electronic Project Manager); Rachel Jackson-Stevens, Lynne Rushton and Dilys Silva (Editorial team); Ruth Atkinson (Freelance editor); Alison Greenwood, Nicholas Tims and Lynn Townsend (CD-ROM team) and all the team at Pentacor (book design).

Chris Redston would like to thank the following people for all their help and support: Mark and Laura Skipper, Will Ord, Polly Kirby, Karen Thomas, Natasha Muñoz, Margie Baum, Ali Bond, Albert Hofmann, Katy Wimhurst, Kari Matchett, Joss Whedon, SMG, David B, Rachel Carr-Hill, Matt Groening, Alan Ball, the Hilder family, his sisters Anne and Carol, and his dear father Bill Redston (happy 80th birthday, Dad!). He would also like to thank Dr Dylan Evans for the robots interview in 5A, and all his colleagues for not phoning him before lunchtime.

Gillie Cunningham would like to thank heaven for Richard Gibb and all his contributions, help, support and patience while this book was being written. Continuing love and thanks go to Amybeth and Sue Mohamed for still being there to give unfailing encouragement, and to all those dear friends who have been so understanding and have kept in touch. Special thanks also go to Captain James Kenyon for supplying information about pilot's training for 3A.

The authors and publishers would like to thank the following teachers for the invaluable feedback which they provided:

Isidro Almendárez, Spain; David Barnes, Italy; Julia Blackwell, Germany; Mike Delaney, Brazil; Elizabeth Downey, New Zealand; Hannah Gibbin, Spain; Alison Greenwood, Italy; Madeline Hall, Portugal; David Hill, Turkey; Lisa Jencsok, Australia; Justyna Kubica, Poland; Justyna Martin, Poland; Celia Martínez, Spain; Joe McKenna, Spain; Michelle McKinlay, New Zealand; Paul Mitchell, Spain; Claudia Payer, UK; Candida Penuizic Buxton, France; Matthew Twiggs, UK; Kevin Warham, Australia.

The authors and publishers are grateful to the following contributors:

pentacor**big**: cover and text design and page make-up
Hilary Luckcock: picture research, commissioned photography
Trevor Clifford: photography
Anne Rosenfeld: audio recordings

The authors and publishers are grateful to the following for permission to reproduce copyright material. All efforts have been made to contact the copyright holders of material reproduced in this book which belongs to third parties, and citations are given for the sources. We welcome approaches from any copyright holders whom we have not been able to trace but who find that their material has been reproduced herein.

For the logo in 2A: © McDonald's Restaurants Limited; for the text in 3C: *The Times Magazine*, adapted from 'Someone's got to do it' by Candida Crewe, 5th August 2000, © Times Newspapers Ltd; for the quotation from Ewan